NEW YORK
RANGERS
GREATEST MOMENTS AND PLAYERS

STAN FISCHLER

RESEARCH EDITORS
RINI KRISHNAN
JOE KELLEHER

SPECIAL PHOTOGRAPHY
DAVID PERLMUTTER

Sports Publishing books may be purchased in bulk at special discounts for sales promotion, corporate gifts, fund-raising, or educational purposes. Special editions can also be created to specifications. For details, contact the Special Sales Department, Sports Publishing, 307 West 36th Street, 11th Floor, New York, NY 10018 or sportspubbooks@skyhorsepublishing.com.

Sports Publishing® is a registered trademark of Skyhorse Publishing, Inc.®, a Delaware corporation.

Visit our website at www.sportspubbooks.com.

10 9 8 7 6 5 4 3 2 1

Library of Congress Cataloging-in-Publication Data is available on file.

Cover design by Tom Lau
Cover photo credit AP Images
ISBN: 978-1-61321-825-9
Ebook ISBN 978-1-61321-845-7

Printed in China

SOME OF MY FAVORITE RANGERS NEVER MADE THE HALL OF FAME NOR THE NHL ALL-STAR TEAM, YET THEY PROVIDED ME WITH THRILLS AND FRIENDSHIP. AT THE VERY TOP OF MY LIST IS ALDO GUIDOLIN, WHOM I MET IN 1954-55 WHEN I WORKED IN THE BLUESHIRTS' PUBLICITY DEPARTMENT. ALTHOUGH HE ONLY PLAYED A FEW BRIEF SEASONS IN NEW YORK, ALDO AND I BECAME GOOD FRIENDS AND REMAIN SO TO THIS DAY. THE TWO OF US HAVE A LOT IN COMMON. WE LIKE TO LAUGH, WE ENJOY GOOD HOCKEY AND WE NEVER PARTICULARLY CARED FOR COACH PHIL WATSON; AND THAT'S THE UNDERSTATEMENT OF THE HALF-CENTURY.

TO ALDO, THANKS FOR BEING SUCH A GOOD PAL.

—STAN FISCHLER

CONTENTS

ACKNOWLEDGMENTS

Talk to the coach of any Stanley Cup–winning team, and he'll tell you that success depends on not one player or two, but contributions from everybody on the squad, right down to the twentieth man. The same holds for producing a book of this nature.

It requires extensive research, first-person interviews, the transcription of tapes, and the referencing of previous volumes on the subject.

Without all of these elements, such a book would not be possible. Which brings us to the business of acknowledging all of the good works provided by so many people.

For starters, there were the vital contributions from my office workers: Matt Jackson and Pat McCormack.

The two who orchestrated much of the nitty-gritty so necessary to make the project work defies the highest form of commendation. So I'll settle for a thousand thank-yous for all the help from Rini Krishnan and Joe Kelleher.

Needless to say, all the folks in Rangerville were most cooperative in every way. And that starts at the top with Glen Sather and Tom Renney.

The Blueshirts' P.R. department was always there to help, specifically John Rosasco, Ryan Nissan, Lindsay Ganghamer, and Michael Rappaport. If anyone was forgotten, please accept my apologies.

Many, many other authors have written extensively and expertly on the Rangers and their history. In our research, we found many useful items that helped us in our writing. The following books were of special help:

Madison Square Garden: A Century of Sport and Spectacle on the World's Most Versatile Stage, by Zander Hollander; *Madison Square Garden, 100 Years of History,* by Joseph Durso; *When the Rangers Were Young,* by Frank Boucher; *A Year On Ice, The 1970 New York Rangers Roller Coaster Season,* by Gerald Eskenazi; *Broadway Blues, New York Rangers' Twelve-Month Tour of Hockey Hell,* by Frank Brown; *The Rangers,* by Brian McFarlane; *New York Rangers Seventy-Five Years,* by John Halligan; *Tales from the Rangers Locker Room,* by Gilles Villemure and Mike Shalin; *New York Rangers: Millennium Memories,* Coordinating Editor: Jeffrey Jay Ellish; *Game of My Life,* by John Halligan and John Kreiser; *The New York Rangers: Broadway's Longest-Running Hit,* by John Kreiser and Lou Friedman; *Losing the Edge: The Rise and Fall of the Stanley Cup Champion New York Rangers* by Barry Meisel; and *Hockey Stars Today and Yesterday,* by Ron McAllister.

Old pal Ira Gitler, as well as good friends Hal and Randy Gelman, provided many insights, as did Mike Cosby, whose father, Gerry, was a pioneer in The Game. Michael was kind enough to turn his photo library over to us for use in the book.

Angela Sarro loaned us photos from her library launched by her late husband, Tom, a good friend, a marvelous historian, and a passionate Rangers fan throughout his life.

And naturally, my wife, Shirley, always was there to help and advise on the project, even as it impinged on family space and time. If any others were omitted—and they probably were—our apologies.

Thanks also to a long-ago editor of mine by the name of Peter Weed. I don't know where he is right now, but this wonderful hockey man once commissioned me to write a book called *Those Were the Days,* which was filled with oral histories including several Rangers, some of whose commentary has been included in this book.

I also had the good fortune of ghosting the autobiographies of Brad Park, *Play The Man,* and Bernie Geoffrion, *Boomer,* and co-authoring (with Hal Bock) Rod Gilbert's work, *Goal—My Life On Ice.* I relied on each of these for anecdotes and oral history.

At the expense of issuing the traditional bromide—last but not least—a ton of thanks goes to our thoughtful, insightful, and tremendously helpful editor, Julie Ganz, whose patience and fortitude helped make this possible.

INTRODUCTION

I went to my first Rangers game at the age of 10 in 1942. The Blackhawks were in town and the rain was coming down in torrents. But my father decided that we would make the trip from our Williamsburg, Brooklyn, home, and so we landed in the ninth row of the side balcony at the old Madison Square Garden, which was located on Eighth Avenue between 49th and 50th Streets.

Since the old Garden was originally built for boxing, the side balcony literally overhung the ice, and that was no fun for many fans.

If you sat in any row beyond the second one, you couldn't see the sideboards directly below or about five feet of ice along the boards.

But that didn't curb my enthusiasm, and by the 1946-47 season, I had become a Rangers season ticket holder—only this time in the end balcony, which afforded a great view of the ice.

As a matter of fact, I still have an original stub of my MSG end balcony seat: October 30, 1949, Section 337, Row F, Seat 6. The ticket cost a dollar and a quarter.

And I loved every game of it.

But my real love affair with the Rangers didn't begin until the 1952-53 season. By that time I was going to Brooklyn College and was looking to get a job in hockey somehow, anyway I could.

Luckily, the club's publicist, Herb Goren, had just organized a Rangers Fan Club, which I eagerly joined.

The club actually became a springboard for my career. Along with RFC members Jerry Weiss and Fred Meier, I started the club newspaper, the *Rangers Review*. This gave us entree to interview players, the first of whom was Ed Kullman, who Freddie and I cross-examined in his suite at the Belvedere Hotel.

I worked hard for the fan club, and in 1954, after graduating from college, Goren recognized my potential and hired me as his assistant.

To this day—more than a half-century later—I can assure you that Herb's phone call telling me I would be working for the Broadway Blueshirts was one of the greatest thrills of my life.

Although that 1954-55 edition of the Rangers didn't make the playoffs, it provided me with enough experience to get a job as a full-time writer with the *New York Journal-American*, which was then the leading evening newspaper in New York.

At the time, Dave Anderson was the Rangers beat writer, but when he left for the *New York Times* in 1954, I moved onto the Rangers beat; and from that time on, my hockey-writing career took off.

Some sixty-one years later, I'm still intensely involved with The Game, and loving it as much as ever. Thus, it's no surprise that I was tickled to receive the assignment for a book of this kind. My aim was to capture the great moments and players of the past while blending them with contemporary Rangers history.

One of the most significant aspects of the book is what I term the "Oral History." This includes interviews that I had done over the years with Hall of Famers and other significant people involved with the hockey club. And naturally, I have featured profiles of players past and present.

To sum it up, I have attempted to present as total a picture of the Rangers, their personalities, and their environment—from Day One in 1926 to the present—as possible.

I hope you enjoy the result.

—STAN FISCHLER
June 2015, New York, NY

PAST
RANGERS

A celebration scene in the dressing room at Toronto after the 1940 Stanley Cup win. *From the Stan Fischler Collection*

ANDY
BATHGATE

1 9 5 3 - 1 9 6 3

If there is one word that describes Andy Bathgate as both a player and person, that word is class. Like Montreal Canadiens majestic center and captain Jean Beliveau, Bathgate was the penultimate role model for young fans.

He was the epitome of artistry. He played the game cleanly but was also an excellent fighter when the occasion demanded rough stuff.

Two episodes among many stand out when one considers Andy Bathgate's seasons as a Ranger.

In 1959 Bathgate fired the shot that ripped into Montreal goalie Jacques Plante's face, causing the netminder to don a mask for the first time in NHL annals. The second episode involved a critical penalty shot taken by Bathgate against Detroit goalie Hank Bassen that helped propel the Rangers into a 1962 playoff berth.

How good was Bathgate?

He has been favorably compared to Bill Cook, who is considered the greatest of the early Rangers right wings.

Bathgate was the consummate performer. He combined the art of stick-handling and shooting to near perfection. His shot, which he endlessly practiced, became so devastating that it was in a class with the mighty blasts of Bobby Hull and Bernie "Boom Boom"

Geoffrion, both of whom were his contemporaries.

Bathgate wasn't quite as flashy as Hull nor blessed with all-star teammates as Geoffrion was, but he was good enough to win the Hart Trophy as the NHL's most valuable player in 1959 and was voted to the First All-Star Team at right wing in 1959 and 1962 as well as the Second Team in 1958 and 1963.

The Bathgate bloc could detail a litany of beauteous plays executed by its hero. One that qualifies among his best was a one-on-one play: Bathgate vs. the Chicago goaltender, Glen Hall.

At the time, Hall, alias *Mister Goalie,* was the best netminder in the business. On this occasion, Bathgate received a

---

ANDY BATHGATE

BORN: Winnipeg, Manitoba Canada; August 28, 1932

POSITION: Right Wing

NHL TEAMS: New York Rangers, 1953-63; Toronto Maple Leafs, 1963-65; Detroit Red Wings, 1965-67; Pittsburgh Penguins, 1967-68, 1970-71 Vancouver Canucks (WHL) 1968-70; Vancouver Blazers (WHA), 1974

AWARDS/HONORS: Hart Memorial Trophy, 1959; NHL First Team All-Star, 1959, 1962; NHL Second Team All-Star, 1958, 1963; NHL All-Star Game, 1957-64; Hockey Hall of Fame, 1978

pass directly in front of Hall and slightly to the right of the net. Rather than simply shoot the puck, Andy performed a 180-degree pirouette, appearing at the left side of the cage with the puck still on his stick. Hall remained with Bathgate until Andy completely reversed the move with another pirouette, this time ending up precisely where he had begun. By this time, Hall's body was so contorted that he was literally unable to move, whereupon Bathgate deposited the rubber in the empty right corner for a goal. It was vintage Bathgate, and a play that few, if any, could duplicate.

Andy had been tabbed a future big-leaguer when he was still a teenager playing for the Guelph (Ontario) Biltmores in the Ontario Hockey Association's Junior A division. When Guelph won the Memorial Cup, emblematic of Junior hockey supremacy in Canada, a number of Biltmores were earmarked for the Rangers including Bathgate.

Under Phil Watson's coaching, the Rangers made the playoffs three straight years (1955-56, 1956-57, and 1957-58). In March 1958, the club finished second, the highest of any New York club since 1942.

Bathgate earned acclaim as one of the most threatening shooters in the game. "I worked on my shooting for at least 15 minutes every single day," Bathgate explained. "To my mind, shooting practice is one of the most overlooked aspects of the game. I see coaches emphasizing skating all the time, but to me, the most important thing is shooting the puck. When you shoot the puck, it's not how straight it is that counts; it's the quickness

of the release, and that's what I kept working on when I was a Ranger."

Unlike many of his contemporaries, Bathgate was extremely scrupulous about conditioning. "In my entire life, I've never had a drink or a cigarette, and it made me feel good as a player. Some nights I'd go out on the ice and I'd know just by looking at the opposition that I was in much better shape than them; and it was to my advantage both physically and mentally."

Bathgate was also a cut above the average player in terms of intellect. He was thoughtful and sensitive to the needs of his teammates. When a core of NHL players began laying the groundwork for a union, Bathgate was one of the organizers. He believes that his participation in developing a players' association inspired the Rangers to deal him to Toronto at the very apex of his popularity as a Blueshirt.

It was no secret that Bathgate's success in Toronto would vitally hinge on his relationship with the boss, Punch Imlach. At first, all went well. Imlach was more than pleased with Bathgate's efforts in February, March, and April 1964. "Andy did," said Imlach, "exactly what I'd had in mind when I made the deal."

The 1964 Toronto Cup win marked the high point in the Bathgate-Imlach relationship. From then on, it was all a decrescendo, marked by bitterness and an eventual trade. The feud came to a head in the spring of 1965, when Montreal eliminated the Maple Leafs in six games of the Stanley Cup semifinals. "He was a different Bathgate from the guy who had said being traded to Toronto was the biggest break of his life," charged Imlach.

In no time at all, Imlach traded Bathgate, Billy Harris, and Gary Jarrett to the Red Wings for Marcel Pronovost, Ed Joyal, Larry Jeffrey, Lowell MacDonald, and Autry Erickson. "Frankly," Bathgate explained, "I didn't enjoy Punch's method of training. By my second season in Toronto, I just wasn't enjoying playing, so I spoke to Punch and I had to give him a reason to get me out of Toronto. So I said something to one of the reporters. Punch overemphasized it, and I wound up in Detroit."

Andrew James Bathgate was born August 28, 1932, in Winnipeg, Manitoba. He followed his older brother, Frank, east to play first-class amateur hockey in Ontario.

As much as anyone, Andy helped develop the hockey renaissance in New York City during the 1950s, and it seemed almost heretical for the Rangers to trade him to Toronto. After his feuds with Imlach, Andy began to lose his touch. He was drafted by the Pittsburgh Penguins when the Steel City sextet entered the NHL in 1967.

While still displaying flashes of his old brilliance, Andy no longer had the legs to enable him to keep up with the play. He later quit the NHL and competed briefly in Switzerland. When the World Hockey Association planted a franchise in Vancouver, he returned to the ice as a coach, although an eye injury suffered in a home accident in 1973 limited his right-eye vision by 80 percent.

Nevertheless, Andy returned to the action once more in 1974 with the Vancouver Blazers and was actually a dominant factor for the seven games in which he played, but a contract dispute with management finally inspired him to pack it in once and for all.

Bathgate returned to Toronto, where he went into the golf business and also became involved with agricultural investments. He never did completely leave the rinks. He soon joined the Toronto edition of the NHL Old-Timers. Late in the summer of 1981, Andy took part in a hockey tourney with members of the six original NHL teams. "He looked like he could have stepped right back into the NHL today," said tourney director Gerry Patterson, "and been a superstar."

Although Bathgate played elsewhere, in the minds of hockey historians, he will remain a Ranger first and foremost—one of the best to ever grace a Blueshirt.

JEFF BEUKEBOOM

1 9 9 1 - 1 9 9 9

Rangers fans have always appreciated tough, hard-working defensemen. Names that come to mind include Lou "The Leaper" Fontinato, Ching Johnson, and Muzz Patrick.

When Jeff Beukeboom arrived on Broadway in 1991, he maintained the tradition.

A defenseman's defenseman, Beukeboom was applauded for his hard but clean play. Using his large physique to his advantage, Jeff threatened oncoming forwards with thunderous bodychecks and was appreciated by goaltenders for his emphatic crease-clearing and generally smart play behind the blue line.

During the Rangers' 1993-94 Stanley Cup season, Madison Square Garden reverberated with cheers for the history-making Blueshirts. But every once in a while, a lusty "BEUUU!" would sound from the Garden faithful.

In such instances, however, the fans were actually expressing appreciation for Beukeboom.

The chant—in this case, a cheer that referenced Jeff's last name—was heard every time Beukeboom delivered a crushing check or helped kill a penalty. The fans loved their gritty No. 23 and showered him with affection throughout the 1990s—not bad for a player who was just an afterthought at the end of a much bigger trade.

Beukeboom was born on March 28, 1965, in Ajax, Ontario. As a teenager, he played Junior B hockey in Newmarket, where he totaled a whopping 218 penalty minutes *in only 49 games.*

The big guy made a name for himself soon after his start in Junior hockey. The young defenseman joined the Sault Ste. Marie Greyhounds in Ontario, a club that had recently featured such luminaries as goalie John Vanbiesbrouck and "The Great One" himself, Wayne Gretzky.

Jeff immediately established himself as a rock on defense, and slowly but surely his game improved enough to gain notice from Edmonton scouts.

The Oilers chose Beukeboom as the 19th pick of the NHL entry draft in 1983,

and the next year he played for Canada at the World Junior Cup.

Two seasons later, Beukeboom made his debut in professional hockey for the Nova Scotia Oilers of the American League. Given a chance to shine, Beukeboom excelled, playing such stellar defense that he was named to the First All-Star Team. The young defenseman played so well that Edmonton brought him up to dress for one playoff game.

The next year, Jeff was in the NHL for good and continued to shine at hockey's highest level. While stars such as Gretzky, Mark Messier, Paul Coffey, and Jari Kurri received the accolades, Beukeboom's quiet but efficient defending was no less important to the Oilers' continued success. In three of his first four years—1987, 1988, and 1990—Beukeboom helped Edmonton bring home the Stanley Cup.

All signs indicated that Beukeboom would have a long career in Edmonton, but economic circumstances dictated otherwise. By the 1991-92 season, the Oilers' management was ready for a fire sale. Having already dealt Gretzky to the Los Angeles Kings three years earlier, Edmonton now decided to unload its other star, Mark Messier. On October 4, 1991, Messier was headed to Broadway in exchange for Bernie Nicholls, Steven Rice, and Louie DeBrusk. The deal allowed for future considerations on both sides in order to complete the transaction. Five weeks later, the Oilers sent Beukeboom to the Rangers for David Shaw, closing the Messier deal and giving Beukeboom the career break of a lifetime.

Traded from a franchise in decline to one on the rise, Beukeboom was quickly integrated into the New York backline along with a young Brian Leetch. As soon as he stepped onto the ice at the Garden, Jeff made an indelible impression on Rangers fans. At 6-foot-5, 230 pounds, Beukeboom had the prototypical defenseman's body, and he put that body to good use. His crashing bodychecks quickly became a Madison Square Garden staple, and the fans grew to love the brawny backliner.

Over the next two seasons, Beukeboom became the team's enforcer. He accumulated over 100 penalty minutes in every season with New York, except during the strike-shortened 1994-95 campaign. His physical play meshed perfectly with Leetch's expert puck-handling, and the two formed a formidable twosome in front of goalie Mike Richter.

When the Rangers completed their magical run to the Stanley Cup championship in 1994, Beukeboom was a key player. Having won three Cups in Edmonton, Jeff, like Mark Messier, had

the playoff experience so many career Rangers lacked. And while the '94 Cup was Beukeboom's fourth, it was certainly the most historic.

Beukeboom continued his successful play for New York well after the 1994 Cup win, netting a career-high 220 penalty minutes in the 1995-96 season. He made an impression off the ice as well, working for many charities, including the Ice Hockey in Harlem program.

"We all have an obligation to give something back, especially athletes and others who serve as role models for kids," said Beukeboom. "It's extremely important. I was especially lucky to do so much for IHIH, because there I watched kids mature and develop in the sport that I love so much." For his generosity, Jeff was awarded the Rangers Crumb Bum Award for service to local youth in 1996.

The sky seemed the limit for Jeff until he was on the wrong end of a sucker punch delivered by Matt Johnson of the Los Angeles Kings in November 1998. Johnson received a 12-game suspension, but the blow effectively ended Beukeboom's major-league career.

Though Beukeboom returned after a few games, the injury and his physical style of play left him predisposed to more concussions. After suffering another in February 1999, Jeff began experiencing recurrent headaches, memory loss, nausea, and mental fogginess. Doctors diagnosed it as post-concussion syndrome and ordered him never to play hockey again.

With that, Beukeboom's career came to a sudden and sad end. The fallout from the concussion was severe:

JEFF BEUKEBOOM

BORN: Ajax, Ontario, Canada; March 28, 1965

POSITION: Defenseman

NHL TEAMS: Edmonton Oilers, 1985-91; New York Rangers, 1991-99

AWARDS/HONORS: OHL First Team All-Star, 1985

he continued suffering post-concussion symptoms for two years before finally recovering in 2002.

Fortunately, after his post-hockey career, Jeff continued helping others and was a frequent visitor to Rangers games at Madison Square Garden, where fans remembered him for what he was—an honest blocker who brought honor to the Rangers uniform.

FRANK BOUCHER
1 9 2 6 - 1 9 3 8

Perhaps the saddest aspect of Frank Boucher's hockey life is that so little of his exploits are remembered today. Among those most synonymous with the Rangers' success, Boucher ranks in the top rung as both a player and coach.

One could make the argument that no one surpassed Boucher when it came to combining clean play with artistry on the ice. In that regard, he had no equals.

As an intuitive hockey mind, Boucher constantly impressed critics with his endless creativity, first as a center for two Stanley Cup teams and then as a coach piloting the Blueshirts to the club's third Stanley Cup championship in 1940.

In addition, Boucher was most responsible for revising and modernizing the NHL rulebook during the World War II years, when the league added the center red line to increase scoring.

Boucher was more than a super-clean stickhandler. He was also a clutch scorer who steered the Rangers to a pair of division titles, three second-place finishes, and four appearances in the Stanley Cup finals as well as the two Stanley Cups. And he was the pivotal force on what many observers regard as *the* most proficient line in NHL history—Boucher centered for Bill and Bun Cook.

Among other plays, Boucher and the Cooks invented the drop pass. Right wing Bill would steer a puck carrier to Boucher, who would hook the puck away. Bun would then race down to his wing, where Frank would flip the puck to him. "As soon as he crossed the other team's blue line," said Boucher, "he faked a shot, drawing a defenseman to him. Then he left the puck for me, coming in fast behind him."

Frank and the Cooks were part of the original Rangers team that made its NHL debut in the 1926-27 season. Previously, he had played professionally with the Ottawa Senators and the Vancouver Maroons.

When Madison Square Garden decided to add its own team to its original hockey tenant, the New York Americans, Conn Smythe, a Toronto sportsman, was asked to select the talent. Smythe spoke to Bill Cook, who in turn recommended Boucher.

Boucher only weighed 134 pounds when he met Smythe prior to training camp. At that point, the talent scout anxiously eyed the seemingly frail athlete and then asked Frank how much he weighed. Boucher allowed that he was about 135 pounds.

"I paid $15,000 for *you*" Smythe groaned. "Bill Cook must be crazy."

Smythe eventually signed Boucher to a contract but never had a chance to see Boucher grow as a Ranger. Prior to training camp, Smythe had a falling out with the Garden brass and was replaced as Rangers boss by the courtly and insightful Lester Patrick. When the new club convened for training camp at Toronto's old Ravina Gardens, Patrick called Boucher to him and said, "I'm going to try you at center between Bill and Bunny Cook."

Patrick never had cause to change his mind. The unit remained intact in Rangers uniforms for 10 years. Unlike today's units, who take the ice for one-minute stretches and are then replaced, Boucher and the Cooks worked almost the entire game.

Frank Boucher was born October 7, 1901, in Ottawa, Ontario. He and his brothers, George, Carroll, Billy, Joe, and Bobby, learned to skate and play hockey on the snow-bordered Rideau Canal. "We played from dawn until dark," Frank recalled, "and in all kinds of weather, even 40 degrees below zero. It was best after your toes froze; they turned numb and didn't bother you anymore—until later."

It was no accident that Boucher developed a meticulously clean style of play. His idol as a kid was Frank Nighbor, a star with the Ottawa Senators.

LEFT: Frank Boucher met with great success as both a player and coach for the Rangers. *From the Stan Fischler Collection*

FRANK BOUCHER

BORN: Ottawa, Ontario, Canada; October 7, 1901

DIED: December 12, 1977

POSITION: Center

NHL TEAMS: Ottawa Senators, 1921-22; New York Rangers, 1926-38

AWARDS/HONORS: Lady Byng Memorial Trophy, 1928-31, 1933-35 (trophy awarded to him in perpetuity, 1935, and second trophy donated); NHL First Team All-Star, 1933-35; NHL Second Team All-Star, 1931; NHL All-Star Game, 1937; Hockey Hall of Fame, 1958

"Nighbor," said Boucher, "was every young lad's hero in Ottawa those days. He was a magnificent center who rarely lost his temper and who could hook check and poke check like nobody else."

Nighbor's influence must have found its reflection in the years that followed. Playing at a time when hockey was infinitely more rugged than today's game, Boucher engaged in only one fight in his 10-year NHL career—in his very first game at Madison Square Garden against the Maroons. Bill Phillips, a square-set, rugged player, singled Frank out and flattened him early in the game. In the third period, he and Phillips tangled again.

"I had simply too much of him," said Boucher. "We threw aside our sticks and our gloves and went at each other. The crowd was standing and roaring and he knocked me down, and I got up and knocked him down, and he got up and we grabbed each other and swung wearily. When the referee separated us, he sent us off with major penalties—five minutes each. It was as rough as I ever played.

"My philosophy always had been that fighting never solved anything—provided you didn't back down if you had to stand up. I was the one who swung at Phillips. I was the first Ranger ever to get a major penalty. Still, it was my last fight, too."

Boucher continued playing until 1938, when he accepted Lester Patrick's suggestion that he turn to coaching. Patrick gave him control of the New York Rovers, the Rangers' farm club in the Eastern Hockey League. Frank was an instant success as a coach after playing for 17 years, four with the Vancouver Maroons, one with the Ottawa Senators, and 12 with the Rangers. He had led the Rangers in scoring five seasons and was named to the NHL All-Star Team three times.

After one year in which he steered the Rovers to a spectacularly successful campaign, Boucher was named coach of the Rangers, succeeding Patrick, who concentrated on managing the club. "The team Lester gave me," said Boucher, "was the best hockey team I ever saw."

In March 1940, Frank's rookie year as coach, the Rangers won their third Stanley Cup.

Boucher's awesome Rangers club was decimated by World War II and plunged to the bottom of the league. During the 1943-44 season, at age 42, Frank brought himself out of retirement and played 15 games.

His legs were obviously gone, but the creative mind still functioned on the ice, and he managed to produce four goals and 10 assists in 15 games. Although he hadn't played a game in five years, Frank outscored *19* other players the Rangers had tried that season.

Boucher eventually succeeded Patrick as Rangers general manager after World War II and kept the position until 1955. Frank's farm system produced such Hall of Famers as Lorne Worsley, Harry Howell, Andy Bathgate, and Allan Stanley.

Those who had the good fortune to enjoy Boucher's skill never forgot his excellent exploits, including Foster Hewitt, long considered the original dean of hockey announcers. During the Team Canada-Soviet All-Stars series of 1972, Hewitt was asked if he had ever seen anything to match the dazzling Russian skaters.

"There aren't many people around to remember," Hewitt told Canadian columnist Trent Frayne, "but the way the Russians play reminds me of the old Rangers, especially the line of Boucher and the Cooks, They were even better than the Russians. When Frank, Bill, and Bunny were on the ice, it always seemed to me they had the puck on a string."

Frank Boucher was one of the most magnificent hockey players ever to grace an arena. Fortunately, he spent his entire career as a Ranger.

NEIL COLVILLE

Before the United States entered World War II, the Rangers had organized one of the best forward lines in the National Hockey League. It comprised Alex Shibicky and the Colville brothers, Neil and Mac.

The trio was instrumental in leading the Rangers to the 1940 Stanley Cup championship as well as finishing first in the 1941-42 season.

Playing the center position, Neil Colville was the balance wheel of the trio, a tall, stately figure who impressed with his skill as much as his size.

Sportswriters dubbed the trio the "Bread Line," signifying that the three players were the bread and butter in the success of the New York Rangers in the late 1930s and early 1940s. Everyday folk could relate to the nickname, because people suffering during the Great Depression stood on breadlines to get food to eat.

Had the war not decimated the Rangers' lineup more than any NHL team, it is likely that the Colvilles and Shibicky would have emerged as the dominant line in the league.

Unfortunately, all three enlisted in the Canadian Armed Forces, leaving a gap that the Blueshirts were never able to fill throughout the international conflict.

It was the hope of Rangers coach Frank Boucher that, at war's end, the Colville line would regain its pre-war luster and lift the Blueshirts out of the non-playoff morass.

But it wasn't to be.

Both Shibicky and Mac Colville had lost the touch that had propelled them to such heights during the Cup year and thereafter. Each exited the league after a brief flirtation with a comeback.

Without his brother, Mac, and buddy, Alex, Neil Colville returned with a flourish but in a totally new position.

Boucher got the bright idea to insert Colville on defense, and Neil immediately adapted to his new role.

Neil Colville was born on August 4, 1914, in Edmonton, Alberta, and began his minor-league career with the Eastern Hockey League's Brooklyn Crescents. From Brooklyn, Neil moved up to Philadelphia to play for the American League's Ramblers. His final pit stop would be on Broadway in a Blueshirts uniform.

Never the best offensive player on the squad, Neil would always finish in second or third place in the team's scoring race. Throughout his first five NHL seasons, Colville's production improved from 28 points to 36, 37, 38, and a career-high 42 in 1940-41.

During his career, Neil amassed 99 regular-season goals, barely missing the 100-goal plateau. The Edmonton, Alberta, native did not score 20 goals during any season in his career, although he had put the puck behind opposing goaltenders 19 times when the Rangers completed their Stanley Cup–winning 1940 campaign.

Modest regular-season production would not deter Colville from scoring when the Rangers desperately needed goals in the playoffs. In 1940, for instance, he tied Phil Watson as the team's postseason leader in points scored with nine in 12 contests.

In the twilight of his career, Neil enjoyed some of his finest hours due in part to an excellent trade made by Boucher, which brought defenseman Frankie Eddolls to Broadway, where he paired with Colville. It was one of those perfect matches in which their styles blended along with their personalities.

As a result, Neil earned a spot on the NHL's Second All-Star Team. Cool, calm, and collected, Colville had a soothing effect on his teammates when the going got rough.

Thus, it was no surprise that he was named Rangers captain in 1945-46 and retained the "C" through the 1948-49 season.

By then, age had taken its toll, and following the 1948-49 campaign, Neil officially retired.

When the Rangers went to the Stanley Cup finals with Detroit—losing in double overtime in Game 7—Colville's former teammate, Lynn Patrick, was the Rangers' coach.

But in the summer of 1950, Patrick clashed with the team's management over a new contract, leaving the team to coach the rival Boston Bruins. Colville seemed a natural to succeed Patrick and was named head coach of the team.

Patrick's was a tough act to follow, but Colville's problems proved to be even larger. A series of injuries and bad luck took its toll on the team and the coach. Because of health problems, Neil decided that it was best that he retire and left the Blueshirts after the 1950-51 season.

Colville was inducted into the Hockey Hall of Fame in 1967, seven years after his death.

While Neil cannot be compared to legendary Rangers defensemen such as Brian Leetch and Ching Johnson, he nevertheless distinguished himself on the blue line and as a crackerjack forward.

Not many Rangers can make that statement!

NEIL COLVILLE

BORN: Edmonton, Alberta, Canada; August 4, 1914

DIED: December 26, 1987

POSITION: Defenseman/ Center

NHL TEAMS: New York Rangers, 1935-49

AWARDS/HONORS: NHL Second Team All-Star, 1939-40, 1948; Hockey Hall of Fame, 1967

BILL COOK

Contemporary hockey followers hardly know Bill Cook—few have even heard of him—and that's a crying shame. If he wasn't the greatest right wing in Rangers history—and many who saw him think he was—Cook certainly ranks right up there.

Unfortunately, there are precious few observers still around who remember the manner in which Cook delivered sizzling goals, punished foes with bodychecks, and helped the Rangers win their first two Stanley Cups in 1928 and 1933.

Battle-hardened in World War I, Bill Cook was more than ready to take on the ice wars after turning professional in the early 1920s.

As opponents would soon learn, Cook's toughness was matched only by his scoring prowess.

Though he would eventually establish his greatness as a member of the Rangers, Cook originally caught the attention of hockey experts while playing for the Saskatoon Crescents of the Pacific Coast Hockey Association.

Upon signing with Lester Patrick's Broadway Blueshirts, Bill and his younger brother—nicknamed Bun—would become an instant hit on Eighth Avenue.

The glint-eyed, well-proportioned Bill Cook took the game every bit as seriously as legendary Maurice Richard and fought his foes as grimly as the great Gordie Howe. "He was," said Frank Boucher, "the finest all-around player in Rangers history."

Unfortunately, Cook did not make his National Hockey League debut until he was 30, an age at which other players were retiring. He won the NHL scoring championship in his rookie year and repeated in 1933 at the age of 37!

A series of unavoidable circumstances delayed Cook's ascent to the NHL clouds. A farm boy from Kingston, Ontario, his hockey skills were sufficient to earn him a professional invitation by the time he was 20, but duty came first. With the outbreak of World War I, Bill enlisted in the Canadian Army and was assigned to a field artillery unit overseas.

Upon returning home, his reward was a soldier's allotment of land in Saskatchewan. But the life of an agriculturalist was not stimulating enough for him, so Cook resumed his hockey career with Saskatoon of the Western League in

BILL COOK

BORN: Brantford, Ontario, Canada; October 9, 1896

DIED: April 6, 1986

POSITION: Right Wing

NHL TEAMS: New York Rangers, 1926-37

AWARDS/HONORS: NHL First Team All-Star, 1931-33; NHL Second Team All-Star, 1934; Art Ross Trophy, 1927, 1933; Hockey Hall of Fame, 1952

1922. It was fast company—Eddie Shore and Frank Boucher were among other top-flight opponents—and Cook established himself among the best. When Madison Square Garden moguls decided to organize the Rangers and asked Conn Smythe to do the recruiting, Bill and his brother, Bun Cook, were his first choices.

Cook wasted no time establishing his credentials in the club's first game. Skating against the champion Montreal Maroons, the Rangers held them to a scoreless tie until Bill and Bunny broke away against Clint Benedict, the Montreal goalie. Bun took the first shot, but Benedict made the save. He retrieved the rebound and tapped the puck to Bill, who flicked the rubber over the fallen goalie.

As the red light glowed, Benedict crumpled to the ice, momentarily stunned by his crash into the goal post. A short delay was necessary for the netminder to recoup.

"During this lull," Boucher remembered, "the crowd stayed on its feet, cheering and clapping for the Cooks and refusing to sit until Benedict returned to finish the period."

Bill had scored the winning goal in a match that tickled the fancy of New York hockey fans and instantly gave the Rangers, along with their rivals, the New York Americans, credibility. The Rangers had one advantage, and that was the Cooks-Boucher line, which combined like perfectly meshed gears.

Although Boucher and Bunny were critical to the line's success, Bill had the commanding personality and gave the unit a Pattonesque leadership.

"When the three of us got together to discuss strategy," said Boucher, "Bill would give the orders. Once, he said, 'When I want that puck, I'll yell for it, and you get that damn puck to me when I yell.'

"On the ice, Bill's cry was the most amazing half-grunt, half-moan, half-yell that I ever heard. He'd let this weird sound out of him, meaning that he was in the clear."

Cook, who was a superior player to brother Bunny, was named to the NHL First All-Star Team in 1931, 1932, and 1933. In any debate over the best forward line in hockey history, the Cooks-Boucher line would, at the very worst, rank among the top three and certainly would obtain votes as *the* best. Both Bunny and Boucher were good shooters, but Bill's shot was more potent than his linemates'.

"Bill didn't have a bullet shot," Boucher explained, "or at least not a *long* bullet shot like the golf-style slap shot Bobby Hull perfected. But he had a very hard wrist shot from close in and could score equally well backhand or forehand."

Over 11 seasons—at a time when the NHL played a short schedule—Bill scored 229 goals and was a conspicuous contributor to the Rangers' Stanley Cup wins in 1928 and 1933. The most striking similarity between Cook's play and Gordie Howe's was in their aggressive

RIGHT: Bill Cook ranks as one of the greatest right-wingers in New York Rangers history
From the Stan Fischler Collection

nature. Some journalists referred to the right wing as "Bad Bill," who had enough episodes to support the nickname.

The most sinister incident by far involved Cook and Nels Crutchfield, a Montreal Canadiens rookie who had made the jump from McGill University to the NHL. Their fateful collision took place during a playoff game in 1935 after Crutchfield—according to Cook—had committed several fouls without being penalized.

"Crutchfield was interfering with me throughout the game, and the referee wouldn't do anything about it," said Cook. "So I finally caught Crutchfield with the butt end of my stick. Then he hit me right on the bean with his stick. The next thing I saw was a million stars."

Crutchfield's two blows could have killed Cook, but he avoided catastrophe by instinctively deflecting each clout with his arm. "When I finally came around," said Bill, "all I saw was the stockings of the players who were scrapping. I never saw so many people getting belted on the ice."

What Bill didn't see was his brother, Bunny, leading the Rangers' charge over the boards. Boucher sensed that Bunny wanted to murder Crutchfield and rather subtly stuck his skate out, tripping Bun a few feet short of his intended victim. "Frank told me," said Bill, "that he had to stop my brother, or he would have killed Crutchfield."

After eight stitches had been embroidered in Bill's wounds, he returned to the bench. "I was kind of groggy," he admitted, "but I wanted to finish the game."

The Rangers' doctor outfitted him with a makeshift helmet, and Bill finally took his position on the right side of Boucher. Late in the game, he gained control of the puck and bobbed and weaved his way through the Canadiens' defense to score the game-winning goal. Bill maintained that the play ranked in his top two greatest thrills in hockey—the other being the winning goal he scored against Toronto in 1933 to provide the Rangers with their second Stanley Cup title.

The Cooks and Boucher had become popular heroes alongside Babe Ruth and Lou Gehrig in the well-publicized New York sports fraternity. Writing for the *New York Sun,* journalist Harold C. Burr composed this ditty:

"Old adages live because they are true:

If they weren't they wouldn't survive.

But once in a while there are a few That shouldn't be kept alive.

In hockey, where speed and grit hold forth,

Some sayings sound awfully funny.

'Too many cooks spoil the broth.'

Did you ever meet Bill and Bunny?"

William Osser Cook was born October 9, 1896, in Brantford, Ontario, and learned the essential hockey skills on the frozen outdoor tracks near his family's home. The rugged farm life helped steel him for the ice wars ahead and accounted, in part, for Cook's longevity as a professional. He played regularly for the Rangers until 1938, when he was named player-assistant to Lester Patrick at the age of 41.

> "WHEN I WANT THAT PUCK, I'LL YELL FOR IT, AND YOU GET THAT DAMN PUCK TO ME WHEN I YELL."

When a coaching job became available with the Cleveland Barons of the American Hockey League, Bill left the Rangers. In 1951, his old pal, Boucher, who had become Rangers manager, asked Bill to coach the slumping New York sextet. Rangers president General John Reed Kilpatrick hoped that Bill could revive the Rangers, but he couldn't. He was fired in 1952—the same year he was inducted into the Hockey Hall of Fame—on Kilpatrick's orders. Bill blamed Boucher, and for three years, they wouldn't talk until they met one night at a banquet. Bill threw his arms around Boucher's shoulders and said, "What the hell, Frankie, it's been too many years. Let's forget the whole thing."

Nobody should forget that Bill Cook was one of the NHL's definitive right wings.

BUN COOK

1 9 2 6 - 1 9 3 6

Ever since its inception, the National Hockey League has been blessed with excellent brother acts. The Chicago Blackhawks featured two Hall of Fame forwards, Max and Doug Bentley, who skated on the same line. More recently, Bobby and Dennis Hull, one of the best one-two combos ever seen, graced the Windy City.

In some cases—the Hulls are a good example—one brother clearly outshined the other.

This was also the case with Rangers brothers Bill and Frederick, or Bun, Cook.

Considered by many to be the finest right wing in Rangers history, Bill outshone his left-wing brother in terms of goals scored, but that in no way detracted from Bun's major contributions to the team.

The hard-nosed forward did all the "dirty" work on the line, which included excellent back checking and significant physical work at all ends of the ice.

Most importantly, Bun was the perfect third gear on a line that meshed better than virtually any other in NHL annals.

Bill and Bun ideally complemented their artistic, crafty center, Frank Boucher. One could legitimately say that none of the trio could have been successful without the others' contributions.

GREATEST MOMENTS AND PLAYERS

Together, Bill, Bun, and Boucher excelled from the 1926-27 season through the 1935-36 campaign. The three combined to form what was dubbed the "Bread Line," which today stands as the only Rangers line in which each player has been enshrined in the Hockey Hall of Fame.

Bun himself was a deft passer who could muck his way into the corners with the best of them. He was an original Ranger, taking part in the franchise's first 10 seasons from 1926-27 until 1935-36 and playing on two Stanley Cup championship teams.

Frederick received the nickname Bun—short for Bunny—because he had a habit of making hopping motions like a rabbit on his skates in order to gain momentum.

The younger brother of Bill and the older brother of Bud Cook (who also played in the NHL), Bun's influence on the game of hockey is an important one.

Bun is credited with the creation of two important hockey moves. One is the drop pass. Bun once explained, "I had a dream about the drop pass one night, and at our next practice, I told Frank and Bill about it. They thought I was crazy, but they decided to humor me. By gosh, it worked!

"I'd cross over from left wing to center as I moved in on defense. I'd fake a shot and leave the puck behind and skate away from it with Frank or Bill picking it up. We got a lot of goals off the crisscross and drop pass."

Bun's other development was the beginning of the slap shot. Bun did not use the move as often as Bernie "Boom Boom" Geoffrion or Bobby Hull, but he used it effectively and with an element of surprise.

Eight years younger than Bill, Bun was always following in his brother's footsteps. Bill joined the Sault Ste. Marie Greyhounds of the Northern Ontario Hockey Association in 1920. The next year, Bun was also on the team. He would eventually win the Allan Cup with the Greyhounds during the 1923-24 season, but by then Bill had moved on to play for the Saskatoon Crescents of the professional Western Canada Hockey League. Again, Bun was not far behind and joined the Crescents in 1924-25.

This trend was finally broken when the Cook brothers were signed together by then Rangers manager Conn Smythe. In order to buy rights to the duo, the Rangers shelled out $30,000—an investment well worth the price. While Bill put up the better statistics, Bun quietly carved out a niche for himself, playing 433 games in Broadway Blue while scoring 154 goals and 293 points.

BUN COOK

BORN: Kingston, Ontario, Canada; September 18, 1903

DIED: March 19, 1988

POSITION: Left Wing

NHL TEAMS: New York Rangers, 1926-36; Boston Bruins 1936-37

AWARDS/HONORS: NHL Second Team All-Star, 1931; Hockey Hall of Fame, 1995

"I HAD A DREAM
ABOUT THE DROP
PASS ONE NIGHT.
AND AT OUR
NEXT PRACTICE. I
TOLD FRANK AND
BILL ABOUT IT.
THEY THOUGHT I
WAS CRAZY BUT
THEY DECIDED
TO HUMOR ME.
BY GOSH, IT
WORKED!"

Bun had a tremendous influence with the Rangers' first general manager and coach, Lester Patrick. During the already strange 1928 Stanley Cup finals (the Rangers played all of the games on the road because of the circus) when the Rangers played the Montreal Maroons, Bun, along with Boucher, convinced the 44-year-old Patrick to take over in goal when netminder Lorne Chabot was injured and could not continue playing. Patrick only played that one game, but Bun and the Rangers went on to win the Stanley Cup in only the team's second year of existence.

Bun was also a prominent voice in convincing Patrick to sign his youngest son, Lynn, to a contract.

Bun was still with the Rangers when the team won its second Stanley Cup in

1932-33, but was forced out of the lineup a few seasons later. During the 1935-36 season, he was sent to the sidelines by a recurring throat problem, and his last campaign with the Blueshirts was shortened to only 26 games, a career low for appearances in a season.

The Boston Bruins picked up Bun for the 1936-37 season. He appeared in 40 games for Boston during this campaign and then retired.

Bun then moved down to the minor leagues and made a name for himself as a coach in the AHL. First, Bun took a position with the Providence Reds. He spent six campaigns with Providence, winning the Calder Cup twice—including one in his first season behind the bench.

Then, as he had so many times before, Bun followed Bill and took over for his brother as the coach of the Cleveland Barons, where he spent the next 13 seasons.

During this time, the Barons failed to make the playoffs as often as the sun forgets to rise—which is to say, never. Bun led the Barons to eight AHL finals appearances, winning the Calder Cup five times.

Bun Cook was enshrined into the AHL Hall of Fame in 2007 for his magnificent coaching ability. He has more Calder Cup victories than any other coach in history. Bun won this title seven times, shattering the runner-up record of three. He is the most victorious coach in league history with a record of 636-413-122. He is also second in games coached (1,171) and postseason victories (75). According to an AHL announcement when he was inducted in 2007, Bun was "the most prolific coach ever to work an AHL bench."

The inventive player is also a member of two other Halls of Fame. He was placed in the International Hockey Hall of Fame in 1966 and the Hockey Hall of Fame in Toronto in 1995, seven years after his death.

ART COULTER

1 9 3 5 - 1 9 4 2

President Teddy Roosevelt once coined an expression, "Speak softly and carry a big stick." That could well have been Art Coulter's theme when he captained the Rangers to the 1940 Stanley Cup championship.

A tough hombre if ever there was one, Coulter might have continued starring in the NHL had World War II not intervened.

Coulter began his career with the Chicago Blackhawks in 1931, moving to Broadway in 1935 when he was signed by Rangers boss Lester Patrick.

Although he played a solid game, Coulter did not at first seem to be a future Hall of Famer.

The turnabout came when veteran Ranger Frank Boucher noticed that a problem seemed to exist between Patrick and Coulter.

"I asked Lester what was wrong between him and Art," Boucher recalled, "and he said he didn't seem to be able to get through to him. I suggested that Art, being a man of tall pride, should be made captain of the team. If Lester did this and took Art into his confidence, I was convinced the change would benefit Coulter psychologically."

Patrick agreed, and the move seemed to be a tonic to the new Ranger. In no time at all, Coulter became a mountain of strength behind the New York blue line. He was a Second Team All-Star in 1938, 1939 and 1940. Coulter was also a force behind the Rangers' first-place team in 1941-42, the last time the New Yorkers finished atop the National Hockey League.

Tall and muscular and without a trace of fat, Coulter was teamed on defense with Lester Patrick's bruising son, Murray, also known as Muzz. Any forward who attempted to bisect that defense was guaranteed a surplus of black and blue marks.

As tough as Coulter and Patrick were on the ice, they were sweethearts in civilian clothes. Both enjoyed the good life on Broadway, and Art in particular had a reputation as a free spender.

During the Great Depression, the Rangers players were to travel in groups of four in taxis. One of them was named "cab captain" and in charge of the fares. Coulter was one of those cab captains.

One day, after the Rangers had completed a road trip, Patrick invited all his cab captains into his office so that he could review the various receipts that the players were required to obtain from the taxi drivers. Patrick was unmoved as

ART COULTER

BORN: Winnipeg, Manitoba, Canada; May 31, 1909

DIED: October 14, 2000

POSITION: Defenseman

NHL TEAMS: Chicago Blackhawks, 1931-35; New York Rangers, 1935-42

AWARDS/HONORS: NHL Second Team All-Star, 1938-40; Hockey Hall of Fame, 1974

"YOU'VE TOLD US THAT WE'RE IN THE BIG LEAGUES NOW, SO I TIP LIKE A BIG-LEAGUER."

he noted receipts ranging from six to eight dollars, but he did a double take when Coulter handed him a chit that totaled $12.75.

"Art," Patrick inquired, "why is your bill so much large than the others?" "Well, Lester," Coulter replied, "you've told us that we're in the big leagues now, so I tip like a big leaguer." Patrick didn't bat an eyelash. "That's very commendable, Art," he shot back, "but I don't know if the Rangers can afford big tippers like you."

Art chuckled. "Okay, Lester. You have nothing to worry about. I resign my captaincy."

According to journalist Eric Whitehead, who wrote *The Patricks, Hockey's Royal Family,* Coulter retained the captain's "C" on his jersey. This permitted Art to play a part in an extraordinary Rangers conference held the night before the Broadway skaters in 1940 annexed the Stanley Cup at Maple Leaf Gardens in Toronto.

Whitehead described it thusly: "The Blues had finished three points behind Boston in the league race, had ousted the Bruins in the first playoff round, and now had the Toronto Maple Leafs down three games to two in the final round. The superb goal-tending of veteran Davey Kerr and a strong defense anchored by Babe Pratt and Ott Heller had been the principal factors in getting the Blues this far, and now a win in the upcoming sixth game in Toronto with the Leafs would wrap it up."

Frank Boucher, who had become the Rangers' coach, invited his players to the beer parlor of the Ford Hotel. While this may have seemed an unusual place for a team meeting, the gregarious Boucher figured it would set a mellow tone during an anxious time.

"Captain Coulter opened with a toast," wrote Whitehead, "Coach Boucher responded by raising his ale glass, there was a rousing 'hear . . . hear . . .' from the troops, then a reverent silence as the steins were drained. This, oft repeated, was the extent of the team-meeting agenda, laced, of course, with convivial conversation, the odd burst of ribald laughter, and even an occasionally more or less scholarly reference to the upcoming game against the Leafs."

Clearly, the psychology worked. "It was," said Coulter, "a loosener. The team had been playing great hockey and wanted no part of a seventh game in Toronto. The only danger was that of getting a little uptight and pressing too hard."

"The next evening," wrote Whitehead, "everybody was beautifully loose and relaxed as the game started. And at the end of the first period, the Rangers were down 2-0 after fast goals by Syl Apps and Nick Metz. Lester came into the dressing room, sat down on a bench beside goalie Davey Kerr, and said quietly, 'Well, boys, you've had your fun. Now let's get down to business. I've made arrangements for a victory party in the Tudor Room of the Royal York. I'll see you there. Don't let me down.'"

The Rangers rallied to tie the score at 2-2 and then won the deciding game on Bryan Hextall's shot in sudden-death overtime. Understandably, Hextall captured the attention at that stupendous moment in Rangers history, but the bosses, Patrick and Boucher, understood that the New Yorkers would never have made it that far without the leadership and skill displayed by Coulter.

Arthur Edmund Coulter was born on May 31, 1909, in Winnipeg, Manitoba. Like so many Rangers, he honed his hockey skills to sharpness on Winnipeg's outdoor rinks before becoming a professional in 1929.

The Blackhawks signed him in 1931, and ironically, he teamed with one-time Rangers star, Taffy Abel, on the Windy City's blue line. The pair starred on Chicago's first ever Stanley Cup championship team in 1934.

Upon joining the Rangers, Coulter was nicknamed "the Trapper" because he would talk about fishing and hunting by the hour. When Boucher, as coach, introduced a revolutionary offensive penalty-killing team in 1939, Coulter was the anchorman with forwards Alex Shibicky and Neil and Mac Colville. So effective was the system that, over the course of the season, the Rangers outscored their opponents almost two to one when they were shorthanded.

> "IT WAS A LOOSENER. THE TEAM HAD BEEN PLAYING GREAT HOCKEY AND WANTED NO PART OF A SEVENTH GAME IN TORONTO. THE ONLY DANGER WAS THAT OF GETTING A LITTLE UPTIGHT AND PRESSING TOO HARD."

Following the Rangers' first-place finish in 1942, Coulter enlisted in the U.S. Coast Guard at a time when that branch of service had established a hockey team—the Cutters—at its base in Curtis Bay (near Baltimore), Maryland.

NEW YORK RANGERS

A number of experienced hockey professionals, including Frankie Brimsek of the Boston Bruins and Johnny Mariucci of the Chicago Blackhawks, also joined the Cutters sextet, which played in the Eastern Hockey League. Not surprisingly, Coulter was once again at the helm of a championship team; the Cutters finished atop the Eastern League and Art was in vintage form.

The Coast Guard sextet won two straight U.S. Senior Hockey championships before it was disbanded when the sailors went off to war.

Coulter retired as an active player at war's end and eventually moved to Florida. One of the game's genuinely overshadowed heroes, Coulter was elected to the Hockey Hall of Fame in 1974. Few were better at playing tough on the blue line.

JOHN DAVIDSON

1 9 7 5 - 1 9 8 3

Charisma comes in different forms with different athletes—and often has little to do with quality of play.

Charismatic Rangers such as Alex Kaleta and Gene Carr had little in the way of productivity, yet Blueshirts fans took them into their hearts because of the dazzling manner in which they carried themselves on the ice.

But a special class of magnetic players blended high-quality play with the ability to win over the fans. John Davidson was one such individual.

Ever since his Junior hockey days as a teenage prodigy among goaltenders in Calgary, the man they came to call J.D. was intensely eyed by NHL bird-dogs because of his extraordinary puck-stopping potential.

It was the Rangers' good fortune to land the Ottawa native after he enjoyed a brief stint with the St. Louis Blues.

Although he wasn't an instant hit at Madison Square Garden when he arrived in New York in the mid-1970s, he eventually became a strong fan favorite. By the 1978-79 season, it was clear that Davidson had Hall of Fame potential provided he could steer clear of the injury bug.

Clearly, John reached his professional apex in the spring of 1979.

This was the year in which the New York Islanders were—according to many experts—*supposed* to win the Stanley Cup.

Fortified with such stars as Bryan Trottier, Denis Potvin, Mike Bossy, and Bill Smith, the Isles appeared to have the ideal formula. But what they didn't have was John Davidson. The mustachioed Rangers netminder frustrated the Islanders' assault team time and again as the Blueshirts upset their traditional rival in six playoff games.

Davidson was the toast of Times Square as the Rangers marched into the final round against the Montreal Canadiens. The series opened at the Forum in Montreal, and lo and behold, Davidson sparked his club to a 4-1 victory.

JOHN DAVIDSON

BORN: Ottawa, Ontario, Canada; February 27, 1953

POSITION: Goaltender

NHL TEAMS: St. Louis Blues, 1973-1975; New York Rangers, 1975-1983

AWARDS/HONORS: Lester Patrick Trophy, 2004

Visions of a Stanley Cup danced in the heads of New York fans, especially after the Rangers jumped to an early lead in Game 2, also at the Forum.

But the Cup wasn't to be brought to Broadway after all. Montreal rallied to win the second contest and then swept the series.

Few realized it at the time, but Davidson—already bedeviled with injuries—would never be the same star again. He played three more seasons before packing away his pads and turning to a pursuit he never would have dreamed of during his playing days: broadcasting. But we'll get to that in a moment.

The fifth overall draft pick—selected behind Denis Potvin, Tom Lysiak, Dennis Ververgaert, and Lanny McDonald—by the St. Louis Blues in 1973, Davidson, at the tender age of 20, became the first goaltender in history to make the National Hockey League straight from the Junior ranks.

While growing up in Canada, Davidson competed for Calgary of the WCHL and Lethbridge of the AJHL,

playing left wing until he was moved to goaltender at the age of 16.

In 1975, Davidson was traded to the Rangers along with Bill Collins as the Blueshirts shipped Ted Irvine, Bert Wilson, and Jerry Butler to St. Louis. It was a fortuitous trade for New York. Davidson played 56 games in his first season as a Ranger but was not in the spotlight as much as he would be at the start of the 1978-79 season under coach Fred Shero.

He had matured as a goalie by that time, and fans would frequently rock the Garden with chants of "J-D, J-D."

Although he finished the season with 20 wins, 15 losses, and four ties, the black cloud of injury hovered over his career even then.

Injuries notwithstanding, Shero had faith in Davidson and announced that no matter what, Davidson was his number-one goalie. John came back a few weeks prior to the 1979 playoffs and looked simply dreadful. But then, as if by magic, the playoffs began and Davidson delivered the goaltending performance of his lifetime.

In the preliminary round, J.D. held Los Angeles to two goals over the series as the Rangers moved on to face Philadelphia. Again J.D. was strong, recording a shutout and allowing only eight goals as the Rangers moved on in five games.

The Blueshirts then took on the Islanders, the NHL's top point-getters that season, in the semifinals. The Islanders possessed a potent offensive attack with three of the league's top six scorers, but that didn't matter to Davidson. J.D.

held the Islanders to one goal a game in three of the Rangers' four wins, sending the Blueshirts into the finals against Montreal.

However, the Cinderella story lasted only one more game. The Rangers defeated Montreal 4-1 in the opening game of the Stanley Cup finals before dropping the next four.

"That whole spring was the most fun I had in hockey," Davidson once said of the playoffs, in which he had a 2.28 goals-against average.

Not long after he retired, a friend in the television business suggested that J.D. might do well in front of a camera. Although the television field was foreign to him, John decided that it was worth a try. A year after his retirement, he signed on as a guest analyst with MSG Network (1983-84) before joining the distinguished *Hockey Night in Canada* program.

In 1986, J.D. returned to MSG as Rangers color commentator alongside play-by-play man Sam Rosen.

The J.D. and Sam duet produced instant chemistry both on the air and in the living rooms of Rangers fans throughout the continent. And the proof was in their longevity.

The act seemed as if it would go on forever and might have had Davidson not been offered the opportunity to become president of the St. Louis Blues in the summer of 2006.

During his time with the MSG Network, Davidson also picked up other short-term commentating jobs. He covered the NHL All-Star game with NBC and FOX Sports, the Stanley Cup finals with ESPN, and the Winter Olympics with

CBS Sports in 1992, 1994, 1998, and 2002. In addition, he's worked with ABC Sports, was the host of *In the Crease* on NHL.com, was an "After 40 Minutes" panelist on *Hockey Night in Canada,* and covered the 1990 Goodwill Games with TBS.

Davidson's MVP-caliber booth work produced a number of prizes, including four New York Emmy Awards for outstanding on-camera achievement. He was also part of the MSG Rangers broadcast team that won the prominent CableACE award for outstanding live event coverage. It was the first time a regional network had ever won in that category.

By the time the 2005-06 season had ended, J.D. had a difficult decision to make. He was certainly at the top of his game in the broadcast business and for years had rejected offers to become a team executive. But this time the offer was too attractive to reject. He signed on in St. Louis, becoming the seventh president in Blues franchise history.

"I was in a situation where I had to say goodbye to a lot of good friends to make the move. But I knew it was the right move," Davidson concluded.

Davidson revealed that he made the decision to give up broadcasting for the front office during the 2006 Stanley Cup finals.

"When Carolina played Edmonton in the seventh game, it was just a terrific game," said Davidson. "Then at the end of the game, the place erupts in Raleigh and goes crazy. The first two people out of the building were [broadcast partner] Mike Emrick and myself. You don't feel very much for somebody else winning a championship when you're an ex-player.

You want to congratulate them, but as an ex-player, you want to win."

John realized that he had not reached the top of the hockey mountain, although he came close as the Rangers' goaltender in 1979. He still wants to conquer the Stanley Cup and now has that opportunity as boss of the Blues.

But as far as Rangers fans are concerned, Cup or no Cup, J.D. delivered some of the best thrills they have ever experienced.

PHIL ESPOSITO

1 9 7 5 - 1 9 8 1

Guaranteed, a sizable bloc of Rangers aficionados will balk at the sight of Phil Esposito's name in a book of Blueshirts notables.

In a sense, that is perfectly reasonable when one considers that the native of Sault Ste. Marie, Ontario, spent his most productive years as a Boston Bruins center working alongside Bobby Orr and Derek Sanderson. It is a fact of life that Esposito once made it abundantly clear in Boston that he wanted no part of playing in the Big Apple.

But that's ancient history. Although he arrived in Rangerville as a reluctant dragon, Esposito gradually grasped the beauty of the five boroughs and in time embraced the Blueshirts as much as he had the gold and black of the Bruins.

What Rangers fans did get to see was the skill that at one time led experts to suggest that Phil was one of the finest centers ever to skate in the National Hockey League.

They point to the indisputable fact that he regularly led the NHL in scoring, that he was consistently voted to the First All-Star Team, and that the Boston Bruins' renaissance directly coincided with his arrival in Beantown at the start of the 1967-68 season. For further emphasis, the Esposito Marching and Chowder Society is quick to point out that Phil was chief architect of Team Canada's pulsating four-games-to-three victory over the Russian national team in September 1972.

"That series," said Toronto *Globe and Mail* columnist Dick Beddoes, "would not have been won without Esposito's big, rough, relentless leadership. I saw him make what will become a hockey heirloom passing down through the generations."

There are others, however, who insist that when you discuss Esposito, it must be in the past-perfect tense; he was knocked out of the 1973 Stanley Cup playoffs with a bodycheck from Ron Harris, a third-string New York Rangers defenseman. The anti-Esposito clan then emphasizes that Phil seemed to have lost his scoring touch in the clutch when Boston skated in the 1974 and 1975 playoffs.

This proves more than anything that there are at least two sides to the Esposito controversy. However, absolutely no one doubts that he was a superstar. Just the fact that he was able to recover from a near-crippling 1973 knee injury to win the 1973-74 scoring title—his fifth in six

PHIL ESPOSITO

BORN: Sault Ste. Marie, Ontario, Canada; February 20, 1942

POSITION: Center

NHL TEAMS: Chicago Blackhawks, 1963-67; Boston Bruins, 1967-75; New York Rangers, 1975-81

AWARDS/HONORS: Team Canada, 1972; Hart Trophy, 1974; Art Ross Trophy, 1971-74; NHL First Team All-Star, 1969-74; NHL Second Team All-Star, 1968, 1975; Lester Patrick Trophy, 1978

years—is testimony to the man's superiority and gumption.

When Phil first broke into professional hockey, no one expected that he would be the superstar he became. In fact, it took him two years to even make the NHL.

In 1962, Phil played for the St. Louis Braves of the Central Hockey League (CHL), racking up 90 points in a mere 71 games. As the 1963 season approached, Esposito waited expectantly to be called up by the Chicago Blackhawks, the team that owned his rights. But the call never came, and Esposito began the '63 season in the CHL. The angry center responded by scoring an incredible 80 points in the team's first 43 games before the red-faced Hawks finally called him up.

Playing alongside the inimitable Bobby Hull, Phil matured admirably in his first three seasons, scoring over

20 goals in each campaign. But Chicago coach Billy Reay never warmed to the budding superstar, and Esposito was sent to the Bruins in 1967.

In Boston, Esposito found his stride, becoming the most prolific scorer the league had ever seen. Beginning in 1968, Espo scored at least 40 goals in seven consecutive seasons, including at least 55 *every year* from 1970 to 1974. In the 1970-71 campaign, Phil had the greatest offensive season in NHL history, scoring an unbelievable 76 goals to set the league mark. He added 76 assists that year to set the total scoring record as well with 152 points. It was the greatest season for an offensive player in league history, and it remains one of the greatest individual seasons of all time.

Because he worked with two burly and gifted wingmen, Ken Hodge and Wayne Cashman, Esposito was virtually unstoppable in his favorite camping ground outside the face-off circle about 15 feet from the net. One scouting report analyzed Esposito in this way: "Esposito combines reach, strength, intelligence, and competitiveness to the degree that the only way he can be countered is with superbly coordinated defensive play."

In the early 1970s, no team could stop Esposito, not even the vaunted Soviet squads of the era. In 1972, Phil was the only member of Team Canada the Soviet defensemen could not handle.

"I'll tell you how good Phil Esposito is," said Maple Leafs manager Punch Imlach. "When you're playing against Espo, you start at least one goal down." There's nothing vague about that, yet many experts have a considerable problem defining Esposito's style. Unlike ex-teammate Bobby Orr and the flamboyant Bobby Hull, Esposito relied more on subtle skill.

"You can't compare Orr and me or Hull and me," said Phil. "They brought people to their feet. They are spectacular players. Orr was the best player in the game; I know it and admit it. I also know that my role was to score goals, to pick up loose pucks and put them behind the goaltender any way I could. So that's what I tried to do—and the people still call me a garbage collector."

While Phil's ex-teammate, Bobby Hull, built his reputation on a booming slap shot, Esposito concentrated on a deadly accurate quick wrist drive, though Phil rarely looked directly at the net. "I've developed a feel for where it is, just as John Havlicek of the Celtics has a knack of knowing where the basket is," Phil once said. "Besides, taking even the quickest look wastes precious time."

Philip Anthony Esposito was born in Sault Ste. Marie, Ontario, on February 20, 1942. Growing up on the frozen ponds of Canada, Phil honed his shot against his younger brother, Tony, who would go on to be one of the superior netminders in NHL history.

Along with Orr, Esposito led Boston to two Stanley Cup victories in the early 1970s. But nearly all of Esposito's goals were forgotten when the Philadelphia Flyers knocked off the Bruins in six games in May 1974 to become the first expansion team to win the Stanley Cup.

Unlike most opponents, the rambunctious Flyers completely manacled Esposito, who was topped in every department—especially face-offs—by the tenacious Bobby Clarke. Even more grating were the words of Bruins coach Bep Guidolin, who singled out Esposito and other Boston skaters for lack of effort. "Determination and second effort are what beat us," said Guidolin. "Our big players should have worked harder to put out more. Too much money is being paid to some individuals."

The suggestion was clear that Esposito had become one of several Boston fat cats, and some advised general manager Harry Sinden that it would be wise to trade Esposito while the big pivot still had some value.

When Esposito heard that he was trade bait and that he might even be dealt to New York, he confronted the Bruins' high command. He was assured that no such deal was in the works.

But it was, and on November 7, 1975, Esposito was shaken right out of his skates when he learned that, after eight seasons with the Bruins, he was being traded to the hated Rangers along with Carol Vadnais for Brad Park, Jean Ratelle, and Joe Zanussi.

The blockbuster deal stunned Phil to his very core, and he was slow to acclimate himself to the Great White Way. These were tumultuous times for the Rangers, who had been on a downslide from their high pinnacle when they reached the Stanley Cup finals in 1972 against Espo's Bruins.

A year after he arrived at Madison Square Garden, Phil was named captain over the popular Rod Gilbert and soon warmed to his responsibilities.

Perhaps the most significant change for Phil occurred at the coaching level in 1978, when Fred Shero was imported as general manager and coach.

Shero believed that Phil could perform at optimum ability if he was not the captain—and the coach was right. In addition, Shero inserted a system that allowed Phil the kind of success he had enjoyed in Bean town. Sure enough, Phil became the Espo of old and the Rangers began a remarkable ascent.

With Phil sparking the team, the Rangers entered the 1979 playoffs as a hot club getting hotter each round. By their third playoff series, the Rangers had upset the Islanders in six games and moved onto the finals, where they were defeated by the Montreal Canadiens.

By this time, Espo had captivated Rangers fans with the same charisma of past aces such as Bryan Hextall, Don Raleigh, and to a certain extent, Jean Ratelle.

Phil retired in 1981 with 717 career goals and 1,590 points and was an easy choice for the Hall of Fame.

A natural on television, Espo worked behind the mike for MSG Network, but garnered even more attention as Rangers general manager from July 1986 through May 1989.

His many deals earned him the nickname "Trader Phil."

Espo later campaigned for an NHL expansion team in Tampa Bay. Although many in the business believed it to be a pipe dream, that dream was eventually realized, and Phil became the club's chief executive in its formative years.

More recently, he has returned to broadcasting again, occasionally revisiting Madison Square Garden, where he is greeted more warmly than he ever thought possible on the day he learned he had been traded from Boston to New York.

MIKE GARTNER

1 9 9 0 - 1 9 9 4

"Kid Lightning" would be an appropriate nickname for Mike Gartner, whose play was synonymous with the NHL's symbol as "the fastest team sport on Earth." For nearly two decades, Gartner graced the NHL with a mixture of stickhandling and shooting prowess that eventually earned him entrance into the Hockey Hall of Fame.

Although Gartner's sojourn with the Rangers lasted a relatively short time—from 1990 through 1994—he had a profound impact on New York fans.

In his career, Gartner was traded three times at or around the trade deadline. In his 35 games with new teams during the seasons in which he was traded, Gartner notched 24 goals, had 18 assists for 42 points, and collected a plus-16 rating.

One of his stops during this trend was on Broadway. The sniping forward was dealt to the Rangers from the Minnesota

North Stars near the end of the 1989-90 campaign.

In his first game with the Rangers, Gartner set off the lamps twice against Philadelphia and continued to score goals the rest of the season. In the final 12 games of the season, including the Philadelphia game, Gartner netted 11 goals and had five assists. During that time, he had a seven-game goal-scoring streak from March 12 through March 27, helping the Blueshirts clinch the Patrick Division and the Presidents' Trophy.

Gartner was up to his tricks again in the playoffs, picking up eight points in 10 games, but the Rangers eventually bowed out in the division finals to the eventual Stanley Cup champion Pittsburgh Penguins.

What made Mike tick?

Obviously, his speed was a major asset, but more importantly, the manner in which he utilized his speed and synchronized it with his shooting talents made him special.

That was evident in 1990 throughout his seven-game goal streak.

He again accomplished the feat between January 30 and February 13 in 1991. During both streaks, he put the puck across the goal line eight times.

Gartner was the first Ranger to score at least 40 goals in three consecutive seasons, 1990-91 to 1992-93, and was selected to his sixth All-Star game in 1993. During that midseason exhibition contest, he scored four goals and was named the game's MVP. He also won the 1991 and 1993 NHL Fastest Skater competition.

During the 1991-92 season, Gartner was the first player in NHL history to reach his 500th goal, 500th assist, 1,000th career point, and 1,000th career game in the same season.

Gartner's 500th career goal came on October 14, 1991, against his first NHL team, the Washington Capitals; his 500th career assist was one of two he notched on April 16, 1992, against the Pittsburgh Penguins; his 1,000th NHL point was achieved March 20, 1992, against the New Jersey Devils; and his 1,000th career contest was on March 20, 1992, at Detroit, where he notched two goals including the game winner.

One of Mike's most stirring moments occurred at the Garden on December 23, 1993. Skating against the Devils, Gartner was sitting at 599 career goals when he received a pass from Alexei Kovalev and stuffed it past Devils goalie Chris Terreri to bring the Garden crowd to its feet. The game was delayed for several minutes as the Rangers bench emptied onto the ice to congratulate only the sixth player

MIKE GARTNER

BORN: Ottawa, Ontario, Canada; October 29, 1959

POSITION: Right Wing

NHL TEAMS: Washington Capitals, 1979-89; Minnesota North Stars, 1989-90; New York Rangers, 1990-94; Toronto Maple Leafs, 1994-96; Phoenix Coyotes, 1996-98

AWARDS/HONORS: NHL All-Star Game, 1981, 1985-86, 1988, 1990, 1993, 1996; Hockey Hall of Fame, 2001

NEW YORK RANGERS

in NHL history to reach 600 goals. Even Rangers goalie Glenn Healy made his way to the Devils' end of the ice to give Gartner a hug. The Rangers won the game in a landslide, 8-3.

"I was someone who loved playing the game," Gartner said. "I competed hard every night. I used my speed to create a lot of opportunities. In the early part of my career, I used my speed to drive wide and used my shot that was pretty accurate and fairly hard. I like to think that I was a fairly dangerous player when I had the puck."

During the 1993-94 campaign, Mike posted 28 goals and 24 assists in 71 games, helping the Rangers win the Presidents' Trophy for the second time in four seasons. But Gartner was not a favorite of coach Mike Keenan, who demanded that general manager Neil Smith stock the team with more gritty—if not skilled—players.

Smith obliged before the March 1994 trade deadline, dealing Gartner to Toronto for Glenn Anderson and a draft pick.

Despite the trade, Gartner went on to finish the season with 34 scores, setting an NHL record for most consecutive seasons with 30 or more goals. He accomplished this feat in 15 straight campaigns, and the streak only ended due to the work stoppage that shortened the 1994-95 season in which Mike totaled 12 goals in only 38 games.

Gartner said of his accomplishment, "There aren't many NHL records that Wayne [Gretzky] doesn't have, but I have a couple: the consecutive 30-goal seasons and total 30-goal seasons, which is

something I'll always remember. It was just one of those things. I tried to show up to play every night and tried to contribute to the team.

"I stayed relatively healthy throughout my career, and before you knew it, I was in my ninth, 10th, 11th season, and somebody said, 'That's your 10th year in a row in which you've scored 30 goals. Do you know the record is 13?' I said, 'No, I really didn't know that.'

"I was given a certain amount of talent, and I wanted to do the best that I could every time I stepped onto the ice. I really strived for that consistency, and as a result, I was able to have that consistency."

Gartner is no longer the only holder of this record. During the 2006-07 campaign, another Ranger, Jaromir Jagr, achieved his 15th straight 30-goal season.

Mike went on to have two more 30-plus goal seasons in 1995-96 with Toronto and again after being picked up by the Phoenix Coyotes in 1996-97.

He retired following the 1997-98 campaign after playing in 1,432 NHL contests, making him the player to have participated in the most total games without reaching a Stanley Cup final.

Following his retirement, Gartner remained close to the game he loves and soon made a mark as an NHL Players' Association official when he became the union's director of business relations.

In 2001, he was enshrined in the Hockey Hall of Fame. Gartner still recalls the phone call he received from Hall of Fame official Jim Gregory.

"Actually, I'm not too often at a loss for words," said Gartner, "but I was for several seconds, and Jim [Gregory] said to me, 'Are you still there, Mike?' I said, 'I'm here, Jim; I'm just a little taken aback by this whole thing.'"

Through the 2004-05 work stoppage, Gartner remained affiliated with the players' union and assisted in its reorganization when play resumed.

One of the most likeable personalities in the ice business, Gartner is still remembered affectionately on Seventh Avenue for his contributions to the Rangers before their 1994 Stanley Cup run.

EDDIE GIACOMIN

1 9 6 5 - 1 9 7 5

Over the years, the Rangers have been blessed not only with first-rate goaltenders but also netminders extraordinarily popular with the often-critical gallery guards.

Davey Kerr, Charlie Rayner, Sugar Jim Henry, and Mike Richter rank among those guardians of the pipes.

But when it comes to an unmitigated love affair between the crowd and the crease-minder, none equals the deliriously happy match between Ed Giacomin and Blueshirts supporters.

No episode exemplifies the quality of this affection more than Giacomin's departure from New York in 1975, when he returned to Madison Square Garden as a member of the visiting Red Wings. Eddie was cheered so loudly

that it appeared as if he was still on the Rangers.

This was an amazing turn of events, considering Giacomin's original trip to the NHL almost began as a joke. Though not identical twins, Eddie and his brother, Rollie Giacomin, were both goalies. When Peanuts O'Flaherty, the coach of the Eastern League's Washington Lions, invited Rollie to come down for a tryout, the elder Giacomin was working a shift at an Ontario lumber mill and asked his kid brother, Eddie, to stand in for him.

Upon Eddie's arrival in Washington, the coach looked at him, discovered he was not Rollie, and was unimpressed. O'Flaherty's Lions, however, lost their next three games. With nothing to lose and only six games left in the season, the coach gave Eddie the go-ahead to play. The Lions won all six.

The following year Giacomin was invited to the American League Providence Reds' training camp, then spent the season playing for various minor-league teams in the East.

Unusual for a goalie at that time, Giacomin was good at stickhandling. My nickname for him was "Goalie A Go-Go."

Eddie attributed these skills, which earned him two assists in a 5-3 win over the Toronto Maple Leafs in 1972, to Hall of Fame defenseman and Reds coach Fernie Flaman.

In 1960-61, Giacomin was called back to the Reds in midseason and toiled for them over the next four years. Finally, the Rangers stepped in and made a major trade. Then general manager Emile Francis sent four players, including former number-one netminder Marcel

Paille, to the Reds. On May 17, 1965, Giacomin was signed by the Rangers.

Giacomin's first year in Manhattan was a shaky one. Playing behind a last-place team and wanting to show off his stickhandling abilities, Giacomin often got himself into trouble and compiled a lowly record of 8-19-7. After his poor rookie showing, Rangers management sent him to the Baltimore Clippers of the AHL, a Rangers farm club. Replaced by Cesare Maniago, Giacomin was hurt by his demotion but vowed to return.

But Francis, who made the deal that brought Eddie to Broadway in the first place, had faith in his prospect. Once Giacomin returned to the big club, Francis staked everything he had on him.

As the old song goes, "Love Is Lovelier the Second Time Around." And so it was with Francis and Giacomin. Eddie was given the starting assignment and finished the season with a 2.61 goals-against average and a league-leading total of nine

EDDIE GIACOMIN

BORN: Sudbury, Ontario, Canada; June 6, 1939

POSITION: Goaltender

NHL TEAMS: New York Rangers, 1965-75; Detroit Red Wings, 1975-77

AWARDS/HONORS: Vezina Trophy, 1971; NHL First Team All-Star, 1967, 1971; NHL Second Team All-Star, 1968-70; NHL All-Star Game, 1967-71, 1973

shutouts. The Rangers made the playoffs and Giacomin was given a berth on the First Team All-Star squad.

In 1970, the Rangers lost in the Stanley Cup quarterfinals for the fourth straight year. Analysts surmised that the Rangers wilted in May because Giacomin was fatigued as a result of playing in excess of 60 games in an era of coast-to-coast scheduling.

After 11 years as an intrepid, bare-faced goaltender, Giacomin decided to wear a facemask when he returned to the Rangers' training camp in Kitchener, Ontario, the following season. While there, he learned that he would be sharing the goaltending chores with Gilles Villemure, a veteran of seven minor-league seasons who had already had a few stints with the Rangers.

Giacomin disapproved of the two-goalie system. He insisted that he needed the extra work to stay his sharpest. He vehemently denied charges that he had been tired at season's end and had failed in the playoffs. He had no choice, however, but to abide by Francis' decision.

The two-goalie system worked well, and by the end of the 1970-71 campaign, Giacomin had captured the coveted Vezina Trophy along with Villemure. Eddie finished with a goals-against average of 2.15, the best of his professional career.

In the playoffs, the Rangers clambered past the quarterfinals, beating the Toronto Maple Leafs in a hard-fought, six-game series. They then battled the Blackhawks in a seven-game series before losing in the semifinals.

ABOVE: Eddie Giacomin makes a kick save as Red Berenson (9) of the St. Louis Blues and assistant captain Harry Howell both look to jump on any rebounds. *From the Stan Fischler Collection*

A year later, Giacomin's average was a respectable 2.70. He starred in a victorious quarterfinal series against the defending champion Montreal Canadiens, but he damaged his knee against the Blackhawks in the first game of the semifinals. Villemure temporarily replaced him and played well enough that the Rangers reached the finals for the first time in 20 years. Next came the classic 1972 confrontation between New York and Boston, but Giacomin couldn't stop the Bruins—Bobby Orr was simply too much for the Blueshirts to handle. The Rangers were eliminated in six games.

Eddie suffered early-season problems in 1972-73, but midway through the year, he found himself and played several contests in which he averaged less than a goal per game. He also recorded his 41st career shutout, surpassing Hall of Famer Chuck Rayner for a Rangers record.

By the mid-1970s, it appeared to some observers that Giacomin's playing career was nearing its end. This point was reinforced when the upstart Islanders beat Giacomin and the Rangers in the opening round of the 1975 playoffs, knocking them out of Stanley Cup contention.

The Rangers' troubles continued as the 1975-76 campaign started.

In fact, the club's slide was so troubling to the high command that they deemed some key moves had to be made to improve the club. Difficult as the decision was for him, Francis stunned Rangers fans by putting Giacomin on waivers. Eddie was claimed by Detroit on Friday, October 31, 1975, and the following night skated onto Madison Square Garden ice in a Red Wings uniform.

No one at the Garden that night would forget the sight of Eddie wiping away the tears as his loyal fans, in an expression of pure love, cheered for their hero.

"From Friday night until game time to the time they started cheering me in warm-ups, I had a funny idea that after the cheering stopped, I would skate out, shake hands with all the Rangers, thank the fans, and then just leave the ice and retire," said Giacomin. "I've never been an emotional man, but I couldn't hold back the tears. When the people started cheering me at the beginning, the tears came down my face. A couple of times, I thought I would collapse from the emotion."

The Garden crowd often chanted, "Ed-die, Ed-die," during the contest, ignoring the home team. The Red Wings won the game 6-4, but even the Rangers players wanted to address Giacomin one last time.

"They were talking to me on the ice, saying things like, 'Good luck,' and, 'Give my best to the family.' One guy [Wayne Dillon] even said, 'I'm sorry,' after he scored a goal," recalled Giacomin.

Giacomin appeared in 539 games for the Blueshirts, posting a record of 267-174-89. He had a 2.73 goals-against average and holds the Rangers record for shutouts with 49. The acrobatic goalie is second in team history in wins and third in appearances.

The Red Wings, a team in turmoil, began making wholesale changes and released Giacomin in 1977. His career over, Eddie briefly joined the New York Islanders as a goalie coach and broadcaster in 1978.

The man himself will tell you that he never completely fulfilled his aspirations as a Blueshirt. "Not winning the Stanley Cup is the thing that hurts most," he remembered prior to having his No. 1 retired in 1989. "But I go to outings and stand next to Bill Gadsby, who played 21 seasons and never won a Stanley Cup, and I don't feel so bad." In 1987 Giacomin was inducted into the Hockey Hall of Fame.

That, plus the endless adulation heaped upon him by Rangers fans, should satisfy the "Goalie A Go-Go" for a lifetime.

ROD GILBERT

1 9 6 0 - 1 9 7 7

Few NHL rookies have made a more stirring debut before the home crowd than Rod Gilbert did at the old Madison Square Garden, which was located on Eighth Avenue between 49th and 50th streets in Manhattan.

This was the spring of 1962, and after a playoff drought, the Rangers were facing the Toronto Maple Leafs in the opening Stanley Cup round.

Riddled with injuries, the Blueshirts had lost the first two games in Canada and were now regrouping on Manhattan ice. What player-coach Doug Harvey needed most of all was reinforcements, particularly on his forward line.

It was then that general manager Muzz Patrick dipped into the Rangers' farm system and promoted a French-Canadian ace named Rodrigue Gilbert.

To say that Gilbert made a sensational debut would be an understatement. The peach-faced rookie proved to be a tremendous catalyst, sparking his new club to two straight victories. It was enough to virtually cement his career in the NHL.

During the 1961-62 season, the Rangers had a formidable outfit and were about to gain a playoff berth. Gilbert already had assumed that he wasn't in the Rangers' plans, especially since he had already been called up to the NHL club early in the season just to sit idly on the bench.

So Gilbert was not surprisingly caught off guard when he received a call from Rangers GM Muzz Patrick, informing him that he needed to take the next plane to New York; he might be used in the playoffs.

The Rangers' regular right wing, Ken Schinkel, had broken a toe in the second game of the playoffs series against the Leafs, and the Rangers needed a quick replacement.

While trying to convince himself that he was going to sit on the bench as he had

before, Gilbert was called into Rangers player-coach Doug Harvey's office.

"I'm going to play you regularly on a line with Dave Balon and Johnny Wilson," said Harvey, according to Gilbert.

Rod worried that this was an April Fool's joke as Game 3 of the series was to be played on April 1. But this was no jest.

In Game 3, Gilbert spent the first two periods getting used to the flow of the NHL game. In the third period, he made a game-defining play. Rod found an open Balon, who put the puck past Leafs goalie Johnny Bower, and the Rangers won the game 5-4.

With the Rangers now behind 2-1 in the series, Gilbert stepped up his play in Game 4. The Balon-Wilson-Gilbert line started the game for the Rangers, and just 41 seconds in, Rod scored his first career goal.

He netted his second career goal toward the end of the first period. Wilson and Balon were passing the puck back and forth like a yo-yo. The puck then ended up on Gilbert's stick, and he flipped it past Bower. The Rangers were up 2-0.

The score was eventually tied 2-2 when Gilbert passed to Balon, who scored the go-ahead goal. The Rangers had evened the series with a 3-2 victory.

However, despite Gilbert's heroics, the Leafs took the next two games to win the series 4-2.

Ironically, Gilbert's NHL career almost ended before it started. Playing for the Guelph Royals in the Ontario Hockey Association (OHA), he skidded on an ice-cream container top thrown on the ice by a fan and injured his back. A few days later, an opponent leveled Gilbert

ROD GILBERT

BORN: Montreal, Quebec, Canada; July 1, 1941

POSITION: Right Wing

NHL TEAMS: New York Rangers, 1960-1977

AWARDS/HONORS: NHL First Team All-Star, 1972; NHL Second Team All-Star, 1968; Team Canada, 1972; Bill Masterton Trophy, 1976; Hockey Hall of Fame, 1982; Patrick Award, 1991

with a strong check, and he fell to the ice, his back broken. The first operation on his spine was a near disaster; his left leg began to hemorrhage and the doctors seriously considered amputation.

Rod was lucky enough to survive the calamities, but was never truly home free when it came to injuries. During the summer of 1965, the bone grafts in his back weakened, and he needed another operation. Rod, now with the Rangers, saw his career was in jeopardy; he played 34 games in a restrictive brace and then submitted to surgery.

After these injuries, Gilbert thought his career might be over.

"To me, [the injuries] have seemed like an eternity," Gilbert recalled. "Many times during the past week I thought my career was over."

But the forward's grit, determination, and ability to recover paid off, and happily, Rod's story was uphill to fame after that.

The second operation cost Gilbert half of the 1965-66 season. However, he rebounded in 1966-67 with 28 goals as the Blueshirts made the playoffs for the first time in five seasons. It was also the first of back-to-back 77-point seasons for the deceptively fast skater.

Later in his career on February 24, 1968, at the Montreal Forum, Gilbert established himself as a NHL star, scoring four goals against Rogatien Vachon and setting an NHL-record 16 shots on goal.

Gilbert reached the 30-goal mark for the first time in 1970-71, but that was just a warm-up for one of the finest Rangers lines, the Goal-A-Game, or GAG, Line: Gilbert, Jean Ratelle, and Vic Hadfield.

The GAG Line amassed 139 goals and 312 points in 1971-72, of which Gilbert was responsible for 43 goals and 97 points. The line finished third, fourth, and fifth in NHL scoring that campaign and was selected to be part of Team Canada that summer. During the season, however, Ratelle broke his ankle, and Rod was hindered by pinched nerves in his neck; otherwise, the Rangers might have taken the Stanley Cup from Boston.

That same season, Gilbert was the first Ranger in eight years to garner a First Team All-Star nomination.

In 1974, Gilbert passed Andy Bathgate as the Rangers' all-time leading scorer, and the milestone goal was celebrated by a five-minute, deafening ovation.

Gilbert owns several team records, including most seasons played, 18, career goals, 406, and career points, 1,021. He is the only player with more than 400 goals and 1,000 points while sporting a Rangers uniform.

During his career, Gilbert set or equaled 20 Blueshirts team scoring records. Rod amassed 12 20-goal seasons, and when he retired, he was second only to Gordie Howe in NHL career points.

One of Broadway's most prolific scorers accomplished this with a blazing slap shot. Some in the media thought he should change his play by taking more wrist shots, but Gilbert and coach Emile Francis disagreed.

"I told Rod not to slap the puck," recalled Francis. "It would have been like telling Bobby Hull to stop slapping. It was a helluva weapon—the kind you didn't discourage an offensive player from using."

The Montreal Canadiens once expressed major interest in the prolific Ranger, but when it came time to make a deal, the Rangers wouldn't allow it. This made Gilbert happy because he was loyal to the team that had provided him an opportunity to play in the NHL—something not often seen among today's professional athletes.

What appeared to be a storybook career turned sour for Rod in 1976. At that point, his former on-ice nemesis John Ferguson took over the Rangers, and the two remained distant. Ferguson did everything to put Gilbert down, including passing him over for the club's captaincy.

However strong the tensions in the Rangers' organization may have been at that time, the rivalry could not detract from Rod Gilbert Night on March 9, 1977. Before that evening's contest, an emotional Gilbert addressed a capacity Garden crowd: "My friends, and I think all of you here tonight are my friends,

you have given me a home, friendship, respect, and love, and that's more important than fame. For these things, I will always be grateful."

Gilbert then went on to score a goal, helping the Rangers defeat the Minnesota North Stars.

As it turned out, 1977 would be Gilbert's final full season, and he concluded it with 75 points in 77 games.

But Rod got off to an unimpressive start the next season with nine points in 19 games and was in the midst of a contract dispute when Ferguson dismissed him from the team. Gilbert then moved to the front office, where he became a goodwill ambassador.

Many thought that when Fred Shero came to the Rangers in 1978, Gilbert would play again. When this fact became known, Ferguson was reported to have asked an NHL club for a one-game contract so he could face Gilbert on the ice one last time. Gilbert, however, had retired for good.

On October 14, 1979, Gilbert, No. 7, became the first Ranger ever to have his number retired.

The Montreal native made Manhattan his adopted home, and to this day remains in the Rangers' front office as the director of special projects and a community relations representative.

He was inducted into the Hockey Hall of Fame in 1982.

As a player, Gilbert was everything New York could have wanted. He was a battler on and off the ice. Unable to give up his true love, hockey, he overcame life-threatening injuries to become one of the greatest Rangers of all time.

ADAM GRAVES

1991 - 2001

He wasn't the best Rangers player of all time, but Adam Graves certainly was the most popular when it came to interacting with fans and New York's man on the street.

It was hard not to like Adam, who extended himself to the public whether the object of his interest was the mayor or a garbage collector.

The peripatetic forward was a splendid player and goal scorer *par excellence.*

Graves was not the original NHL power forward, but he did redefine that style of play from the time he came to the New York Rangers in 1991 to the Blueshirts' victory over the New Jersey Devils in the 1997 playoffs, when he scored an overtime winning goal.

The quintessential gentleman off the ice, Graves became one of the most beloved athletes in New York history for his unparalleled charity work and noble efforts in the rink. Adam became so much a part of New York's fabric that it's hard to believe he actually started his NHL career in Edmonton.

In his early years as an Oiler, Graves was part of a youth movement that followed the dynastic Edmonton teams of the 1980s, which featured the likes of Wayne Gretzky, Grant Fuhr, and Mark Messier. As an Oiler, Graves played for a Stanley Cup–winning team in 1989-90, but was to enjoy even greater success after being dealt to New York.

The 1994 championship season showcased Graves more than ever. He tallied 52 goals, breaking the previous Blueshirts record for goals in a single season, set by Vic Hatfield in 1971, and helping the Rangers electrify New York en route to a Presidents' Trophy and the club's first Stanley Cup since 1940. The record held for 12 seasons until Jaromir Jagr netted 54 goals in 2005-06.

"Gravy" would not score at that rate again, but he consistently delivered 22 or more goals in each season from 1995-96 through 1999-2000 while earning respect across the NHL.

The 1997-98 season saw Graves lead the Rangers with 23 goals in 72 games. During that campaign, he carried the team in the absence of Messier.

Graves' second proudest moment occurred on January 14, 2001, when he achieved his 300th goal in a 4-2 victory over the Minnesota Wild.

Many believed that it would be most appropriate for Adam to finish his career in New York, but it wasn't to be.

On a day that broke the hearts of Rangers fans everywhere, Graves, the Rangers' third leading goal scorer with 280 goals in 772 Blueshirts appearances, was traded at the 2001 entry draft on June 24 to the San Jose Sharks for Mikael Semuelsson and Chris Gosselin. Graves' career was renewed on a veteran Sharks team that challenged Western Conference perennial powerhouses Detroit and Colorado for league supremacy.

Looking backward, nobody should be surprised that Adam was a success on the ice and off it.

GREATEST MOMENTS AND PLAYERS

ADAM GRAVES

BORN: Tecumseh, Ontario, Canada; April 12, 1968

POSITION: Left Wing

NHL TEAMS: Detroit Red Wings, 1988-89; Edmonton Oilers, 1989-91; New York Rangers 1991-2001; San Jose Sharks, 2001-03

AWARDS/HONORS: King Clancy Memorial Trophy, 1994; Bill Masterton Memorial Trophy, 2001; NHL Second Team All-Star, 1994; NHL All-Star Game

After a Junior hockey career in which he averaged more than a point a game, Graves broke into the NHL with the Detroit Red Wings. Unable to recreate his Junior success in the NHL, he was dealt to Edmonton during the 1989-90 campaign.

Graves won the King Clancy Memorial Trophy in 1994 and the Bill Masterton Memorial Trophy in 2001 for facilitating charity work in the New York metropolitan and San Jose areas.

In 2000, Adam received the NHL Players Foundation Award, which recognizes "the NHL player who applies the core values of hockey—commitment, perseverance, and teamwork—to enrich the lives of the people in his community."

Graves, who has been acknowledged by several other organizations for his charity work, retired in April 2004 and then returned to Broadway on July 19, 2005, to become part of the Rangers' front office.

He has taken on the dual role of prospect and community development, giving back to the Rangers by training prospects and helping the Rangers give back to the community and fans.

If there was one play Rangers fans could pinpoint as defining Graves' career, it took place in the final game of the Devils-Rangers playoff in 1997 at the Meadowlands. With the scored tied in overtime, Graves captured the puck at the right side of New Jersey's net and barreled around the cage with defenseman Scott Stevens in pursuit. One of the strongest backliners in the game, Stevens was unable to halt the Rangers forward. Graves forced his way past the defenseman and then beat goalie Martin Brodeur to cement the series.

"Not everybody is as lucky as I have been," Graves admitted while summing up his life in the NHL. "I love hockey. I love playing the game—love everything about it—but it's not real, is it? It's not real at all. Helping people is what's real. That is life."

Whether on the ice or off, Adam Graves' life has always been impeccably pure; every Rangers fan knows it and loves him all the more for what he brought to the New York sports scene.

NEW YORK RANGERS

RON GRESCHNER

Although many Rangers rooters may not appreciate the comparison, in many ways Ron Greschner's play was very reminiscent of an earlier New York defense stalwart, Brad Park.

It was Park's misfortune—if one could call it that—to play most of his career in the shadow of the indomitable Bobby Orr.

In a sense, it was unfortunate that Greschner did likewise while the Islanders captain, Denis Potvin, dominated the National Hockey League as a backliner.

Certainly, Greschner was in his own way as valuable to the Blueshirts as Potvin was to the Nassaumen. And there were several instances in which Greschner overshadowed his Islanders counterpart.

This was made evident during the 2006-07 season, when a trivia question was posted during a Rangers-Islanders telecast on MSG Network: "Who scored the winning goal for the Rangers in the sixth and final game of the 1979 series between the Rangers and Islanders?"

This was a terribly significant episode since the win—one of the most arresting upsets in Rangers history—catapulted the Blueshirts into the Stanley Cup finals.

The goal was scored by Greschner, who in a remarkably quiet way emerged as a titan among Rangers defensemen.

It was New York's good fortune that Ron could play his position both ways at a very high level. He was clever behind his blue line, adroit with a poke check, and able to play physical when necessary. He was equally proficient on the attack.

In another playoff game against the Islanders, he broke down the right side of the rink and cruised over the enemy blue line, where he was confronted by none other than Potvin himself. Greschner deftly out-feinted his foe before delivering a laser shot past another Hall of Famer, goalie Bill Smith.

This was the essence of Greschner, who was respected by critical New York fans on many counts, not the least of which was the fact that he wore the Blueshirt throughout his 16-year big-league career.

When it came to hockey, Ron Greschner was always ahead of the curve.

As a 12-year-old growing up in the distant community of Goodsoil, Saskatchewan, Greschner played in a senior league with skaters in their 20s and 30s.

"There were only about eight kids my age when I started in hockey," he said. "The only way I could play enough was in a senior league."

Then he played Junior hockey for the New Westminster Bruins in the West Coast Hockey League, where he grew to be a dominant player in three seasons. Gresch's Junior career consisted of 179 games in which he scored 56 goals and had 126 assists for 182 points.

His Junior performance caught New York's eye, and he was drafted 32nd overall by the Rangers in the second round of the 1974 NHL Amateur Draft. After seven games and 11 points scored for the Providence Reds of the AHL, a 19-year-old Greschner found himself on Broadway.

RON GRESCHNER

BORN: Goodsoil, Saskatchewan; December 22, 1954

POSITION: Defenseman

NHL TEAMS: New York Rangers, 1974-1990

AWARDS/HONORS: NHL Challenge Cup All-Star, 1979; NHL All-Star Game, 1980

Ron played in 70 games his rookie season, setting the record for assists by a rookie defenseman with 37, and added eight goals to his resume.

In his second season, Greschner hit a sophomore slump. After the success of his rookie year in which he contributed 45 points, his passing was often below average, he had little puck control, and he only tallied 27 points.

"I was trying to do so much, and I was getting burned," said Greschner concerning his sophomore difficulties. "I wasn't thinking right. I'd do certain things without thinking, like sleeping too much in the afternoon, and it would hurt my game at night."

His performance during the 1975-76 season declined so much that the Garden faithful became boo-birds whenever Greschner touched the puck.

"I don't think the booing affected me that much," said Greschner. "Everybody gets booed sometime. I didn't get down, but I knew I had to work hard mentally."

After the disaster that was his second season, Greschner rebounded and established himself as a favorite among the Blueshirts.

The handsome defenseman avoided injury early in his career, let his swift skating and smooth stickhandling speak for itself, and became the general for the Rangers' attack.

"With Ron on defense," defensive teammate Dave Farrish said, "it's like there are four forwards on the ice. From back there, he can see the play shaping up and can set up plays better than if he were playing center or wing." Over the next five seasons, Greschner accumulated 298 points in 288 games. Along the way, he was part of the 1978-79 team that lost to Montreal in the Stanley Cup finals and became the highest scoring Rangers defenseman when he assisted on a Dave Silk goal in 1981. This was just one of many records Greschner held for Rangers defensemen until Brian Leetch found his way into Rangers blue.

Greschner's offensive play was so good that the defenseman occasionally found his way onto a forward line. During the 1986-87 season, Gresch was moved from the blue line to center for the majority of the season. The results of the experiment weren't outstanding, but they weren't bad, either. He posted six goals and 34 assists for 40 points in 61 games. The next season, Greschner was moved back to his natural defensive position.

Although Ron had many highs in his career, his play was not always flawless. Greschner did make mistakes, but early on he was surrounded by enough talented players, including Anders Hedberg and Phil Esposito, for the team to pick up the slack.

Said Greschner, "I did a lot of things wrong. You make one mistake, you don't want to make it again. . . . But it was easy for me breaking in. If I had gone to an expansion team, it might have been different. I played with a good team where the forwards backcheck. And if they got in trouble, they just didn't throw [the puck] to me and say, 'Here, do something.'"

Because of the enormous ice time he logged, Ron was inevitably assailed with injuries. In the 1978-79 and 1984-85 seasons, he suffered from separated shoulders, and from 1981 to 1983, he faced back problems. While the former did not cost Greschner much playing time, the latter did. During the 1981-82 and 1982-83 seasons, he played in only 39 contests.

Greschner continued to play well the next few years, but in 1987-88 his production severely declined. From 1987-88 to 1989-90, he netted just 27 points in 164 games.

By 1990, Ron's days in the NHL were numbered, and he was released by general manager Neil Smith. He was just 18 games shy of playing in his 1,000th career NHL game. Unfortunately, no other team showed interest in signing him, and his 982 regular-season games rank him fourth in games played in Rangers history. While he was one of the better offensive defensemen to play the game on Broadway, he was also a physical player who committed many penalties. The 6-foot-2, 205-pound defenseman registered 1,226 penalty minutes in his career, still a club record.

Greschner played all 16 of his seasons on Broadway. The big city did not intimidate the small-town Canadian, and he learned to enjoy the Big Apple.

"I think somebody who has something negative to say about New York doesn't deserve to play here," he said late in his career. "It's a fascinating city; there's always something going on."

Ron not only played for the Blueshirts, but was also the co-owner of New York restaurants and was involved in charity work as well. The city reciprocated his love when he won the Rangers Good Guy award in the 1985-86 season.

It's a long way from Goodsoil, Saskatchewan, to Times Square, but Ron Greschner executed the move as smoothly as anyone—probably as well as Denis Potvin did from Ottawa, Ontario to Uniondale, Long Island!

WAYNE GRETZKY

1 9 9 6 - 1 9 9 9

New York being the Big Apple, it has always been the goal of the city's impresarios to bring the world's finest acts to Broadway—and that includes the sports realm as well as legitimate theatre. It explains why Yankees owner Jacob Ruppert lured Babe Ruth from the Boston Red Sox and why other major-league stars have always wanted to play on the Great White Way.

Thus, it was no surprise that the Rangers always had their eyes on the greatest star of his era, Wayne Gretzky.

But bringing him to Manhattan would not be easy. After all, "The Great One" was originally signed by the Edmonton Oilers and only switched to Los Angeles after Kings owner Bruce McNall made an offer that was impossible for Glen Sather—then Oilers boss—to refuse.

Somehow, Wayne also signed a contract with the St. Louis Blues before he eventually made his home in Madison Square Garden.

Neil Smith was general manager of the Rangers when Gretzky became available in 1996. Even though it was apparent by then that Wayne was on the downside of his career, Smith made it abundantly clear that the opportunity to bring such a personality to the Gotham was simply impossible to refuse.

His arrival as a Ranger made worldwide headlines, particularly since he would become a teammate of his Edmonton buddy, Mark Messier. Gretzky's tenure with the Blueshirts did not produce another Stanley Cup, but his artistry did not fail him, and New York fans were tickled to have "The Great One" in their midst.

"We are thrilled to be fortunate enough to have the greatest player in the history of the National Hockey League as a member of the New York Rangers," Smith explained during a news conference to introduce the superstar.

In Gretzky's inaugural season with the Blueshirts, he showed flashes of brilliance. And in the postseason, he tallied a hat trick against the Florida Panthers in a second-round playoff victory before New York lost to the Philadelphia Flyers in the Eastern Conference finals.

WAYNE GRETZKY

BORN: Brantford, Ontario, Canada; January 26, 1961

POSITION: Center

NHL TEAMS: Edmonton Oilers, 1979-1988; Los Angeles Kings, 1988-1996; St. Louis Blues, 1996; New York Rangers, 1996-1999

AWARDS/HONORS: Hart Memorial Trophy, 1980-1985, 1987, 1989; Lester B. Pearson Trophy, 1982-84, 1985, 1987; Conn Smythe Trophy, 1985, 1988; Art Ross Trophy, 1981-87, 1990, 1991, 1994; Lady Byng Memorial Trophy, 1980, 1991, 1992, 1994, 1999

Although his numbers as a Ranger were not as high as they were with the Oilers, Kings, or Blues, Wayne still contributed admirably, considering that he was near the end of his playing career. The greatest offensive center in NHL history averaged more than a point per contest while with the Rangers.

Gretzky was born on January 26th, 1961, in Brantford, Ontario. He developed into an amazing talent at a very young age. By the time he was 10, he had accumulated 517 points in a single season for his pee wee team. Of course, no professional hockey player had ever neared this mark. It signaled the beginning of a legendary career for the young star.

From that point forward, Gretzky astonished hockey scouts as he led the Canadian World Junior Hockey club with

17 points to a bronze medal finish. His accomplishments would continue into the World Hockey Association (WHA) with his first club, the Indianapolis Racers. He was eventually traded to a developing NHL franchise, the Edmonton Oilers.

As a lad growing up, Gretzky idolized NHL legend Gordie Howe. However, the most prolific scoring center of all time was denied the opportunity to wear his idol's No. 9 jersey because it had been taken by former OHA teammate, Brian Gualazzi. He chose to commemorate his hero by wearing a double nine (No. 99) instead. Gretzky's jersey number would eventually be retired by every team in the National Hockey League.

During his first NHL season with Edmonton, Gretzky astounded many as he led the NHL with 137 points. What's striking is that he did not win the Art Ross Trophy for scoring the most goals, but rather Marcel Dionne seized the honors. However, in the next six seasons, Gretzky took his aggression out on opposing netminders by finding twine more than 50 times each year, including an NHL-record 92 goals in the Oilers' 1981-82 campaign.

Not only did the siren go off for Gretzky, but other Oilers found the back of the net after dazzling passes from "The Great One" as well. In four of the six seasons following his rookie year, Gretzky amassed more than 200 points, including a record 215 in the 1985-86 season. In each of these six years, Gretzky also won the Hart Trophy as most valuable player in the NHL.

With Gretzky's leadership, the Oilers were able to brake the success of four consecutive Stanley Cup championships by the New York Islanders. The Edmonton squad won the team's first Cup in 1984. The Oilers would dance to the top twice more with the assistance of Gretzky.

But after the 1987-88 season, the financial status of the Oilers worsened. In order to fix the difficulties within the club, drastic moves were necessary. The dealing began with perhaps the biggest trade in sports history: the greatest scorer in hockey was traded to the Los Angeles Kings along with Marty McSorley and Mike Krushelnyski for Jimmy Carson, Martin Gelinas, $15 million, and first-round draft picks in 1989, 1991, and 1993.

Wayne's arrival in California brought more hockey fans into the Great Western Forum, which was primarily considered a basketball home for the Los Angeles Lakers. In his first season with the Kings, No. 99 led his team to the playoffs and helped spark interest for the sport in the Southwest.

After the Rangers signed Gretzky, he spent three full seasons wearing Broadway Blue. "The Great One" served as the alternate captain to Mark Messier and posted superior numbers at the end of his playing career. During his first two seasons with the club, Gretzky did not miss a single game and racked up 97 and 90 points, respectively. After a slower season in 1998-99, Gretzky left the Rangers and retired from the playing side of professional hockey.

In 2000 he became the alternate governor and managing partner of the Coyotes and began coaching Phoenix after the 2004-05 lockout.

Any further comments about Gretzky would be roughly equivalent to painting the rose or gilding the lily.

He was one of a kind, and the Rangers were most fortunate to have him, if only for three precious seasons.

VIC HADFIELD

1 9 6 1 - 1 9 7 4

Few players in the history of professional hockey have endured a more positive metamorphosis than Vic Hadfield.

When he entered the National Hockey League in 1961, the best thing you could say about the left wing was that he was big and enthused.

His skating was awkward—one might even call it clumsy—and for a time, he appeared to be wearing snowshoes instead of blades.

Most critics believed that the best one could expect from the Ontario-born forward was that he would be an effective fourth-line enforcer. If nothing else, Vic could fight.

Those who saw him as a rookie still find it hard to believe that his game grew to the point that in one season, 1971-72, he actually totaled 50 goals.

The 6-foot, 190-pound Hadfield was originally drafted by the Chicago Blackhawks and played most of three seasons in the Ontario Hockey Association (OHA) and American Hockey League (AHL) for the St. Catharines Teepees and the Buffalo Bisons. In the 1960-61 season, just before Hadfield's career in the NHL would blossom, he developed a physical presence, drawing 111 penalty minutes for the Bisons.

In the waiver draft, the Blackhawks showed no interest in retaining Hadfield's rights. This was a huge mistake from which the Rangers would benefit after acquiring the young battler.

Vic's evolution as a Rangers ace was slow but sure, a testament to his perseverance and ability to hone his skills to sharpness.

It didn't hurt that Vic eventually was placed at left wing alongside right wing Rod Gilbert and center Jean Ratelle. Hadfield was the final piece in an offensive puzzle that would confound enemy goalies and defensemen for many years. Both Gilbert and Ratelle were classy skill players who avoided intense physical play.

For the line to succeed, a rough presence was necessary to take the load off the two French-Canadian aces. Hadfield was an ideal choice, especially since his skating had remarkably improved and he had mastered the slap shot to the degree that it had become one of the most lethal in the league.

Despite his success as an offensive talent, Vic remained an intimidating force. Some of his battles were classic, including several with Montreal's gritty Henri "Pocket Rocket" Richard. In one such encounter, Hadfield attempted to climb over a plexiglass barrier separating the two penalty boxes so he could resume his battle with the "Pocket Rocket."

ABOVE: Vic Hadfield (right) charges at Toronto defenseman Bob Baun, The Ranger's upraised stick suggests that the Maple Leafs defenseman is going to get a crosscheck in the head. At the very least, it would be a near miss. Referee John Ashley, pictured in the background, will decide on the legality of Hadfield's maneuver. *From the Stan Fischler Collection*

In the 1963-64 season, the veteran of three years accumulated over 150 penalty minutes. At the same time, Hadfield's offensive production increased as he competed more. Eventually, as his penalties lessened, he stayed on the ice more and took advantage of the opportunities he had.

By the beginning of the 1970s, he had come into his own. He set the team's playoff points record with 13 while netting eight goals, including a hat trick against the Toronto Maple Leafs.

His growth and maturity led to special times for Hadfield and the Rangers organization as this Blueshirts leader became the 14th captain of the club after the prior one, Bob Nevin, was traded to Minnesota in the summer of 1971. With greater responsibility, Hadfield stepped up to the plate, picked a pitch, and rocked it over the centerfield wall. Rather than becoming a Hank Aaron, Hadfield developed into a magnificent goal scorer with the assistance of his new linemates (Ratelle and Gilbert).

With the GAG Line combination, the Rangers tandem fared exceptionally on the ice and in their wallets: Vic Hadfield was the first Ranger to make the siren sound 50 times in one season. The record was not broken until Adam Graves contributed 52 scores in the 1993-94 Stanley Cup championship year. Former Pittsburgh Penguins and Rangers right wing Jaromir Jagr, who currently plays for the Florida Panthers, now owns the record for most goals in a season with 54 in 2005-06.

Stark differences remain among Hadfield, Graves, and Jagr. For one, they are of different nationalities: Hadfield and Graves are Canadian, and Jagr is from the Czech Republic. Hadfield and Graves were solid offensive players and physically agitating, whereas Jagr is a superstar who helps other players on his team produce. The Czech also has the ability to use his body to forecheck and create mismatches with opposing defenses. Two

similarities exist, though: all three are right wingers and prolific on the power play.

Jaromir Jagr stands at the right point with the man advantage and receives passes for one-timers that often end up in the back of the net.

Graves was an excellent power play forward used in front of the net to utilize screens and deflections for scoring opportunities.

Hadfield scored using a similar approach to Jagr's. With Ratelle and Gilbert feeding him the puck, Hadfield set the team mark with 23 power-play goals in 1972 while earning Second Team All-Star honors.

What distinguishes Hadfield from the others is his physical play. He found the opposition, punished other players with checking, and followed the puck to score.

After his All-Star game appearance, Hadfield continued dominating as he compiled his first and only 100-point campaign in the 1971-72 season.

The next year, Hadfield had difficulty continuing his astonishing play. During the two seasons after the team's run to the Stanley Cup finals, Hadfield's production plummeted to 28 and 27 goals, respectively, his point total remaining only half of what it was during the 1970-71 season. Also, Hadfield's aggressive nature seemed to dissipate as he spent less time in the penalty box.

Vic's declining play led the Rangers to deal him and his $100,000 salary to the Pittsburgh Penguins. Hadfield never again established his dominance, and his

VIC HADFIELD

BORN: Oakville, Ontario, Canada; October 4, 1940

POSITION: Left Wing

NHL TEAMS: New York Rangers, 1961-74; Pittsburgh Penguins 1974-77

AWARDS/HONORS: NHL Second Team All-Star, 1972; Team Canada, 1972; NHL All-Star Game, 1965, 1972

knees buckled over the years, forcing his retirement in 1977.

Interestingly, two New York heroes wore No. 11 for the Rangers. Hall of Famer Rod Gilbert makes an interesting comparison. "I've always said that Vic Hadfield is No. 11 to me, my era," said Gilbert, "But . . . Mark Messier doesn't need a number. You could have a banner up there with no number that just says, 'Messier,' and it would still be Messier."

Hadfield remained in hockey as a Rangers scout, and to this day is a regular at alumni functions.

"I enjoy coming back," said Hadfield. "I still have ties to New York." These ties include his involvement with the Ice Hockey in Harlem program and other charitable organizations.

In retrospect, Vic's numbers speak eloquently about the manner in which he evolved from goon to giant among Blueshirts. He scored 262 goals and 572 points and accumulated 1,036 penalty minutes in 13 seasons. He also participated in the Olympics for Team Canada in 1972.

Off the ice, Hadfield was a humble, witty, intelligent man who became a professional golfer and businessman. But most of all, he was a Ranger who demonstrated that he could use his brains as well as his brawn.

DOUG HARVEY

1 9 6 1 - 1 9 6 4

One of the most depressing three years in Rangers annals occurred between March 1959 and October 1961.

In mid-March 1959, the Blueshirts had a seven-point lead in the playoff race over fifth-place Toronto. However, by the final night of the season, the Maple Leafs had caught the New Yorkers and edged them out of the fourth and final playoff spot.

The following year, 1959-60, was no better, nor was the season after that.

General manager Murray, or Muzz, Patrick knew that the club desperately needed a catalyst who could inspire the team to a playoff berth, but at the time, nobody could have imagined that the long-sought Lochinvar would turn out to be one of the best defensemen ever to step on to an NHL rink.

That catalyst was none other than Doug Harvey. Without question, Harvey had been one of the most important players on the greatest dynasty of all time, Montreal's Canadiens, the only team to win five consecutive Stanley Cups (1956-60).

After watching Harvey in action—and later coaching him—Scotty Bowman, the world's winningest coach, unabashedly labeled Harvey the greatest defenseman that he'd ever seen, and that included Bobby Orr, et al.

Harvey's confidence was supreme to the point that he was one of the few players

DOUG HARVEY

BORN: Montreal, Quebec, Canada; December 19, 1924

DIED: December 26, 1989

POSITION: Defenseman/ Coach

NHL TEAMS: Montreal Canadiens, 1974-61; New York Rangers, 1961-64; Detroit Red Wings, 1966-67; St. Louis Blues 1968-69

AWARDS/HONORS: James Norris Memorial Trophy, 1955-58, 1960-62; NHL First Team All-Star, 1952-58; NHL Second Team All-Star, 1959; NHL All-Star Game, 1951-62, 1969; Hockey Hall of Fame, 1973

who ever defied Montreal's legendary coach, Toe Blake, a fact that Doug's Hall of Fame partner, Tom Johnson, vividly recalls.

"Doug took a lot of chances," said Johnson. "Toe would tell him, 'Look, I don't want you in front of [our] net handling the puck.' Well, some games, if we were winning, he'd be out there in front of the net and look right over at the bench. It drove Toe nuts.

"He'd take his hands—and his fingers were so long, they were like a bunch of bananas—and he'd just wrap them around one of our guys' throats if they did something wrong. Didn't matter who it was."

But after the Habs won their Cup in 1960, Harvey fell out of management's

favor, and by the end of the 1960-61 season, managing director Frank Selke Sr. decided that he'd had enough of Doug's shenanigans and, in a startling move, dealt him to the Rangers for erstwhile New York hero Lou Fontinato.

Not only was Harvey to become a defenseman, but Patrick decided that Doug would take on the head coaching assignment as well.

The move shocked the hockey world, because Harvey had never been a head coach before. The burden of the dual assignments seemed staggering in every way.

Nevertheless, Harvey took on the challenge head first and with his usual aplomb.

The results were amazing, and the defenseman's confidence and championship demeanor instantly rubbed off on the Rangers. They not only became competitive but made a rare run for the playoffs.

In addition to his stellar defensive play, Harvey could also turn on the offense when necessary. For example, the Blueshirts once were losing 2-1 in the third period in a contest against the Blackhawks. Harvey set up the tying score and then scored a goal to lead the team to a 4-2 victory.

Even after he reached the age of 37 midway through the season, Harvey continued to play 35 to 40 minutes a game.

During Harvey's inaugural season, the Rangers started off hot, going 6-4-2 in their first 12 contests. By midseason, the Blueshirts had cooled off and suffered a few losing streaks, including one that lasted 10 games.

ABOVE: This battle of the titans features Rangers defenseman "Leapin' Louie" Fontinato (8) and Canadiens backliner Doug Harvey, considered by many at his position to be the greatest defenseman of all time. Harvey, who rarely fought, is flanked by teammate Tom Johnson on the left and New York's Camille Henry on the right. Goalie Gump Worsley watches from the goal crease. *From the Stan Fischler Collection*

On the final Thursday night of the season, the race for fourth place reached its peak at Madison Square Garden, where the Red Wings challenged the Blueshirts for the final playoff spot. Early in the game, the immortal Gordie Howe blew past Harvey, putting the visitors ahead.

Nonplussed, Doug rallied his troops, and the Rangers skated to victory on Andy Bathgate's penalty-shot goal, which propelled New York into the playoffs for the first time since 1958.

With Doug in command, the Rangers again rallied from a two-game deficit against the Maple Leafs to tie the series before bowing in six contests.

One of the most remarkable aspects of Harvey's adjustment to New York was his ability to relate to his players, even those such as Red Sullivan, who was once a bitter enemy.

Five years prior to becoming a Ranger, Harvey had had a run-in with Sullivan while Doug was playing for the Canadiens.

It had been Harvey's contention that Sullivan, never lauded for his lily-white play, had developed an obnoxious, not to mention dangerous, habit of "kicking skates." Any time Harvey and Sullivan would pursue the puck into the corner of the rink, Sullivan would kick Harvey's skates out from under him, making it very easy for Doug to fall on his head.

Several warnings failed to impress Sullivan, so Harvey decided to escalate the war. During one game, Harvey and Sullivan once again appeared to be on a collision course when Harvey planted the pointed blade of his stick in Sullivan's gut. The Rangers center was taken to the hospital with a ruptured spleen.

For a time, Sullivan's condition was so grave he was given the last rites of the Catholic Church. Fortunately, Sullivan recovered, and when the two rivals were united on the same team, they didn't have to deal with each other's animosity for long.

When Sullivan and Harvey met at training camp, they buried that hatchet—thankfully, not in each other's backs—and a rare harmony existed on the team as it entered the season. The ability to orchestrate such a pleasant atmosphere was merely a product of Doug's overall personality on and off the ice.

Sadly, though, neither Doug nor the Rangers were able to reignite the spark that had existed throughout the successful 1961-62 season.

Much of that had to do with Doug's personal life. His family had remained in Montreal, and he often felt lonely in Manhattan. Despite his success, he seriously considered retiring after the 1961-62 triumph.

But as the 1962-63 campaign approached, Patrick realized he needed Harvey in the lineup and offered the defenseman a contract he couldn't refuse.

Doug could skip practice whenever he wanted to fly home to Montreal to see his family or attend to business. In addition, even with his reduced workload, Harvey received a salary boost to about $30,000.

Harvey was dealing with a failed restaurant at the time, and often took advantage of his contract benefits to skip practice and visit his hometown. The excessive amount of travel left Harvey out of shape, and he played inconsistently throughout most of the season.

Eventually, Sullivan was brought up to coach the team. It was then that Harvey became more committed to New York. He missed fewer practices, and it showed in his play: he ended the season leading all Blueshirts defensemen in points.

The Rangers failed to make the play-offs, and the team and Harvey seemed to be parting ways when the Rangers did not protect him in the offseason during the NHL entry draft.

This hurt Harvey, but after he wasn't claimed by any other team, he returned to the Rangers at a reduced salary. Patrick told Harvey that he could have a roster spot if he came to training camp in the same shape he had the pervious season.

However, due to ongoing complications pertaining to his failed restaurant, Doug was unable to make it to training camp and was instead sent to the Rangers' farm team.

His play earned him a trip back up to the NHL club just five games into the season, but Harvey was still not in good condition. His play suffered, and after just 14 games with the Rangers, he was told that his days on Broadway were over.

Although he was given the option to play for the team's AHL club, the Baltimore Clippers, while retaining his NHL pay level, Harvey asked for his outright release to become a free agent.

Doug found it difficult to pull the curtain on his career. He took part in a few AHL seasons before briefly resurfacing in the NHL. He played two games for the Detroit Red Wings in 1966-67 and then joined the St. Louis Blues for a playoff run in 1967-68. While skating for Scotty Bowman, who was in his first NHL stint as a head coach, Doug remarkably regained much of the form that had made him an All-Star. Along with former Montreal teammate Dickie Moore, he helped the expansion team make the Stanley Cup finals in its first year of existence. The Blues kept him on for one more season before he called it a career.

Harvey will most certainly be remembered as one of the best defensemen of all time and for his work with the Canadiens, with whom he won six Norris Trophies and five straight Stanley Cups from 1956-60. However, his contributions to the Rangers must not go unnoticed. In the span of eight seasons, from 1958-59 through 1965-66, the Blueshirts only made the postseason once—and it just so happens that player-coach Harvey took them there, winning himself yet another Norris Trophy.

ANDERS HEDBERG

1 9 7 8 - 1 9 8 5

The World Hockey Association (WHA), which was organized in 1975, did the Rangers a big favor, even though it considered itself a major-league rival of the National Hockey League.

The WHA was special in that it unhesitatingly signed European players, while its NHL counterpart tended to focus almost exclusively on North Americans.

Arguably the most outstanding European forward to grace the WHA was a Swedish right wing named Anders Hedberg, who played for the Winnipeg Jets alongside former NHL ace Bobby Hull and countryman Ulf Nilsson.

The line's razzle-dazzle play arrested the attention of NHL scouts, including those at Madison Square Garden. Meanwhile, Hedberg's WHA numbers over four seasons explain why his progression to the NHL was inevitable. Hull repeatedly stated that the two Swedes were the best linemates he'd ever had. Considering that he scored his 1,000th career goal with them, this may be true.

In that time, Anders never failed to score less than 100 points. His 458 points with the Jets rank fifth in WHA history. He led the league in the 1976-77 season with 70 goals in 68 games and added 61 assists to round out his 131 total points.

By Hedberg's fourth WHA season, NHL and WHA officials had begun discussing the possibility of merging the two leagues or, at the very least, allowing the NHL to absorb some teams from the rebel circuit.

One of the individuals heading the merger talks was Rangers president Bill Jennings, who held behind-the-scenes discussions with WHA president Howard Baldwin. The friendly relationship enabled Jennings to engineer one of the most meaningful acquisitions in his club's history.

Shortly before the WHA folded, Hedberg brought his tremendous skating speed and scoring power to New York when he and Nilsson signed with the Rangers on June 5, 1978. However, their signing was not without controversy.

The Swedish pair had it written into their WHA contracts that they could negotiate with any NHL team as long as they gave the Jets a chance to retain their services if Winnipeg presented a contract within $20,000 of the NHL team's offer.

When Hedberg and Nilsson began talking with NHL teams during the 1977-78 season, a bidding war ensued as the Swedes received offers from many teams, including the St. Louis Blues, Vancouver Canucks, Philadelphia Flyers, and Chicago Blackhawks. However, it soon became clear that the Rangers were willing to pay handsomely for the duo.

Once the WHA owners learned that Hedberg and Nilsson planned to jump to the NHL, they panicked. At one point, each team in the association offered up $50,000 for a total of $400,000 to keep both players for two more years. It was a futile effort compared to what the Rangers were offering—a $2.4 million two-year package, or $600,000 a year for each player. That made Hedberg and Nilsson the highest paid players in the sport at the time.

Nevertheless, some on the NHL staff, including then-president John Ziegler, criticized the deal. Many owners were worried that the contract would drive up salaries at a time when the NHL was trying to curb them.

For the Rangers, signing the pair turned out to be a glass half full when Nilsson suffered a serious injury that sidelined his career. On the plus side, Hedberg thrived on Broadway. In his inaugural season, Anders scored 33 goals and led the Rangers with 78 points, helping the team to the 1979 Stanley Cup finals. En route, Hedberg played a major part in the Rangers' six-game upset victory over the New York Islanders in the third playoff round. The Blueshirts lost to Montreal four games to one in the finals.

Hedberg's success was in direct contrast to the handful of other European players with whom the Rangers had experimented.

ANDERS HEDBERG

BORN: Ornkoldsvik, Sweden; February 25, 1951

POSITION: Right Wing

NHL TEAMS: New York Rangers, 1978-85

AWARDS/HONORS: Bill Masterton Memorial Trophy, 1985; NHL Challenge Cup All-Star, 1979; NHL All-Star Game, 1985

Often known in Sweden as the "New Tumba," a name originally derived from the Swedish sensation Sven "Tumba" Johansson, Hedberg electrified the Rangers faithful with dazzling stickhandling displays without playing the violent game typical in North America at that time.

Many NHL viewers feared that Hedberg would not survive this style of play. But Anders had an answer to that. "When somebody tried to run me and got a penalty," said Hedberg, "I'd get even by scoring goals. That was the best revenge."

What's more, Anders proved to be a money player in the more important games—particularly in the playoffs, when he scored 22 goals and 46 points, 16 of which came in 14 games during the 1981 postseason.

It is noteworthy that Hedberg, who lost all but four games in the 1981-82 season to a knee injury, never scored less than 20 goals or less than 50 points in any of his six complete seasons with the Rangers before retiring as an active player in 1985.

Hedberg totaled 465 games for the Blueshirts, scoring 172 goals. A marvelously clean player, Anders served only 144 minutes in the penalty box. His 397 career points are a testament to the wisdom of the Rangers' high command that signed him.

Hedberg's career highlights on Broadway are many. One of his finest NHL games occurred on October 27, 1980, against the Detroit Red Wings in the Garden. The Swede banged home four goals, paving the way to a 7-6 victory.

Hedberg scored the first goal of the game, but the Rangers soon lost the lead. The Wings moved ahead 2-1 and then 4-2. The Rangers' Mike Allison scored and Hedberg tied the game, but Detroit would pull ahead again. Hedberg then found the net twice in the final 74 seconds to give the Rangers the win.

The combination of his skill, overall clean play, and good works off the ice explains why, in the final year of his career, Hedberg was awarded the Bill Masterton Trophy—an award that can only be given to a player once in his lifetime—for "perseverance, sportsmanship, and dedication to hockey."

Following his retirement, Hedberg became an assistant to Rangers GM Craig Patrick. He continued his management career, taking over Stockholm's AIK hockey team before becoming a scout for the Toronto Maple Leafs in 1991. After serving as Toronto's chief European scout for six seasons, he moved into the front office as assistant general manager and director of player development until 1999.

Then, after a brief stint as the Edmonton Oilers' director of European scouting, Hedberg took over as GM for the Swedish national hockey program from 2000 to 2002 and Team Sweden at the 2002 Olympics. Anders followed that position by signing on as the director of player personnel for the Ottawa Senators before returning to the Rangers as head professional European scout in the summer of 2007.

Some would argue that Hedberg belongs in the Hockey Hall of Fame, but he has not yet been nominated and may never attain that accolade. However, during the 1997 World Championship in Finland, Hedberg, along with "Tumba" Johansson, among others, were inducted into the European Hockey Hall of Fame.

Many Swedes have starred in the NHL—Nicholas Lindstrom, Henrik Lundqvist, and Mats Sundin, to name a few—yet Anders Hedberg was in a class by himself not only on Broadway, but throughout the hockey world.

CAMILLE HENRY

1 9 5 3 - 1 9 6 4

Camille Henry earned distinction with the Rangers on several counts, not the least of which was becoming the National Hockey League's first "designated hitter," so to speak—or, to be more specific, the NHL's first exclusive designated power-play specialist. Rare was the occasion that this remarkably frail performer ever took a regular turn when the sides were even during his premiere big-league campaign.

When Henry made his debut with the Rangers in 1953, he was deemed too fragile for full-time duty. Manager Frank Boucher decided that it would be best to simply limit the French Canadian's workload to the power play alone.

Henry had the good fortune to work alongside Max Bentley, then an aging superstar who was arguably the best power-play specialist of all time.

Bentley's guidance was invaluable to Henry, who soon earned the nickname "Camille the Eel."

Those who had seen Henry perform in Junior hockey were not surprised. After all, Henry had succeeded the legendary Jean Beliveau as a star with the Quebec Citadelles.

What Beliveau had in size, Henry had in brains. Never was there a craftier forward who could thread the needle with a puck if need be. Henry put up such impressive goal totals in Juniors and the minors that Boucher had no choice but to bring him up.

Henry was an instant hit in the NHL. When Boucher gave him a shot with the team in 1953, the "Eel" not only scored 24 goals—20 of them on the power play—but also won the Calder Trophy as Rookie of the Year.

It is a testament to the French Canadian's clutch ability that he scored some of his biggest goals against the very best goaltenders.

One such netminder was the immortal Terry Sawchuk of the Detroit Red Wings, a prideful performer who resented giving up even one goal a game. Imagine, if you will, how furious Sawchuk was on the night of March 13, 1954. Playing at Detroit's Olympia Stadium, Henry delivered a hat trick plus one against Sawchuk. It is believed that the four goals may have cost Sawchuk his third Vezina Trophy.

The "Eel" remembered the event very vividly.

"That four-goal night won the Calder Trophy for me," Henry recalled. "It also

CAMILLE HENRY

BORN: Quebec City, Quebec, Canada; January 31, 1933

DIED: September 11, 1997

POSITION: Left Wing

NHL TEAMS: New York Rangers, 1953-64, 1967-68; Chicago Blackhawks, 1964-65; St. Louis Blues, 1968-70

AWARDS/HONORS: Calder Memorial Trophy, 1954; Lady Byng Trophy, 1958; NHL Second Team All-Star 1958; NHL All-Star Game, 1958, 1963-64

knocked Sawchuk out of all the honors [the Vezina Trophy and a First Team All-Star nomination] he practically had in his pocket."

Soon after, Henry suffered some hardship as well. During the athlete's sophomore year, general manager Frank Boucher sent Henry down to the minors because of sub-par play. The Rangers placed him on waivers more than once that year, but no team would budge because of his hefty $15,000 contract.

It wasn't until Phil Watson became coach of the Blueshirts in the mid-1950s that Henry hit his stride with the New Yorkers. In the 1956-57 season, Camille proved that he could take a regular turn as well as work the power play and finished with 29 points in 36 games.

The Rangers' high command believed the skinny sharpshooter would be even more effective if he fattened up considerably. Management sent him home with

specific orders that he add as many thick malted milks to every one of his meals possible.

Dutifully, Camille obliged, and when he returned to training camp in September, the New York staff eagerly awaited the moment when Henry would step on the scale. They expected him to have added a minimum of at least 10 pounds to his physique.

Alas, the "Eel" didn't add one ounce, and that was the end of that grand plan.

Like many of his teammates, including Andy Bathgate, Gump Worsley, and Dean Prentice, Henry feuded with Coach Watson from time to time.

Regardless, Camille became an integral part of the Rangers team that gained a playoff berth in each of the 1955-56, 1956-57, and 1957-58 seasons.

Often battered by the bigger, tougher opposition, Henry managed to prevail because of his superior savvy and goal-scoring skills. But by the early 1960s, the physical toll had worn him down, and during the 1964-65 season, he was traded to the Chicago Blackhawks.

The deal was denounced by Rangers fans who had taken the thin man to their hearts, and the Blueshirts briefly reclaimed him before trading him again, this time to the St. Louis Blues.

The player who many critics claimed was too frail for big-league hockey certainly proved them wrong. He finished his career with 279 goals and 249 assists while competing for the Rangers, Blackhawks, and Blues.

During his most productive years, Henry totaled more than 50 points five times and even reached 60 in 1962-63. He also earned All-Star honors in three of his 11 seasons on the Blueshirts' roster.

After his playing career ended, the Eel had a short-lived stint as head coach of the World Hockey Association's New York Raiders.

From that point on, Camille's life was a disaster.

Many of the players on the Raiders—some of whom were NHL rejects—took advantage of Henry's good nature, breaking curfews and otherwise ignoring the coach's requests. The demoralized "Eel" finally decided to give up the job and move back to Canada, where he was an occasional TV analyst.

Meanwhile, his health deteriorated severely, and in 1997, Camille died at the age of 64.

A hero to the Garden's gallery gods, Camille Henry will always be revered for defying the odds to become not only one of the most productive Rangers in a short time but also one of the most beloved.

BRYAN HEXTALL

1 9 3 6 - 1 9 4 8

Had the advent of World War II not intruded on his playing career, there's no telling what heights Bryan Hextall might have achieved as a National Hockey League right wing. While he will always be remembered as the person who scored

the game-winning goal during the Rangers' 1940 Stanley Cup championship run, Hextall is also known as a dominating physical force who has blood lines in hockey circles.

As it was, the man his teammates called "Hex" proved a valiant attacker and contributed to one of the most important goals in New York's franchise history.

Hextall did not know it at the time, but the goal he scored to win the Rangers the Stanley Cup grew in stature to become a veritable legend in Manhattan with each passing season, simply because the Rangers did not win another championship for 54 years after "Hex" beat pudgy Toronto goalie Walter "Turk" Broda.

Hextall recalled his sparkling moment as a Ranger: "I received a pass from Dutch Hiller and Phil Watson. The puck came out from behind the net, and I took a backhand shot to put it past Broda."

The 1939-40 season preceded the advent of television and widespread media coverage. As a result, Hextall's stunning overtime goal was only momentarily acknowledged on radio and for one day in the newspapers. There were no video replays or Sportscenter television shows, and as a result, Hextall's melodramatic moment essentially became a footnote in Rangers history.

RIGHT: Bryan Hextall played 11 strong years with the New York Rangers. *From the Stan Fischler Collection*

The goal clearly signaled that "Hex" was a right wing to be reckoned with, a galvanizing force playing alongside left wing Lynn Patrick and either Phil Watson or Wilfred "Dutch" Hiller at center. Hextall would spearhead the Rangers through the 1941-42 season, when the Blueshirts finished first in the seven-team league—the seventh team being the New York Americans, who shared the Garden with the Rangers.

Hextall was more than just a member of the championship squad and the person who provided the Cup for native New Yorkers. "He was," said Herb Goren, who covered the Rangers for the *New York Sun*, "the hardest bodychecking forward I have seen in more than 40 years of watching hockey."

While he was never the captain of the Rangers, he led the National Hockey League in scoring in 1942, was a First Team All-Star in 1940, 1941, and 1942, and made the Second Team in 1943.

Like so many Rangers, Hextall joined the Canadian Armed Forces during World War II at the very height of his career. By the time he returned to the team at war's end, he was a shade of his former self. He played a few more less than spectacular years before retiring.

Bryan Aldwyn Hextall was born July 31, 1913, in Grenfell, Saskatchewan. He commanded attention during the early 1930s while playing for the Vancouver Lions of the Western Hockey League, a league originally established by Lester Patrick. The Rangers noticed Bryan after he led the Lions to a first-place finish. Two years later, he appeared on Broadway not for a show, but to succeed as a Blueshirt whose patriarch was Patrick, the Western Hockey League innovator himself.

At the time Hextall arrived, Patrick was in the process of dismantling an aging club and rebuilding it with youth. Patrick eventually inserted Bryan alongside the likes of newcomers Alf Pike and Alex Shibicky.

When Frank Boucher became head coach in the fall of 1939, he created a line that included Hextall, Lynn Patrick, and Watson, who alternated with Hiller. It would become one of the hottest units in the league.

To his credit, Bryan continued to play hard hockey after World War II and managed to crack the 20-goal mark during the 1946-47 season—one of seven occasions he achieved that feat.

"Hex" amassed 187 goals and 362 points in 449 games during his 11-year tenure with Broadway's Blueshirts. "I scored 20 goals for seven straight

BRYAN HEXTALL

BORN: Grenfell, Saskatchewan, Canada; July 31, 1913

DIED: July 25, 1984

POSITION: Center

NHL TEAMS: New York Rangers, 1936-48

AWARDS/HONORS: Art Ross Trophy, 1942; NHL First Team All-Star, 1940-42; NHL Second Team All-Star, 1943; Hockey Hall of Fame, 1969

years," Hextall recalled proudly. "Twenty goals was a big thing then."

In reviewing Bryan's career, one must keep in mind that seasons comprised 48 games during most of his playing days. One year he participated in 50, and when the NHL continued to develop after World War II, he joined in 60 games.

The three-time All-Star won the scoring title in the 1941-42 season with 24 goals and 56 points in 48 games. He was among the top 10 in scoring on four other occasions.

After his retirement, Bryan started a lumber yard and hardware business, but his love for hunting inspired him to open a commercial shooting lodge near his home in Poplar Point, Manitoba.

He proudly watched his sons, Bryan Jr. and Dennis, make their way to the NHL. Each of them had an adequate, albeit brief, stint with the Rangers.

In 1969, Hextall was enshrined in the Hockey Hall of Fame for his excellence and contributions to the sport. He died on July 25, 1984, just six days before he would have turned 81.

HARRY HOWELL

1 9 5 2 - 1 9 6 9

Over the years, the Rangers developed several successful developmental teams. These include the New York Rovers, Winnipeg (Junior) Rangers, New Haven Ramblers, and the Springfield Indians. But none could top the Junior A team playing out of the small hat-manufacturing city of Guelph, Ontario, a short drive from the metropolis of Toronto.

Created in the post-World War II years, the Guelph Biltmore Mad Hatters were coached by Alf Pike, a former Rangers star from the 1940 Stanley Cup-winning team. By the start of the 1950s, the Biltmores had become a major force in Canadian Junior Hockey circles. In 1951-52 they reached their peak, winning the Memorial Cup emblematic of Canadian Junior Hockey supremacy.

The Biltmores were led by forwards Andy Bathgate, Dean Prentice, Lou Fontinato, and Ron Murphy, but arguably the best player of all was defenseman Harry Howell, who played a versatile game blending hard hitting with an occasional offensive foray.

Howell was so good that he averaged 45 to 50 minutes a game with the Biltmores. He was so precocious that the Rangers gave him a one-game tryout in the American Hockey League before promoting him to the big club in the fall of 1952.

In his early NHL years on Broadway, Howell was clearly rough around the edges, skating for a struggling Rangers team that failed to make the playoffs from his debut in 1952 until the 1955-56 season, when many of his Guelph teammates had matured into NHL aces under coach Phil Watson.

Howell's evolution as a Ranger was met with peculiar irony. The better he played, the less fans liked him. In a sense, Harry was following the same unfortunate saga of Allen Stanley, a Rangers defenseman who was traded to Chicago in 1954 when Howell was just learning the ropes.

Although each defenseman eventually made it to the Hockey Hall of Fame, both were unappreciated because Garden fans demanded a more energetic, robust style that simply was not part of the Howell or Stanley persona.

Objectively speaking, Harry did all the Rangers management wanted of him. He was intelligent, courageous, and a thorough team man and quietly responsible for some of the club's major triumphs.

Howell spent 22 years in the NHL. Seventeen of those years were spent with the Rangers, for whom Howell played 1,160 games, a team record. For his 1,000th game, the Rangers honored him with a memorable Harry Howell Night at Madison square Garden.

How did Howell become a Ranger?

Having played organized hockey since the age of 12, Howell had already been scouted as a player before entering the Junior ranks.

Said Howell, "The NHL had the reserve list, and I remember when it came time to play Junior hockey, I got a call from New York and they said, 'We understand you want to play Junior hockey. You're

HARRY HOWELL

BORN: Hamilton, Ontario, Canada; December 28, 1932

POSITION: Defenseman

NHL TEAMS: New York Rangers, 1952-69; Oakland Seals, 1969-70; Los Angeles Kings, 1970-73

AWARDS/HONORS: James Norris Memorial Trophy, 1967; NHL First Team All-Star, 1967; NHL All-Star Game, 1954, 1963-65, 1967-68, 1970; Hockey Hall of Fame 1979

going to play in Guelph.' I said, 'Now why would I want to play Junior hockey in Guelph?' It wasn't bad because it wasn't very far from home [in Hamilton], but Frank Boucher, the general manager of the New York Rangers, said, You have to play in Guelph because you've been on our reserve list since you were 14.'"

With Guelph, Howell was part of the 1951-52 Memorial Cup–winning squad. The next season, a 19-year-old Howell, who had only played one game in the AHL in his career, was called up to the Rangers three games into the season.

"Actually, I was still playing Junior in Guelph," Howell remembered. "After five games [into the OHL season], I got a call from New York. 'We've got a couple of defensemen injured,' I was told, and of course, they started the season with a five-game road trip as usual because of the rodeo at Madison Square Garden. They were going to Toronto, and Boucher said,

'You can come down and fill in for us in Toronto and then you go back to Guelph.'

"I went to Toronto and played with Leo Reise, who was a big help to me. Leo was a great veteran and taught me an awful lot. During that [first] game, we played every second shift. After the game, Boucher said, 'Well, you've never been to New York. I think you'd better come down and just spend the week with us practicing with the team, and then you can go back to Guelph.'"

As it turned out, Howell never did go back to Guelph. Instead, he finished the 1952-53 season with the team as well as the next 16 campaigns, during which the "Iron Man" defenseman missed only 40 of the Rangers' 1,200 regular-season games.

Howell quickly established himself as one of the game's best defensive defensemen with his subtle—some deprecatingly called it dainty—style of play.

Although he actually managed to accumulate 101 minutes of penalty time one year, his play was so habitually void of vengefulness that the Madison Square Garden fans took to mocking him with names such as "Harriet" and "Sonja." Fans overlooked the fact that his bodychecks were effective, timely, and often lowered opposing players' morale.

Howell remembered one of his solid performances: "We were playing the Canadiens," he recalled, "At the time, they had big 'Spider' Mazur up front. Well, one night he comes down my side, thrown a deke, but I get him good with my shoulder—clipped him right in the teeth—and half his molars fall on the ice. I had a notion he might be going." Asked how Mazur reacted to the hit, Howell said, "He looked up at me with the sorriest look you can imagine and said, 'Geez, Harry, I wish you hadn't done that.'"

Howell posted his best offensive year in 1966-67 with 12 goals and 28 assists for 40 points. This accomplishment along with his strong defensive play garnered him a nomination to the NHL All-Star squad in 1967 as well as the Norris Trophy as the league's best defenseman—and this was the year that Bobby Orr made his debut with the Bruins.

"I'm glad I won it this year," Howell said prophetically when he earned the Norris. "I think some other guy is going to win it for the next decade."

And while eight years is not a decade, Orr did take home the award the next eight seasons.

Howell was the youngest Blueshirt ever to be given captaincy. At age 23, he was given the "C" for the 1955-56 season. However, Howell gave up the position to Red Sullivan after the 1956-57 campaign, saying, "I was just too young for it. I know that after Sully took over, I had a good year with that off my mind. We finished second that year, too."

During the 1968-69 season, Harry was afflicted with back problems, and the Rangers began to move in a new and younger direction.

"My back went bad on me in my 17th and last year in New York," he explained. "It was determined that I needed to have a spinal fusion. I had my choice—either have the spinal fusion and feel better or don't have it and don't play anymore. I did have the fusion. [Rangers GM] Emile Francis came in to see me at the hospital. He said, 'We're going to make a move.

NEW YORK RANGERS

We don't think you should be playing because of your back and we'll get you a job in the front office or coaching.' I said, 'I didn't go through this operation to sit in an office or coach.' Emile asked me where I'd like to go, and I said, 'How about the West Coast?' He made a deal with Oakland and there I was."

Howell was sent to the Oakland Seals for an undisclosed amount of cash believed to be over $30,000 by a *New York Times* article that ran one day after he was traded.

He played two years with in Oakland and was then traded to the Los Angeles Kings, with whom he played three more years before moving around the World Hockey Association for a few seasons. In 1977, Harry became general manager of the Cleveland Barons, and when the club merged with the North Stars in 1978, he was named coach of the team. But coaching wasn't for Harry, and his health began to suffer shortly after the start of the 1978-79 season. He resigned to become a scout with the North Stars and, more recently, with the Rangers.

Howell was voted to the Hockey Hall of Fame in 1979 and continued as an NHL scout. He also won the Rangers Fan Club's Frank Boucher trophy for being the most popular player on and off the ice three straight times from 1965 to 1967. This feat has been accomplished by only three other Rangers: Andy Bathgate, Rod Gilbert, and Mark Messier.

And yet fans who were not members of the fan club took issue to that with their booing.

CHING JOHNSON

1 9 2 6 - 1 9 3 7

Before the Rangers were created prior to the 1926-27 season, they were preceded in New York by another NHL team called the Americans. Because the Rangers arrived a season later, it was important for the new, upstart club to make inroads into the New York fan base.

Since the Americans had a number of colorful players such as "Shorty" Green and Roy "Shrimp" Worters, Rangers manager Lester Patrick pursued as many attractive youngsters as possible.

One such defenseman was a rugged backliner from Winnipeg named Ivan Wilfred Johnson, better known to his compatriots as Ching.

He proved just the colorful competitor the Rangers needed in the late 1920s when they were trying to establish a following in the Big Apple.

His robust play was a perfect metaphor for hard hockey. A swashbuckling defenseman if ever there was one, Ching helped sell the still foreign game of hockey to New Yorkers during the Roaring Twenties with his gregarious personality.

RIGHT: Ching Johnson was one of many colorful characters on the Rangers' first teams. *From the Stan Fischler Collection*

CHING JOHNSON

BORN: Winnipeg, Manitoba, Canada; December 7, 1897

DIED: June 16, 1979

POSITION: Defenseman

NHL TEAMS: New York Rangers, 1926-37; New York Americans, 1937-38

AWARDS/HONORS: NHL First Second Team All-Star, 1931, 1934; Hockey Hall of Fame, 1958

He was 28 years old when he made his debut on Broadway with the Rangers. It was also the debut for the Blueshirts, who were launching their National Hockey League franchise in the 1926-27 season against the powerful Montreal Maroons.

Before the game, Ching suffered doubts about the Rangers' ability to withstand the mighty men from the North. The game itself was billed as the best against the worst. Johnson was teamed on the blue line with his sidekick, Taffy Abel. Their names—Taffy and Ching—would soon become household words to New York's hockey fans.

Johnson was a big, rawboned hunk of man with a bald head and an extremely positive view of life. "He always wore a grin," said teammate Frank Boucher, "even when heaving some pour soul six feet in the air. He was one of those rare warm people who would break into a smile just saying hello or telling you the time."

Abel was heavier and rounder than Johnson. It was said that when Taffy hit a foe, it was like being swatted with a fat pillow. When Ching connected, it was like being hit by a train. Ching hit often, but he was also the recipient of many hits, and that opening game against the Maroons was a good example of what was to come.

In the first period, the Maroons chose to intimidate the Rangers; hard-nosed Nels Stewart went after Johnson, hooking him over the eye with his stick when they clashed along the boards behind the Rangers' net. Referee Lou Marsh gave them both penalties, and Ching went to the dressing room, where five stitches were placed in the wound. He soon returned to the fray wearing a white patch over the eye. Ching played more effervescently than ever, and the Rangers scored an upset victory over the Maroons.

Johnson gave New York fans a million bucks worth of entertainment during his career. He was a First All-Star Team member in 1932 and 1933 and made the Second Team in 1931 and 1934. With Ching starring on defense, the Rangers finished first in the American Division and a season later won their first Stanley Cup.

Johnson helped the Rangers to a second Stanley Cup in 1933.

"Ching," said Boucher, "loved to deliver a good hoist early in a game because he knew his victim would likely retaliate, and Ching loved body contact. I remember once against the Maroons, Ching caught Hooley Smith with a terrific check right at the start of the game. Hooley's stick flew from his hands and disappeared above the rink lights.

"He was lifted clean off the ice and seemed to stay suspended five or six feet above the surface for seconds before finally crashing down on his back. No one could accuse Hooley of lacking guts. From then on, whenever he got the puck, he drove for Ching, trying to outmatch him, but each time, Ching flattened poor Hooley. Afterwards, grinning in the shower, Ching said he couldn't remember a game he'd enjoyed more."

Johnson was not counted on as an offensive threat, though he did add the occasional goal. The numbers that tell the most about his style of play are his penalty minutes: 798 in 403 games. Johnson led the team in penalty minutes in eight of his 11 seasons with the Blueshirts, including seven of the first eight—in 1934-35, he had only 34 penalty minutes, but they came in just 26 games as he missed most of the season with injuries.

Ivan Wilfred Johnson was born on December 7, 1897, in Winnipeg, Manitoba. He was nicknamed Ching because he wore a wide grin on his face whenever he bodychecked the enemy. In those pre-politically correct days, friends believed that his eyes gave him an Oriental look when he smiled; therefore, they called him Ching, as in "Ching-a-ling-Chinaman."

Johnson was discovered by Conn Smythe when the hockey entrepreneur was scouting for the Rangers prior to their entry into the NHL. Both Ching and his buddy, Taffy Abel, were playing semi-pro hockey in Minneapolis. Smythe liked them both, but found Johnson a hard bargainer.

"I must have reached an agreement with Ching 40 times," Smythe recalled. "Each time, when I gave him my pen to sign, he'd say, 'I just want to phone my wife.' Then there'd be a hitch, and he wouldn't sign. In my final meeting with him, I said before we started, 'Ching, I want you to promise that if we make a deal, you will sign, and then you'll phone your wife.' He promised. We made a deal. He said, 'I've got to phone my wife.' I said, 'You promised!' He said, 'Okay, Connie,' and signed."

Smythe was unloaded by the Rangers before the opening season had begun and was replaced by Lester Patrick.

Johnson played for the Rangers until 1937, when he was ironically dealt to the rival New York Americans. He completed his NHL career in 1938 and briefly coached in the minors before he turned to officiating. While calling a game in Washington, D.C., he committed a memorable gaffe.

"I was calling this game," Ching recalled, "when some young forwards broke out and raced solo against the goalie. Instinctively, I took this player down with a jarring bodycheck. Following the game, I apologized to his team. I don't know what made me do it, but I did it I guess it was just the old defenseman's instinct."

Johnson eventually went into the construction business and remained in Washington, where he occasionally attended games played by the NHL's Washington Capitals. He was elected to the Hockey Hall of Fame in 1958. Johnson died on June 16, 1979.

DAVEY KERR

1 9 3 4 - 1 9 4 1

If ever there was a Mike Richter before Mike Richter became the Rangers' goalie, it would be Davey Kerr. Like Richter, Kerr was a primary reason why the Rangers won a Stanley Cup. And like Richter, Kerr was small in stature but big between the pipes.

Unfortunately, his major-league career was relatively short, and as such, he is often overlooked when historians consider the legendary Rangers.

The Rangers acquired the rights to Davey Kerr from the Montreal Maroons on December 14, 1934, and he immediately filled in as the Blueshirts' starting goaltender. The nimble netminder played only 37 contests in the 1934-35 season, but went on to miss only one more game—substitute Bert Gardiner was called on to replace Kerr in Kerr's sophomore season—throughout the rest of his career.

Before he retired following the 1940-41 season, Davey played 324 regular-season games for the Rangers, posting a record of 157-110-57 with 40 shutouts and a goals-against average of 2.07. He also played a significant role in taking the Rangers to two Stanley Cup finals appearances, including a quite memorable one in his finest season, 1939-40.

"Davey was tremendously important to the 1940 team," recalled former coach Frank Boucher. "He was always in fantastic shape and was really an inspiration for the other fellows to stay in shape. We relied on him a lot, and the fans really liked him."

During that season, the Rangers set a franchise-high 19-game unbeaten streak behind Kerr's solid netminding. The streak began when the Rangers played a 1-1 tie with the Canadiens on November 23, 1939, and ended when Kerr became the first goalie pulled from the net on the fly. Coach Frank Boucher believed the streak could have been extended to 25, but those Rangers were too smart for their own good.

"We were playing Chicago in the 20th game of the streak," said Boucher, "and playing rings around them. It was the kind of game we should have won hands down, but for some strange reason, we couldn't score a goal and were down 1-0 going into the third period."

During the intermission, Boucher came up with a revolutionary idea. If the Rangers hadn't tied the score by the final minutes, New York would pull Kerr, but not in the usual way. In those days, a team waited for a whistle and a face-off before replacing the goaltender with a sixth skater. This, of course, enabled the opposition to prepare for the extra man.

"We decided," said Boucher, "that it would be better to pull the goalie without making it obvious—to do it on the fly."

Chances are it would have worked, but Boucher neglected to inform general manager Lester Patrick of the plan.

Normally this wouldn't have mattered, since Lester rarely occupied the bench. But on this night in Chicago, he was rinkside with the players. Lester was mistrustful of the Chicago timekeeper,

ABOVE: Netminder Davey Kerr helped lead the New York Rangers to the Stanley Cup, *From the Stan Fischier Collection*

who was located between the two teams' benches.

"By this time," said Boucher, "we had the puck in their end. The signal was given for Kerr to come off the ice and the extra forward to go on. And that's exactly what happened. Nobody in the rink realized what happened but my players—and then Lester, except he didn't know that Kerr was removed."

Believing that Boucher had made the mistake of allowing too many men on the ice, the frantic Lester beseeched Boucher to remove the sixth skater before the referee saw him.

"Paul Thompson, the Chicago coach, heard him," Boucher recalled, "and when he saw six men in his zone, he started screaming. We were about to put the puck in the net when the referee blew his whistle to give us a penalty. Then he turned around and saw Kerr was out and there shouldn't be a penalty at all. But it was too late. The attack was stopped and we lost the game 1-0."

In the 1940 playoffs, Kerr reached his peak. During the Rangers' semifinal series with Boston, he posted three shutouts, including two consecutive 1-0 victories when the Rangers were behind in the series two games to one.

"He was our leader," recalled stalwart defenseman Ott Heller. "It was as simple as that."

In the finals, the Blueshirts took on the Maple Leafs and won 4-2, allowing Kerr to lift the Stanley Cup in his hometown, Toronto. It was the Rangers' third Stanley Cup in franchise history, Kerr was awarded the Vezina Trophy for his work throughout the championship season.

Kerr also led the team to the finals during the 1937 Stanley Cup playoffs. The Rangers posted 2-0 series victories against both the Toronto Maple Leafs and Montreal Maroons before falling to the Detroit Red Wings three games to two. During the run, Kerr set a Rangers record for most shutouts (four) in one playoff year. Mike Richter eventually tied this record during the 1994 playoffs.

The first NHL player to appear on the cover of TIME magazine, Kerr was as agile as a ballet dancer. He could do splits with one skate firmly anchored against one goal post and the other skate stretching across the goalmouth to the other post.

During practice, Davey would also lay his stick across the goalmouth in front of the goal line and prop his left skate against the right post, thus extending his body across

DAVEY KERR

BORN: Toronto, Ontario, Canada; January 11, 1910

DIED: May 12, 1978

POSITION: Goaltender

NHL TEAMS: Montreal Maroons, 1930-31, 1932-34; New York Americans, 1931-32; New York Rangers, 1934-41

AWARDS/HONORS: Vezina Trophy, 1940; NHL First Team All-Star, 1940; NHL Second Team All-Star, 1938

much of the net. This would leave his two hands free to catch the puck and his stick to deflect pucks along the ice. Kerr would then dare his teammates to beat him. According to Frank Boucher, they never did.

Boucher studied the goalie's style carefully on the ice and once offered this analysis of the NHL ace: "Kerr was gifted with an excellent right hand that picked off shots like Bill Terry playing first base for the Giants. He was deliberate and methodical in everything he did. Davey retired long before his time, when he was at his peak and only 30 years old. In a commanding way, Davey was able to shout at his defensemen, giving them guidance without offending them and getting them to do the job he wanted done in front of him, talking continually when the pick was in our end. I don't even remember Dave accusing a defense player for a mistake when a goal was scored against him. He always assumed the blame."

EDGAR LAPRADE

1 9 4 5 - 1 9 5 5

One of the great pleasures when watching the Rangers during the Post–World War II years was the sight of Edgar Laprade stickhandling through and around enemy defenses before skimming an accurate pass to one of his linemates.

A clean player with amazing puck control, Laprade's career actually began a couple of years later than it should have because of Edgar's affection for his hometown of Port Arthur, Ontario.

He had been a top-drawer hero in the amateur set and star of the Port Arthur Bear Cats. He led the Cats to the Allan Cup in 1939 and to the Western Canada, or Allan Cup, finals in each of the next four seasons. Newsmen referred to him as "a bearcat on the prowl."

Rangers manager Frank Boucher spent a couple of summers working on Laprade and finally persuaded him to turn pro in time for the 1945-46 season. Edgar was an instant hit, and for good reason. As noted in the yearbook, Inside the Blueshirt, Laprade was the hockey player's hockey player.

The yearbook put it this way: "Popular and respected in every rink in the league, he's one of the most skilled stickhandlers in the business, exceedingly proficient at breaking up an enemy offense."

Laprade was one of those rare athletes with a plan. He knew at an early age just how he wanted his hockey career to go,

and he set out to achieve his goals. While playing for the Bear Cats, Laprade was awarded the Gerry Trophy as the league's top athlete in 1939 and 1941.

Laprade refused to turn pro until he served a two-year stint in the Canadian Air Force, where he played on the Montreal Royal Canadian Air Force team. When he was discharged in 1945, Laprade finally signed a contract with the Blueshirts, and three weeks after his 26th birthday, Laprade made his NHL debut.

Laprade's Rangers teammates quickly discovered that their new center was worth waiting for. Impressing his coaches and peers with his dogged work ethic, Edgar earned the nicknamed "Beaver" from his colleagues. At the end of his first season, he had 34 points in 49 games and earned Calder Trophy honors as the league's best rookie.

Over the next three seasons, Laprade continued to impress, anchoring the Rangers' front line during a series of lean years. Edgar had finished third in team scoring in his first season and would finish in the top three in each of the next four years. In the 1948-49 campaign, Laprade took his place among the Rangers greats of the past when he shared the team MVP award with goalie Chuck Rayner.

"IT WAS THE BIGGEST DISAPPOINTMENT OF MY CAREER."

But Laprade had even more in store for New York. His most memorable season

GREATEST MOMENTS AND PLAYERS

came in 1949-50, when he tallied 22 goals and added 22 assists to lead the team in scoring while winning the Lady Byng Trophy. Laprade also had three goals and eight points in the Rangers' near-championship playoff run to the seventh game of the finals.

A smooth skater and an expert stickhandler, Laprade possessed only one shortcoming: a terribly weak shot. Equally impressive was Laprade's ability to avoid confrontations with the opposition and stay out of trouble with the refs.

Over his entire NHL career, Edgar amassed just 46 penalty minutes including playoffs. On three separate occasions, he tallied zero penalty minutes in a season, a remarkable achievement for an everyday player.

But by no means was Laprade a weak competitor; his back-checking and penalty-killing abilities were superior. Although he would frequently find himself in scoring position only to shoot ineffectively, either weakly or wide of the mark, Laprade's playmaking emerged as one of the jewels of a relatively lackluster New York team.

"I've always felt that he missed the general acclaim he deserved," said Boucher, "because it was his misfortune never to be cast with a winner."

Laprade starred for the Rangers during their vain effort to win the Stanley Cup in 1950. The Blueshirts fought hard to send the Stanley Cup finals series with the Red Wings to a Game 7, but fell when Detroit left wing Pete Babando buried the puck in the second overtime.

"It was the biggest disappointment of my career," said Laprade, whose only

EDGAR LAPRADE

BORN: Mine Center, Ontario, Canada; October 10, 1919

DIED: April 28, 2014

POSITION: Center

NHL TEAMS: New York Rangers, 1945-55

AWARDS/HONORS: Calder Trophy, 1946; Lady Byng Trophy, 1950

other playoff appearance came in 1948 when the Red Wings ousted the Rangers in six games in the semifinals.

Laprade retired following the 1951-52 season at the relatively young age of 32. He compared his decision to that of boxer Joe Louis, since Louis also left the game while he was on top. Laprade, whose family owned a sporting goods business in Port Arthur, also wanted to go out on his own terms. His motives were strictly to spend more time with his business and family.

Edgar, however, was too good for the Rangers to let go without a fight. When the Rangers suffered a slump in 1953-54, Boucher went up to Port Arthur and, though it took over two months of cajoling, finally convinced Laprade to come back to Broadway. He played on a line with the aging Max Bentley. The two veterans meshed well together, and Laprade

RIGHT: Edgar Laprade excelled at stickhandling for the New York Rangers. *From the Stan Fischler Collection*

played a key role in one of the most poignant moments in Rangers history: the reuniting of Max and Doug Bentley.

That night, Laprade was shifted to right wing, and fans were skeptical of his ability to blend with the sometimes unpredictable Bentley brothers. The fans' fears were groundless, as the line of Laprade and the Bentleys accounted for a whopping four goals in the first two periods. In the third period, Edgar was part of one of the most beautiful goals in Rangers history.

The shot was chronicled in Metro Ice in these words: "Flanked by the brothers, Laprade swiftly crossed the center red line, then skimmed a pass to Doug on the left, who just as quickly sent it back to Laprade as he crossed the Boston blue line. By now only one Bruins defenseman was back, trying to intercept the anticipated center slot pass from Laprade to Max speeding along the right side. Laprade tantalized the Boston player, almost handed him the puck, and when he lunged for it, Edgar flipped it to Max, who was moving on a direct line for the right goalpost. Laprade meanwhile had burst ahead on a direct line for the left goalpost, ready for a return pass. Both goalie Jim Henry and the defenseman— and possibly even Laprade—expected Max to relay the puck back to Edgar. So Henry began edging toward the other side of the net as Max faked and faked and faked the pass, but continued to move toward the goal until, without even shooting the rubber, he calmly eased it into the right comer."

Laprade retired at the end of the 1954-55 season after playing his 500th game, a milestone that only four previous Rangers

had reached. Edgar returned to Thunder Bay, Ontario, where he became a sporting goods dealer and village alderman.

He was inducted into the Hockey Hall of Fame in 1993.

In retrospect, if this wonderful performer could be described in one word, that word would be elegant.

BRIAN LEETCH

1988 - 2004

Some have called Brian Leetch "the greatest Rangers defenseman of all time." While that issue is debatable, there's no question that the Connecticut-reared backliner ranks, at the very least, near the top of the list. Brian Leetch was the New York Rangers' primary defenseman for well over a decade.

The two-time Norris Trophy–winner was the linchpin of the Blueshirts' lineup following his arrival after the 1988 Olympics and remained so until he left Broadway in 2004.

Smooth, clean, and calm in both zones, Leetch metamorphosed into a perennial All-Star, frequently appearing at the top of scoring races among defensemen with contemporaries Ray Bourque, Paul Coffey, and Larry Murphy.

The Rangers had been waiting more than a decade, since the trade of Brad Park in 1975, to acquire or draft a quality defenseman in the Park mold. However, in 1986, they drafted Leetch (ninth overall). Leetch spent one year at Boston College before leaving behind his amateur career for the bright lights of midtown Manhattan.

In his first full season, 1988-89, Leetch took the NHL by storm with 23 goals and 48 assists and won the Calder Trophy as the NHL's top rookie. He markedly improved in his own zone as the Rangers built their franchise around the dynamic Leetch, young goaltender Mike Richter, and, beginning in 1991-92, the game's premier leader, Mark Messier. Messier's arrival that year lifted Leetch to a career-high 102-point season and a Norris Trophy as he played a key role in the Blueshirts' division title.

A broken ankle would hinder Brian's progress during the next season and prevent the Rangers from earning a spot in the playoffs. However, he would prove durable afterward. He experienced just one abbreviated season through the end of the century, playing only 50 games in 1999-2000 as the Rangers again failed to make the playoffs.

During the Rangers' magical postseason of 1993-94, Leetch led all players with 11 goals and 23 assists in 23 playoff matches en route to becoming the first American to win the Conn Smythe Trophy as MVP of the Stanley Cup playoffs. His finest moment may have been the goal he scored in Game 7 of the Stanley Cup finals against the Vancouver Canucks. Leetch took a pass from the point and lifted the puck top-shelf as goalie Kirk McLean sprawled on his front side, helping the Blueshirts to win their first Stanley Cup in 54 years.

Leetch was regarded as one of the key pieces in the championship puzzle. "Brian is not only one of the best players to ever play for the New York Rangers, he's a classy individual," said Rangers president and general manager Glen Sather, expressing his appreciation of the team's star defenseman.

How does one make a case for Leetch as the best Rangers defenseman of all time?

For starters, his numbers are staggering, outpointing every other Rangers backliner, including Brad Park.

For another, unlike Park, Leetch played on a Stanley Cup–winning team.

Although outstanding Rangers defensemen such as Ching Johnson, Art Coulter, and Harry Howell were significantly stronger in their own end of the rink, it is clear looking back that they did not come close to matching Leetch's offensive stats.

Few could ever match Leetch's offensive style, let alone his ability to orchestrate the tempo of the game to suit his team. In that sense, Brian emulated the inimitable Doug Harvey, who won the Norris Trophy in 1961-62 as Rangers player-coach.

Then there was his power-play work. Teaming with Sergei Zubov, Leetch provided the Rangers with their best-ever double-dip power-play combination.

Likewise, Leetch made a better player out of his even-strength defensemate Jeff Beukeboom, who achieved his finest moments working alongside No. 2.

But Brian was far from perfect behind his own blue line.

Because he was not a hard hitter and lacked the size of a heavyweight

BRIAN LEETCH

BORN: March 3, 1968

POSITION: Defenseman

NHL TEAMS: New York Rangers, 1988-2004; Toronto Maple Leafs, 2004; Boston Bruins, 2005-06

AWARDS/HONORS: Calder Memorial Trophy, 1989; James Norris Memorial Trophy, 1992, 1997; Conn Smythe Trophy, 1994; NHL All-Rookie Team, 1989; NHL First Team All-Star, 1992, 1997; NHL Second Team All-Star 1991, 1994, 1996; NHL All-Star Game, 1990-92, 1994, 1996-98, 2001-02

defenseman, he could be knocked off the puck, but he was quickly able to rebound from mistakes.

It was also Brian's good fortune to play with some of the finest Rangers, including Mike Richter, Mark Messier, Adam Graves, and "The Great One" himself, Wayne Gretzky.

The 1996-97 campaign featured the addition of Gretzky, an appearance in the Eastern Conference finals, and a second Norris Trophy for Brian. Messier abruptly departed to Vancouver that summer, and Leetch assumed the captaincy. Sadly, Brian never appeared comfortable in the role, often overcompensating for his underachieving team, and the drop from a plus-31 rating to a minus-36 proved the point. But when Messier returned in 2000-01, Leetch was rejuvenated and turned in a vintage 79-point performance.

Despite being teamed up with several veteran players and continuing to play in the most skilled fashion, Leetch was unable to lead his team to the playoffs in his final seven years on the Rangers.

The decline and fall of Brian as a New York Ranger was not pretty. A player who loved Manhattan—he had a Broadway apartment on the Upper West Side—Leetch felt losses as intensely as any athlete. There was no doubt that by the year 2003, he was no longer the dominant figure he had been in the 1990s.

This presented a most difficult decision for general manager Glen Sather, particularly since most experts had forecast a labor work stoppage for the 2004-05 season.

Sather wrestled with the issue and finally decided that the time had come to trade the high-priced defenseman. He found a partner in the Toronto Maple Leafs.

On March 3, Sather dealt Leetch to Toronto for Maxim Kondratiev, Jarkko Immonen, and a 2004 NHL entry draft first-round selection, giving the Blueshirts a second pick that year, the best of which was goalie Al Montoya, followed by Lauri Korpikoski. The Rangers also received an additional 2005 NHL entry draft selection in which they selected Michael Sauer and Marc-Andre Cliche.

In answer to critics, Sather explained why he made the move.

"As we proceeded down the path, we feel we did very well with the players we got and the draft choices we got. We felt that going as far as we did go with Toronto was as good as we could get," said Sather.

As for the Maple Leafs, general manager John Ferguson Jr. believed that he had received an amazing player with tremendous potential who could lead the team to the Stanley Cup playoffs and beyond. "Brian has been a premier defenseman in this league since first coming into the league. We look forward to having a player with his great credentials joining our group," said Ferguson of his acquisition.

But the Maple Leafs were unable to win the Cup, although Leetch and Bryan McCabe proved to be an excellent power-play combination, not unlike the Zubov-Leetch pairing during the Rangers' glory years.

One of the worst things to happen to Brian's career was the NHL lockout, which stopped play for the entire 2004-05 season. The last thing a player his age needed at that time was to be deprived of work when he still had his legs left.

Once the new collective bargaining agreement was signed, Brian accepted an offer from the Boston Bruins and played reasonably fair hockey for them, but not good enough to lead them into the playoffs. During the summer of 2006, he wrestled with the idea of playing one more season—possibly even with his favorite team, the Rangers—but ultimately decided that, at 39, he'd rather spend more time with his family, and that's precisely what he did.

How will historians regard Leetch among hockey's greatest stars?

Some have labeled him as the foremost American-born defenseman.

This much is certain: he scored 247 goals and had 781 assists over 1,205 career-games, mostly in his 17 seasons as a Ranger. He was also responsible for 97 points in 95 postseason appearances.

The numbers speak volumes as to why those who saw Leetch in action have no problem comparing him with New York's very best, a list that includes Park, Howell, Coulter, and, on Brian's best nights, even the legendary Doug Harvey.

MARK MESSIER

1991-1997; 2000-2004

In a city filled with legendary characters, only a precious few hockey players can be counted as genuine Big Apple icons. Without question, Mark Messier emerged as just such a hero of heroes.

All things considered, it's hard to believe in retrospect that Messier spent only a decade—over two different periods—in a Rangers uniform.

Messier eventually departed from the Big Apple as one of the city's most revered sports heroes, right up there with Joe Namath, Jackie Robinson, Willie Mays, Joe DiMaggio, and Willis Reed.

Many reasons exist for this extraordinary turn of events, not the least of which is the fact that Messier—as captain—spearheaded the Rangers' march to their last Stanley Cup in 1994.

Not only did he wear the "C" with distinction, but Messier, in one of those extraordinarily rare moments of leadership, actually "guaranteed" a victory at a time when many Rangers fans thought it impossible.

Even more noteworthy, Messier captivated New Yorkers during the twilight of a glorious professional career that actually began in the World Hockey Association when the WHA was still a rival of the NHL.

As was the case with many future Hall of Famers, Messier was the beneficiary of a second "major league." The WHA was born in 1972 and managed to steal such legendary performers as Bobby Hull, Gordie Howe, and Gerry Cheevers from the NHL.

By the 1978-79 season, the upstart league was staggering but still alive and quite willing to gamble on young talents who had been overlooked by the NHL. One reason for this was that the senior league hesitated to sign any player under 20. This meant that future aces such as Wayne Gretzky and Mark Messier filled a rich talent pool from which NHL bird-dogs could feast.

Although he was extremely raw talent-wise, Messier enjoyed stints with two teams—the Indianapolis Racers and Cincinnati Stingers—during the 1978-79 season.

Since the Edmonton Oilers were also members of the WHA at the time, scouts and boss Glen Sather were able to appreciate Mark's potential.

A year later, the Oilers—but not Cincinnati or Indianapolis—entered into the NHL as part of a marriage between the elder circuit and the WHA. Thus, Messier had reached the top rung on his professional ladder, and despite a modest start point-wise, he hit the NHL running.

Mark was in good company. Not only was Wayne Gretzky a teammate, but such young stallions as Kevin Lowe, Glenn Anderson, and Grant Fuhr also graced the Edmonton roster.

"Winner" would be the most appropriate word to describe Mark Messier. He was the ultimate power forward of his era and retained that reputation until his retirement in 2004. Known in New York as "The Messiah," and "The Captain," Mark bore striking similarities to Gordie Howe and many go so far as to say that Messier was a better all-around player than his former Edmonton teammate, Gretzky.

"Numbers don't tell you everything you have to know about hockey players," said Lou Vairo, author of an in-depth hockey manual and assistant coach of the 2002 U.S. Olympic Team. "There are intangibles that can be seen and felt but can't be calculated with a computer."

The intangibles are vital elements that can never truly be measured by statistics. These include energy, toughness, checking, fighting ability, and desire.

With Messier and Gretzky a part of the squad, Edmonton conquered four Stanley Cups. It is significant that while Gretzky never won another Cup after he left Messier's side, Mark captured the Mug again as an Oiler in 1990 and still one more in 1994 as a Ranger. Thus, Messier totaled six championships in his career.

In his prime, Messier tore down a rink like a speeding locomotive. Shadowing him was virtually a waste of time and manpower.

"When Mark got going, it was impossible to stop that man," said former

MARK MESSIER

BORN: Edmonton, Alberta, Canada; January 18, 1961

POSITION: Center

NHL TEAMS: Edmonton Oilers, 1979-1991; New York Rangers, 1991-97, 2000-04; Vancouver Canucks, 1997-2000

AWARDS/HONORS: Conn Smythe Trophy, 1984; Hart Trophy, 1990, 1992; Lester Pearson Trophy, 1990, 1992; NHL First Team All-Star, 1982-83, 1990, 1992; NHL Second Team All-Star, 1984

Montreal Canadiens coach Jacques Demers, now a television and newspaper analyst.

The transformation of Messier from foot soldier to superstar did not come overnight, nor did the evolution of the Oilers as a major-league hockey dynasty.

After playoff setbacks in the early 1980s, the gears meshed during the 1982-83 season, during which Edmonton reached the Stanley Cup finals against the New York Islanders, who had already won three consecutive championships.

Although the Oilers went out in four straight games, they fought hard and well at times and seemed capable of winning any one of the matches.

"One of our greatest lessons," Mark remembered, "was after the final game as we headed out of Nassau Coliseum.

"To get out of the building, we first had to walk past the Islanders' dressing room. We could hear all the celebrating, and we knew how hard they had worked to get to the top. Right then and there, we knew that we had to work harder and improve our game a bit more."

It didn't take very long for that to happen. Just a year later, the Oilers and Islanders again collided in the finals. It was then that Messier took over as a leader and dynamite scorer.

The finals moved from Long Island to Edmonton when the series was tied at one game apiece. With future Hall of Famer Bill Smith in goal, New York took the lead in Game 3 and appeared Cup-bound again.

Then came the goal that would ultimately determine the game and the eventual outcome of the series.

Messier snared the puck at center ice and barreled over the enemy blue line, going one-on-one with defenseman Gord Dineen. As the bromide goes, Mark left Dineen standing there like a cigar-store Indian.

Messier followed that bit of devilry with a laser-like wrist shot that left goalie Smith mummified as the puck hit the twine. Edmonton won the game and the next two to take the Cup—its first of four in five years.

Despite all the fuss and fanfare over Gretzky, it was Messier who won the Conn Smythe Trophy as the postseason's most valuable player in 1984. Mark had totaled 26 points in 19 playoff games.

After Gretzky was dealt away in 1988, Messier inherited the captaincy. Although hampered by injuries, he rose to the occasion as never before and carried the Oilers to their fifth championship in 1990. Mark also won the Hart Trophy as the NHL's most valuable player.

In a sense, this was Messier's most arresting triumph. The Oilers were an underdog team loaded with youngsters and were, of course, without "The Great One."

By this time, the Oilers were beset by economic problems, and the franchise's fiscal situation was worsening by the season.

Large-market teams were acutely aware of this and attempted to pry Messier loose from the Oilers, particularly since he had become one of the higher-salaried players in the league.

Finally, on October 4, 1991, what was once thought unthinkable happened. Messier was traded to the Rangers with future considerations for Bernie Nicholls, Steven Rice, and Louie DeBrusk. Edmonton was in mourning because Messier had captured a top slot in every offensive category in its team's history, including games played (second with 851), goals (fourth with 392), assists (second with 642), and points (third with 1,034).

Having seen enough of Messier to know how special he was as a player and a personality, New Yorkers greeted him with open arms.

In no time at all, Mark became a New Yorker through and through. He moved into a lavish apartment on 57th Street right next to Carnegie Hall and soon became a coveted member of Manhattan's social set.

He endured a few bumps on Broadway before reaching the coveted Cup terminal.

Sparks emerged between Mark and coach Roger Neilson. Messier objected to Neilson's style, and eventually the feud went public.

Messier, who had been knighted as soon as he arrived in New York, won the battle, and Neilson was replaced by Mike Keenan. The new coach and Mark worked well together.

Anyone who played alongside the captain invariably improved his game, but no one more than Adam Graves. During the 1993-94 season, Graves broke Vic Hadfield's Rangers single-season goal-scoring record with 52 tallies. In addition, the Rangers won the Presidents' Trophy for most points in the season.

But this was a prelude of even better things to come. The Rangers steam-rolled through the first two playoff rounds before running into a surprisingly hot, young New Jersey Devils team.

For a time, it appeared that the long-standing "Curse of 1940" would remain intact. The Devils had taken a three-games-to-two lead and were up 2-0 in the second period of Game 6.

Few Rangers fans were hanging their hopes on the "guarantee" delivered by Messier to the papers that morning, which assured the faithful that the Rangers would prevail.

Who could have dreamed that the victory would be manufactured with Messier's three-goal hat trick? But it was!

New York went on to capture the seventh game in double overtime before facing Vancouver for the championship.

In Game 7 of the finals, No. 11 scored what turned out to be the game-winning goal in a 3-2 victory over Pavel Bure and the Canucks.

Messier and company were hailed like no other Rangers team in history. Crowds lined the Canyon of Champions in a memorable ticker-tape parade.

To some, Messier's heroics went beyond the meaningful goals and raucous celebrations.

Unbeknownst to Messier, a young Rangers fan was holed up in Manhattan's Columbia-Presbyterian Hospital, dying of a heart ailment. The patient, Brian Bluver, desperately required a transplant. The lad's father, Bill Bluver, contacted a hockey broadcaster, asking if a Ranger was available to visit and bolster his son's spirits.

A phone call was made to the Rangers' public relations office, where team publicist Barry Watkins took the message but promised nothing because of the intense round of celebrations that transpired all week.

"I'll see what I can do," said Watkins and left it at that.

A few days later, a limousine pulled up in front of the hospital in the Washington Heights section of Manhattan. Out stepped Messier, carrying the Stanley Cup. The captain delivered the silverware to the intensive care unit and the bedside of the ailing Bluver. Despite his critical condition, the youngster responded positively to the Rangers leader, who delivered telling words of encouragement.

"It was a tremendous boost for my son," said Brian's father, Bill. "We couldn't thank Mark and the Rangers enough!"

The Bluver family was further encouraged when Brian received a new heart and recovered to lead a normal life.

Eventually, Brian left the hospital, returned to school, and in time earned a law degree. He never forgot Messier's visit and actually enjoyed a reunion with his hero many years later at Madison Square Garden.

Other fans' dreams came true when Wayne Gretzky was reunited with Messier in the 1996-97 season. The pair spearheaded the Blueshirts to a playoff berth before being ousted by the Philadelphia Flyers.

That just about ended Mark's rosy years in Manhattan. The Rangers were on a downward spiral that not even he could reverse, and he was dealt in 1997 to the Vancouver Canucks.

It didn't seem possible that Messier would return to New York as a player, but in 2000, the 40-year-old warrior headlined an MSG press conference heralding his homecoming. Despite his advanced years, Messier collected 67 points and was one of four Rangers to play every game during that season—the second time in his career that he had competed in all 82 games. But the gas finally ran out of Mark's tank prior to the 2003-04 season and he called it a career.

The future Hall of Famer owned dynamic credentials.

He amassed 694 goals, 1,193 assists, 1,887 points, and 1,910 penalty minutes in his regular-season career. During the playoffs, Mark produced 109 goals, 186 assists, 295 points, and 244 penalty minutes.

The capper for Mark in Manhattan occurred on January 12, 2006, when a gala Mark Messier Night preceded an Oilers-Rangers match at the Garden. The captain's No. 11 was officially retired, never to be worn by a Ranger again. Tears of joy along with endless applause filled the venerable arena.

Nobody summed up Messier's qualities better than the man who nurtured him as a rookie in Edmonton in 1979.

"Mark had that look in his eye," explained Glen Sather. "It's a look that I had only seen once before in a great hockey player, and that was Maurice Richard. But Mark had it even more. At critical times in the playoffs, he'd give everyone that look in the dressing room, and away we'd go!"

Perhaps it is redundant to add that Messier was inducted into the Hockey Hall of Fame in the summer of 2007. "Mark represents the epitome of hockey excellence," said NHL commissioner Gary Bettman. "His career was distinguished by his skill, by his drive, and by his refusal to accept anything less than the best."

Al MacInnis, who was also named to the Hall along with Messier, played against Mark for many years. The defenseman summed up his feelings about his longtime foe this way: "Mark's reputation is the right one as far as maybe being [one of the best], if not the best, leaders in the game for many, many years. . . . [A] complete player, he could change the momentum of a game with his skill level and his physical attributes.

"He was one of the top players ever to play the game."

MURRAY MURDOCH

1 9 2 6 - 1 9 3 7

It's been said that hockey's foot soldiers are often as valuable to their teams as the glittering superstars. This was never more true than in the case of Murray Murdoch.

When the original Rangers team was being organized in 1926, Murdoch had just graduated from the University of Manitoba. When Conn Smythe was scouting players for the Rangers, he liked what he saw of the lad, although he couldn't have imagined how durable he would prove to be. Murdoch was living in Winnipeg when Smythe was signing other would-be Rangers in Duluth, Minnesota.

Murdoch, who was a newlywed, received a telegram from Smythe: "MEET ME HERE IN DULUTH STOP ALL EXPENSES PAID."

To that, Murdoch wired back, "IF YOU WANT TO SEE ME COME TO WINNIPEG."

Decades later, Murdoch recalled the fateful rendezvous: "Smythe came to Winnipeg, we talked, and he offered me a $1,500 signing bonus and a $5,000 salary. I remember sitting in the lobby of the Fort Garry Hotel thinking it over, and I was just about to say no when Conn leaned over a coffee table and slowly counted out $1,500 in $100 bills. That clinched it. For a young guy just married and with a summer job selling insurance, that looked like an awful lot of money."

MURRAY MURDOCH

BORN: Lucknow, Ontario, Canada; May 19, 1904

DIED: May 17, 2001

POSITION: Left Wing

NHL TEAMS: New York Rangers, 1926-37

AWARDS/HONORS: Lester Patrick Trophy, 1974

Although Smythe was in charge of the Rangers before their original season began, he was fired before the opening face-off in a dispute with management and replaced by the less-vitriolic Lester Patrick, who Murdoch appreciated much more.

"Lester never dealt that way. He just made his proposition, and you knew his word was his bond," said Murdoch.

"Lester took over from Conn quietly without any fuss, and after a couple of days, he called a team meeting. 'Gentlemen,' he said, 'when we start playing in the National Hockey League, you're going to win some games and you're going to lose some. I just want to stress this: if you lose more than you win, you won't be around.'"

When Lester Patrick took over as manager and coach, Murdoch became one of the most valuable Rangers. Lester played him on a line with Billy Boyd and Paul Thompson. That Rangers checking unit was one of the best ever at what it did.

"Murray didn't get the buildup that the modern players receive, but he was a superstar in his own right," said hockey historian Kip Farrington. "His iron-man record stood as a tribute to his durability and desire."

John Murray Murdoch was born on May 19, 1904, in Lucknow, Ontario, and was skating shortly after he learned to walk. He originally made his name in the sport while attending St. John's College in Winnipeg, Manitoba.

A superb all-around athlete, Murdoch played tennis, baseball, and football in addition to hockey at St. John's. But he was most comfortable on the ice.

In his senior year, after transferring to the University of Manitoba, Murdoch led his team to the Canadian Junior Hockey championship and the Memorial Cup—emblematic of Junior hockey supremacy in Canada—scoring nine of the team's 14 goals along the way.

Murray played stellar hockey for nearly a decade, anchoring the checking line on the Rangers' Stanley Cup–winning teams of 1928 and 1933. Following the Rangers' 1933 Stanley Cup championship—their second in seven years—Murdoch and other members of the old guard began to falter, yet he still had some success, enjoying the biggest scoring season of his career in 1933-34 with 17 goals. He played capably through the 1936-37 season, his last. In that campaign, he had 14 assists but no goals.

During his 11-year career, Murdoch did not miss a single game. He played in a total of 508 consecutive contests during that span, including every one of the Rangers' 55 Stanley Cup playoff matches.

Murdoch was there from the very beginning and retired with a pair of Stanley Cup rings.

An intense admirer of Murdoch as a player and a person, then Rangers president General John Reed Kilpatrick believed that Murray would make an excellent college coach. Since the General was a distinguished alumnus of Yale, he was in a position to help Murray obtain the job.

From that point on, Murdoch became something of a hockey legend at the collegiate coaching level. "He brought to Yale a quiet dignity and professionalism," said Farrington. "The ruddy-faced Canadian, once a handsome, blond-haired center-man, helped popularize the sport at Yale."

Murdoch coached Yale for 28 years before retiring in 1966. One of Murray's players, Bill Hilderbrand, captain of the 1963 squad, said this of his coach: "Murray was one of the greatest college coaches who ever lived, if just from the standpoint of his knowledge of hockey. He knows the game inside out, but most of all, the players respect him because he's a real man in every way."

In 1974, Murdoch was awarded the Lester Patrick Trophy for service to hockey in the United States.

A distinguished citizen both on and off the ice, Murdoch was revered in every realm of the game, from the amateur level to the Rangers and then as a collegiate coach.

But when it came to the Blueshirts, who else can say—as Murray did—that he never missed a single game from the beginning of his honorable career to its conclusion?

BRAD PARK

1 9 6 8 - 1 9 7 5

Had Bobby Orr not skated onto the NHL stage in the late 1960s, the spotlight would have focused on Brad Park, who was arguably the best defenseman—including offensive play as well as play behind the blue line—in the National Hockey League.

In fact, there was little to distinguish between Park and Orr when it came to analyzing their respective styles, not to mention value to their teams.

However, Park had one missing link in his glittering hockey necklace: a Stanley Cup ring. Orr had two.

The consummate contemporary defenseman, Park was the master of the hip check and an exceptionally accurate shooter who could develop an attack and then retreat in time to intercept an enemy counterthrust. The baby-faced backliner could also play the game as tough as anyone.

Park's game was embellished by a fluid skating style that often underplayed his speed as well as strength, which proved deceptive because of his relatively modest size.

It was Park's misfortune never to have skated for a genuine powerhouse. He was the ice general and captain of a modestly successful Rangers team in the late 1960s and early 1970s, but he never tasted the Stanley Cup champagne.

One of his closest encounters with the Cup came in the 1971-72 season, when his

Broadway Blueshirts reached the Stanley Cup finals.

Facing the Boston Bruins, the Rangers extended the series to six games. The sixth was played at Madison Square Garden, where it appeared that the Blueshirts had an excellent opportunity to win the contest until Orr executed a razzle-dazzle play at the blue line that led to the decisive goal and helped Boston to the championship. Once again, Orr was in Park's way.

By this time, the New York-Boston hockey rivalry had reached a fever pitch and got even steamier after Park decided to write his autobiography, *Play the Man.*

In one chapter, Park delivered some unkind words about Boston and the Bruins, which infuriated both the team and Beantown hockey fans. It seemed incredulous, but Brad had become the number-one villain in Boston.

Whenever he appeared at Boston Garden, Park was singled out for abuse. Just about the last thing anyone would have expected would have been the sight of No. 2 in a Boston uniform.

And then it happened. Because the Rangers failed to win the Stanley Cup during Park's golden years in New York, he became the target of the Madison Square Garden boo-birds and was eventually part of one of the biggest trades in NHL history. On November 7, 1975, Park, who was then the Rangers' captain, and Jean Ratelle, the club's foremost playmaker, were traded to the Bruins for Phil Esposito and Carol Vadnais.

The blockbuster exchange reverberated negatively through New England and New York City. Bruins fans were stunned to the core by the idea of one-time Bruins-hating Park suddenly playing for the black, white, and yellow.

Perhaps the biggest surprise of all was the ease with which Brad made the transition. For that he had to thank the guidance of coach Don Cherry. In no time at all, Park won the hearts of Boston fans with the same kind of dedication and hard work that had made him a hit on Broadway.

With Orr on his way out—he would finish his career in Chicago with the Blackhawks—Park became top banana on the Beantown blue line. With the colorful Cherry behind the bench, Boston played exciting hockey, even though the Bruins were no longer as powerful as they had been during their Cup-winning years.

Because he played in the shadow of some of the most proficient backliners, Park may not have received the media attention he merited, but the experts took due note of his excellence. Brad was

BRAD PARK

BORN: Toronto, Ontario, Canada; July 6, 1948

POSITION: Defenseman

NHL TEAMS: New York Rangers, 1968-75; Boston Bruins, 1975-83; Detroit Red Wings, 1983-85

AWARDS/HONORS: NHL First Team All-Star 1970, 1972, 1974, 1976, 1978; NHL Second Team All-Star 1971, 1973

voted to the First All-Star Team in 1970, 1972, 1974, 1976, and 1978. He made the Second Team in 1971 and 1973.

More than anything, Park was a refreshing player to watch and, in some ways, a throwback to an earlier, more robust era of defensive play.

"One of the glorious aspects of sports," said author Roger Kahn, "is having your spirits renewed by Brad Park." Park's own spirits were occasionally deflated by Orr's presence in the same league. A defenseman like Park, Orr had been regarded by many as the "Most Holy, Blessed Be He" in hockey since the invention of the puck. Playing second fiddle to a superstar like Orr could not have been the easiest thing in the world, but Park made the adjustment.

"If I have to be number two," Brad explained, "I might as well be number two to a superstar like Orr."

Park had been super, or close to it, ever since he became a Ranger in 1968-69. An instant regular, he learned the ropes, took punches in the chops, and scored goals almost immediately.

His career almost ended with similar suddenness. The Rangers were playing the Red Wings, and dangerous Gordie Howe was still playing for the Detroit sextet. Park was guarding Howe, notorious for his great strength, durability, and viciousness. "Watch Howe!" Brad was warned. "He likes to club you with his elbows."

Park remained vigilant, and when Howe confronted him, the young Ranger bodychecked the veteran cleanly, depositing him on the ice. But Brad became less vigilant as the game continued, and a few minutes later, Howe's stick flashed, cracking into Park's Adam's apple.

For an instant, it appeared as if the blow might have ended his career. Brad fell, unable to swallow and gasping for breath. Rangers trainer Frank Paice dashed across the ice and calmed the kid until he was fully revived and able to skate off the ice under his own steam.

As Brad passed Howe, he turned to his assailant and rasped, 'You son of a gun. It could have been my eye. From now on, when you're skating around me, you damn well better keep your head up." Park clashed with the best of foes, especially the Philadelphia Flyers.

The flak was never heavier than in the spring of 1974, when the Rangers met Philadephia in the semifinal round of the playoffs. Dave Schultz, the number-one hitter on the Flyers, made a point of zeroing in on Park early in the third game of the Cup round. First, he bodied Brad heavily in the comer. Then, as play swung up the ice, Schultz charged into Park a second time and knocked him down, straddling the semi-defenseless Ranger and pouring punches at his face.

The Flyers' theory was simplicity itself—beat up on the best Ranger and grind out a series victory. 'You can't be a hitting team 60 minutes a game," countered Park. "It's exhausting."

But it was just as exhausting for Park, mostly because his teammates failed to generate as much zest as he did. As a result, the Flyers edged New York four games to three and advanced to the Stanley Cup finals.

Douglas Bradford Park was born July 6, 1948, in Toronto, and learned the game on the city rinks. For many years, Brad's size worked against him, but he was also tough enough to land a spot on the Toronto Junior Marlboros, a club that usually fed gifted stickhandlers to the NHL.

Normally, Park would have graduated to the Toronto Maple Leafs, but the NHL had instituted a draft rule that enabled the Rangers to land Park. Brad was stunned, to say the least.

When Park arrived at the Rangers' training camp in September 1968, he was not even considered for a position on the New York varsity. The Rangers had a well-rounded defense and had also been grooming a tall, well-built prospect named Al Hamilton as their fifth defenseman. But Park outplayed Hamilton each scrimmage, and the Rangers' braintrust was faced with a dilemma. Management solved the issue by sending Park to the minors and keeping Hamilton with the big club. But Brad played too well to be kept down, and Hamilton couldn't cut it with the Rangers.

The call went out to Park, and he never looked back. Injuries severely braked the career of the star defenseman, but Park continued to play through knee problems, though at a more modest pace.

"In some ways," said Don Cherry, "Brad was a better player after all the injuries because he began to pace himself. He wouldn't take as many chances on offense, and that meant he was in better position on defense, so he was caught out of position much less."

The pain had so troubled Brad that it was freely predicted he would retire by 1980, but he kept coming back. When the 1981-82 campaign began, he was back on the Bruins' blue line, playing as smart a game as he ever had in his life.

Unfortunately for him, a number of younger, flashier defensemen such as Denis Potvin of the New York Islanders and Randy Carlyle of the Pittsburgh Penguins were scoring more than Park, though they didn't necessarily play better defense. But the high-scoring defensemen received the accolades, and Brad, just as he had been during the Orr era, was relegated to the shadows.

Yet the purists remained appreciative of Park's skills, particularly his "submarine" bodycheck in which he'd thrust his hip into the path of onrushing attackers, catapulting them upside down on the ice. In 1977 and 1978, Park was one of the primary reasons the Bruins reached the Stanley Cup finals. The series were close, but Boston ultimately lost; Brad had come in second once more.

Park concluded his career with the Red Wings and was named Detroit's coach in December 1985. Unfortunately, he was the wrong man at the wrong time in the wrong place with the wrong team and was fired at the end of the season.

Brad finally obtained the recognition he deserved in June 1988, when he was elected to the Hockey Hall of Fame.

LESTER PATRICK

1 9 2 7 - 1 9 2 8

If anyone deserved the label "Mister Ranger" on the club's administrative level, it was Lester Patrick. He created the first Rangers team in 1926, coached the first Blueshirts club, and guided them to their first two Stanley Cups in 1928 and 1933 while behind the bench. As general manager in 1940, Lester helped the club to yet another Stanley Cup championship.

When one considers the foremost notables in hockey, not to mention esteemed coaches, Patrick ranks at the very top of the list.

There are those who would argue that Patrick was in a class by himself during both his playing and coaching career, which lasted from 1905 till 1939.

To New Yorkers, it was Patrick the manager and coach who mattered most.

Patrick first made an impact on the game of hockey while playing for a team in Brandon, Manitoba. Patrick was the very first defenseman ever to make a practice of lugging the puck out of his zone and deep into enemy territory. Lester could never comprehend why only forwards were the puck-carriers and, conversely, why defensemen did nothing but engage the enemy attackers.

Said Elmer Ferguson of the Montreal Herald, "He felt that a defenseman should do more than defend, so he rushed the puck as well."

Patrick graduated from Brandon to the powerful Montreal Wanderers in 1903. At that time, organized hockey was dominated by the Ottawa Silver Seven, a club that captured the Stanley Cup in 1903, 1904, and 1905.

The Wanderers finally dethroned the Silver Seven 12-10 in the 1906 two-game total-goal series. Patrick scored the 11th and 12th goals for Montreal.

Imperial looking—many fans said he reminded them of the distinguished actor John Barrymore—Patrick stood 6-foot tall, was slim but solidly built, and had a crown of thick, curly hair. (When the

---

LESTER PATRICK

BORN: Drummondville, Quebec, Canada; December 30, 1883

DIED: June 1, 1960

POSITION: Rover/Defenseman/Goaltender

TEAMS: Westmount (CAHL), 1905; Montreal Wanderers (ECAHA), 1906-07; Renfrew Millionaires (NHA), 1910; Victoria Aristocrats (PCHA), 1912-16, 1919-26; Spokane (PCHA), 1917; Seattle Metropolitans (PCHA), 1918; New York Rangers, 1927-28

AWARDS/HONORS: All-Star Coach, 1931-36, 1938; Hockey Hall of Fame, 1945; Trophy for outstanding service to hockey in United States named in his honor in 1966; Division of NHL named in his honor in 1974

mane grew gray, he was dubbed the "Silver Fox.") Lester had an inimitable knack for striking dramatic poses, tossing his head back, and staring archly at others.

He was actually one of the first high-priced athletes because he knew the value of a dollar and, more importantly, the value of Lester Patrick.

While Lester was starring for the Wanderers, a wealthy group of business-men in Renfrew, Ontario, decided to organize a major-league team and pursued Lester. He eventually signed with them for what at the time was regarded an absurdly high fee for a hockey player—$3,000 for 12 games.

It was a honey of a deal, but Patrick only stayed one season and then abruptly moved to British Columbia with his family when his father established a lumber business in the Canadian Northwest. While logging the giant trees of the Fraser Valley, Lester and Frank came up with an ambitious plan to run their own hockey league along the Pacific Coast. They had only one problem: no natural ice or rinks existed in the area.

Undaunted, Lester borrowed $300,000 from his father and, with Frank's assistance, built a chain of rinks that gave birth to the Pacific Hockey League, including Victoria, Vancouver, Seattle, Edmonton, Calgary, Regina, and Saskatoon. Lester operated the Victoria team while Frank ran Vancouver.

"The Patricks," said Ferguson, "took hockey into an area where no hockey existed, built magnificent rinks, and made a major sport of it. They were the greatest personal factors in 20th-century hockey."

Lester never gave up his skates for the executive suite. He was a one-man gang who owned, managed, coached, and played for his club. Patrick did wonders for the Cougars, especially in 1925, when Victoria met the Montreal Canadiens in the Stanley Cup finals.

"All the sportswriters had conceded the series to Montreal," said Frank Frederickson, a Hall of Famer who played for Victoria. "But they didn't bargain for Lester's analytical mind, and we wound up beating the Canadiens."

The triumph added another ribbon to Patrick's collection, but it was soon dwarfed by his unexpected performance in the 1928 playoffs after he had retired as an active defenseman. It was then that Lester startled the hockey world by going into the nets and playing goal for the New York Rangers against the Montreal Maroons.

"This dramatic moment," wrote Canadian journalist Trent Frayne, "has become a part of the lore of the sport, as legendary as the World Series home run Babe Ruth hit off Charley Root of the Chicago Cubs when he pointed to the distant center field bleachers and then laced the ball there."

Patrick was manager of the Rangers at the time. His regular goalie, Lorne Chabot, had nearly been blinded by a shot from the stick of Montreal Maroons ace Nels Stewart. The Rangers had no spare goaltender, so Lester agreed to put on the pads.

John Barrymore couldn't have played the part better had the playoff been staged in Hollywood. "Lester struck poses in the net," one of his players recalled.

GREATEST MOMENTS AND PLAYERS

"He would shout to us, 'Let them shoot!' He was an inspiration to the rest of us."

The Rangers had scored once, and Patrick had a shutout going until late in the third period, when Nels Stewart finally beat him. The game went into overtime, and Lester foiled the Maroons until Frank Boucher was able to score the winner for New York. At that moment, Lester Patrick became immortalized.

He was half dragged, half carried off the ice by his players as he received a tumultuous ovation from the crowd. It was Lester's final curtain as a player.

Lester Patrick was born on December 30, 1883, in Drummondville, Quebec, not far from Montreal. Although hockey was his forte, Lester was equally gifted at rugby, lacrosse, and cricket. He enrolled at McGill University when he was 17 but quit after a year to devote his energies to hockey. His first raves were received in Brandon, where he led the Manitoba sextet to the provincial championship and then the Stanley Cup round, in which they almost beat the mighty Ottawa Silver Seven. When he became captain of the Montreal Wanderers, they won the Stanley Cup in 1906 and 1907.

"Lester was a classical player in every phase of the game," said Hall of Famer "Cyclone" Taylor, who teamed with Patrick on the Renfrew Millionaires.

It is fascinating to note that a number of Patrick's most glorious moments as a player occurred at a time when most observers figured him to be washed up. He had decided to retire and concentrate on front-office duties in Victoria in 1921, but a year later, two defensemen on his Cougars club were seriously injured.

Lester retrieved his skates and took his position on right defense.

"From the start," one of his opponents commented, "he was a sensation."

The Cougars, who had not won a game in seven starts, won 19-5, and Patrick was never better. He personally won two games, taking a shot to win in an overtime contest against the Saskatoon Sheiks and netting the only goal in a 1-0 victory over the Vancouver Maroons.

Patrick's fertile mind had already brought permanent changes to the game. After watching a soccer match in England, Lester and Frank introduced the penalty shot to hockey. To this day, it remains one of the most exciting aspects of the game. Lester and Frank were the first to put numbers on the players' jerseys. "It was a Patrick innovation," said Elmer Ferguson, "pure and simple. And it has been universally adopted by all major sports."

The Patricks were the first to adopt forward passing and to legalize puck kicking in certain areas as a means to sustain play. They invented the assist and broadened the rules governing goalies. Under the old conventions, a goalie could not legally make a stop while in any position but a vertical one. The Patricks said a goalie could fall to the ice. Today, that's all netminders ever seem to do when blocking the rubber.

RIGHT: After Lester Patrick's classic performance in goal, this photo was taken. Many experts believe it is a phony, with Patrick's head superimposed on that of another goalie. *From the Stan Fischler Collection*

"The Patricks," said Ferguson, "legislated hockey into modernism."

More than that, Lester and his brother brought the professional hockey establishment to its knees. They battled the National League. They organized, reorganized, and then broke up a whole league on the Pacific Coast. When it became obvious that the Pacific League could no longer compete with the NHL, Lester sold his Victoria team to a Detroit group for $250,000.

When the third version of Madison Square Garden was completed in 1925, the first NHL team to play on its ice was not the Rangers but rather the New York Americans. The Amerks, as they were affectionately known, caught the imagination of New York fans.

The new club was owned by one of the most notorious bootleggers, "Big" Bill Dwyer, who just happened to be in jail on opening night. Nonetheless, the Amerks became such a hit that Garden ownership decided it should have a team of its own and sought a recognized hockey personality to help create it.

The organization's first choice was Conn Smythe, who had made a name for himself in Toronto ice circles. Smythe came to Manhattan and began signing players for the Garden's new club, which was named the Rangers.

But the irascible Torontonian clashed so often with management that he was fired before training camp had finished. MSG moguls were advised to replace Smythe with Lester Patrick, and it turned out to be a fortuitous move for both sides.

Lester became manager and coach of the Rangers in the midst of training camp and instantly won over his players with the Patrick blend of discipline and savvy, not to mention tactical brilliance.

It was a testimonial to the "Silver Fox" that he was nominated as outstanding coach in seven of his first eight years from 1930 through 1938. He missed only the 1936-37 season.

The Rangers have won four Stanley Cups since the club's inception, three of them with Patrick as manager.

"Lester," said Babe Pratt, who starred on defense for Patrick, "was to hockey what the legendary New York baseball Giants' manager John McGraw was to baseball."

That is true. One can even substitute the name Babe Ruth, Connie Mack, or Christy Mathewson for McGraw, but that still wouldn't do the "Silver Fox" of hockey enough justice.

BABE PRATT

1 9 3 5 - 1 9 4 2

Among the most likeable and competent skaters ever to don a Rangers uniform, Babe Pratt was the first genuine offensive defenseman to become a star on Broadway.

Like his namesake, Babe Ruth, Pratt was as flamboyant off the ice as he was in the rink, a fact that caused several run-ins with his boss/manager, Lester Patrick.

Nevertheless, Patrick valued Pratt's ability to play sound defense while providing offensive power. Rangers scout Al Ritchie said Pratt was "the finest prospect" he had ever seen, and Ritchie knew what he was talking about.

The Babe replaced veteran defenseman Ching Johnson during the 1937 playoffs against Toronto and made headlines by scoring the winning goal in the deciding game. His presence also paid off in 1940, when the Rangers won their first Stanley Cup in seven years.

Pratt was a defenseman who could rush the puck and score goals in a manner similar to later blue-liners such as Bobby Orr and Denis Potvin. He had a flair for the dramatic and the ability to satisfactorily conclude each project he began.

Later in his career—as a Maple Leaf— the Babe was the architect of one of the most dramatic winning goals in Stanley Cup history. This was in the seventh and final game of the 1945 championship

---

BABE PRATT

BORN: Stony Mountain, Manitoba, Canada; January 7, 1916

DIED: December 16, 1998

POSITION: Defenseman

NHL TEAMS: New York Rangers, 1935-42; Toronto Maple Leafs, 1942-46; Boston Bruins, 1946-47

AWARDS/HONORS: Hart Memorial Trophy, 1944; NHL First Team All-Star, 1944; NHL Second Team All-Star, 1945; Hockey Hall of Fame, 1966

---

against the Red Wings. With the score tied 1-1 late in the game, Pratt fired the puck behind goalie Harry Lumley, and the Leafs triumphed 2-1 to capture the Cup.

By all rights, Pratt should have been a New York Ranger at the time. He had climbed through the Rangers' system, but his off-ice antics finally infuriated Patrick to the point that he finally decided to unload his ace.

Conn Smythe, the Toronto manager, had been watching Pratt for years and dealt for him when he got the chance.

"I remember once," said Smythe, "when Pratt was with the Rangers, and we were tied late in the game. A good Rangers forward got hurt and Pratt was moved up to wing. I thought, 'Aha, here's our chance to win.' Who got the winning goal? Pratt, playing forward."

The Babe won the Hart Trophy as the National Hockey League's most valuable player in 1944 and was a First Team All-Star that same year. A season later, he was voted to the Second All-Star Team. "If he'd looked after himself, he could have played until he was 50," said Smythe in his memoir, *If You Can't Beat 'Em in the Alley*. "But he was [as big a] drinker and all-around playboy as he was a hockey player."

Walter Pratt was born January 7, 1916, in Stony Mountain, Manitoba, but grew up in the city of Winnipeg. His hero was National Hockey League star Frank Frederickson, who lived near the Pratt family's home.

Babe played his early hockey on Winnipeg's numerous outdoor rinks in temperatures as low as 40 degrees below

zero Fahrenheit. When he was 15, he moved up to the Junior hockey level and began demonstrating the moves that would soon attract the attention of major-league scouts. Ritchie, a noted Rangers birddog, was so impressed with Pratt that he reported back favorably to Patrick. The Babe was invited to the Rangers' camp in 1934 and played well enough to win a professional offer, but he chose to return to the amateur ranks for another season.

A year later, he returned to the Rangers' training camp and was signed to a contract. He was farmed out to the Philadelphia Ramblers of the American Hockey League at first but was soon recalled by Patrick as part of a Rangers youth movement.

"By the end of the '30s," said Pratt, "Patrick had really developed a powerful hockey club; we could play terrifically offensively as well as defensively. Conn Smythe, who was then running the Toronto Maple Leafs, said that the 1940 Rangers were the greatest hockey club he'd ever seen. In those days, whenever we came to Toronto, Smythe would advertise us as 'the Broadway Blues, hockey's classiest team.'

"Our club was so well balanced that our first line scored 38 goals, the second 37, and the third line 36 over that season. On that Rangers team, we had three great centermen—Clint Smith, Phil

Watson, and Neil Colville—plus so many good wingmen that we were able to put the pressure on the other team when we were a man short. Our power play was so strong that once the Toronto Maple Leafs took a penalty, we kept the puck in their end of the rink for the entire two minutes and scored two goals."

Pratt's experiences with the club were quite unlike those of hockey players now.

"It was a different kind of game then," recalled Pratt. "Today, they stress board checking and checking from behind— both unheard of when we played. We'd hit a man standing right up, and now the players don't seem to want to take that kind of check. The only check they want is on the first and 15th of the month.

"Sure, we played a tough game, but we also had a million laughs. There was a newspaperman from *The New York World-Telegram* named Jim Burchard who liked to drink, tell stories, and do wild things like swim across the Hudson River. Once, we had [big-time show business star] Ukulele Ike traveling with us, and naturally, Burchard had his own ukulele which he played every night we were in a Stanley Cup round. We also had quite a few jokers on the team. Ching Johnson was one; he was also one of the finest players when it came to working with rookies. Ching was from Winnipeg, too, and he sort of took me under his wing."

When the Rangers later traded the Babe, they accepted an untried rookie, Red Garrett—who was killed during World War II—and a mediocre forward, Hank Goldup. Babe stabilized the Toronto backline and personally

LEFT: Considered the New York Rangers' first offensive defenseman, Babe Pratt always enjoyed a good laugh.
From the Stan Fischler Collection

delivered a Stanley Cup in 1945. But the Maple Leafs floundered the following year, and Smythe decided to go with youth.

Pratt was traded to the Boston Bruins, played one season with them, and was then sent to the minors. Instead of quitting, he played for the Hershey Bears, Cleveland Barons, and New Westminster Royals. After skating for the Tacoma Rockets, he finally called it a career in 1952.

Those who knew and loved the Babe were delighted when the Vancouver Canucks signed him as a goodwill ambassador after they entered the NHL in 1970. Few big leaguers possessed as much goodwill as Pratt, and even fewer possessed his talent.

DEAN PRENTICE

1 9 5 2 - 1 9 6 2

He's not in the Hockey Hall of Fame, but many believe that Dean Prentice is a worthy candidate for the shrine. Certainly those who played alongside the left wing—especially his linemate, Hall of Famer right wing Andy Bathgate—would attest to that. In the late 1950s and early 1960s, Bathgate and Prentice comprised one of the best forward duets in the NHL.

Originally, their line included Bathgate-Prentice-Larry Popein. It later became Bathgate-Prentice-Earl Ingarfield.

Indefatigable, Prentice was known as "Deano the Dynamo" for his tenacious checking and excellent speed. He was as good a two-way forward as the Rangers owned in that era.

Like Bathgate, Harry Howell, and Lou Fontinato, Prentice was a member of the Memorial Cup–winning Guelph Biltmore Mad Hatters, the Rangers' Junior farm team in the early 1950s. Their Cup win took place in 1952.

The Rangers had been missing the playoffs on a regular basis at the time and felt the need for new blood. Prentice was one of the first rushed into the breach straight from the Junior ranks—a move that severely stunted his hockey growth. It wasn't until the 1955-56 season that he had matured into an NHL ace, but from that point on, he remained one of the best and most reliable Rangers forwards.

Prentice's career in the majors lasted 22 years, spanning three decades—the 1950s, '60s, and '70s. Half of his seasons—the first 11—were spent on Broadway.

Prentice learned the hockey trade growing up in Schumacher, Ontario—a gold mining area in Canada. He played for a local juvenile team, the South Porcupine Teepees, which happened to be affiliated with the Rangers' Junior club in Guelph.

The Rangers signed Prentice in 1950 when he was just 17 years old. He was placed on the Biltmores with a group that later became known as the "Guelph Gang."

Early in the 1952-53 campaign, the "Guelph Gang," with the exception of Fontinato, was called up to the Rangers.

Prentice's first two years with the Rangers were statistically unimpressive, but the left winger's hard work on both ends of the ice soon paid off. Along with Bathgate, Popein, and later Ingarfield, Prentice completed the Rangers' most productive line. When he was not out on the offensive prowl, Dean found himself playing strong defense—he was even placed as a forward among defensemen when the Blueshirts were playing with a five-on-three disadvantage.

A fearless skater, Prentice even played the immortal Gordie Howe so thoroughly that a frustrated Gordie threatened to knock out his teeth.

Between the 1954-55 and 1962-63 seasons, Prentice never failed to reach the 30-point plateau with the exception of the 1957-58 season, in which he played only 38 games. However, Prentice still had at least one highlight during the 1957-58 preseason. He netted one goal and two

assists in the All-Star game, earning top honors for the contest.

His best season in New York was the 1959-60 campaign. After missing all of training camp because of surgery to repair torn cartilage in his right knee, Prentice scored 32 goals and had 34 assists for 66 points in 70 games. The Rangers failed to make the playoffs that season, but the Rangers Fan Club awarded Prentice the Frank Boucher Trophy as the "most popular player on and off the ice," ending Bathgate's three-year streak. The Professional Hockey Writers Association also named Prentice the team's MVP.

Dean suffered back problems during the 1961-62 season and was often forced to wear a corset. Nonetheless, in the final week of the 1961-62 season, he was involved in a play that helped send the Rangers to the playoffs for the first time in three years. The Rangers and Red Wings were battling for the fourth and final playoff spot; the winner would clinch the berth.

In the third period, Prentice charged down the ice on a breakaway. Hank Bassen, Detroit's goalie, threw his stick at Prentice, causing a penalty shot to be called. However, Prentice did not take the shot. Referee Eddie Powers had forgotten a rule change that had taken effect that season: penalty shots were now to be taken by the offended player. Powers awarded the shot to Andy Bathgate because he was ruled the last Ranger to have touched the puck.

Bathgate scored on the shot, giving the Blueshirts a 3-2 victory, and moved the team into fourth place with just four games left in the regular season. The Rangers made it, and Detroit did not.

DEAN PRENTICE

BORN: Schumacher, Ontario, Canada; October 5, 1932

POSITION: Left Wing

NHL TEAMS: New York Rangers, 1952-62; Boston Bruins, 1962-66; Detroit Red Wings, 1966-69; Pittsburgh Penguins, 1969-71; Minnesota North Stars, 1971-74

AWARDS/HONORS: NHL Second Team All-Star, 1960; NHL All-Star Game, 1957, 1961, 1963, 1970

Near the end of the 1962-63 season, the Rangers traded Prentice to the Boston Bruins for Don McKenney and Dick Meissner. The pair the Blueshirts received in the trade combined to play 112 contests on Broadway. Meanwhile, Prentice went on to play in another 712 games with Boston, Detroit, Pittsburgh, and Minnesota.

Prentice, a devoted Christian who joined Hockey Ministries International for several years after his playing and coaching days, played in 666 regular-season games for the Rangers, scoring 186 goals and 236 assists.

When Prentice retired at age 41, he had played in 1,378 games, which ranks him among the top 50 in games played in NHL history. He finished with 860 career points, 391 goals, and 469 assists, including 10 20-goal seasons.

After Dean retired from playing, he coached the New Haven Nighthawks for one season, leading the team to a 30-35-11 record and an appearance in the AHL finals.

Prentice played the game as it should be played. He wasn't afraid to go into the corners and dig the puck out; he could skate, stickhandle, pass, and shoot. Though Dean may have lacked size—he was 5-foot-11 and weighed in at around 180 pounds—he was always the consummate team player, displaying both grit and determination.

JEAN RATELLE

1 9 6 0 - 1 9 7 5

Elegant is one way of describing the silky-smooth style that was the hallmark of Jean Ratelle's game. Enemy goaltenders also will cite his splendid shot and the adroit dekes that frequently confounded them.

Whatever the description, the lithe Ratelle was as pure a Hall of Famer as any who ever skated in the NHL.

But Jean was slow to stardom. Very slow! He suffered through a mediocre 1966-67 campaign when he finished with only six goals in 41 games. It wasn't until Rangers GM Emile Francis fired Red Sullivan as coach and inserted Ratelle on a line with buddy Rod Gilbert and Vic Hadfield that Jean was able to silence anyone who doubted his extraordinary, natural hockey ability.

The gears meshed perfectly for Francis' new trio, dubbed the GAG (Goal-A-Game) line, and they quickly emerged as the Rangers' most consistent unit, leading the team to the playoffs for the first time in five years. Ratelle contributed to that 1967-68 campaign with 78 points in 74 games.

The nickname "Gentleman Jean" perfectly described Ratelle. Quiet to a fault, he soon developed into the team's best center between Frank Boucher's retirement and Mark Messier's arrival.

Francis, who had coached Ratelle in Juniors before taking over the Rangers, once said, "Ratelle was the closest thing I had ever seen to Jean Beliveau."

NEW YORK RANGERS

The analogy made sense. Both were tall, rangy centers who were swift skaters, deft passers, and accurate shooters. Like his boyhood friend and longtime linemate Gilbert, Ratelle overcame major back surgery to become a NHL star.

Employing a crisp wrist shot, Jean embarked on a string of three consecutive 32-goal seasons, establishing himself as the NHL's premier centerman. Midway through the 1971-72 campaign, Ratelle was the NHL's leading scorer, outpointing even the fabulous Phil Esposito of the Boston Bruins with 109 points in only 63 games. With the Rangers in first place and Ratelle's line setting all kinds of scoring marks, Rangers fans were flying high.

One of the loudest and longest ovations in Garden history was heard on February 27, 1972, when Jean became the first Ranger to score 100 points in a single season. Ratelle briefly and modestly acknowledged the cascading applause and, looking embarrassed, skated back to the bench.

Less than a week later, disaster struck. While the Rangers were playing the California Golden Seals, New York defenseman Dale Rolfe fired the puck at a maze of players in front of the net.

The shot careened goalward and struck Ratelle on the right ankle. The ankle was badly fractured, disabling him for the rest of the regular season.

He had accumulated 109 points, and with 15 games left, scored 46 goals. Number 50 was clearly in sight, but it was not to be. His value was underscored as the Rangers faltered without No. 19 in the lineup, falling to second place and barely finishing ahead of the contending Montreal Canadiens.

Ratelle briefly returned for the Stanley Cup finals against Boston, but was clearly not the same player. As a result, the Rangers were outclassed by the powerful Bruins in six games. Many contend that Ratelle's injury was the key blow that cost the Rangers the Stanley Cup.

Nevertheless, Jean led his club in scoring and finished third in the league behind Esposito and Bobby Orr. For his efforts and for his sportsmanship on the ice, Jean was awarded the Lady Byng Trophy.

Jean Ratelle was born on October 3, 1940, six months into the Rangers' 54-year Stanley Cup drought. Born and raised in Lac Ste. Jean, Quebec, a small town 300 miles north of Montreal, Ratelle established a name for himself in hockey with the Guelph Biltmore Juniors of the OHA before making his

JEAN RATELLE

BORN: Lac Ste. Jean, Quebec, Canada; October 3, 1940

POSITION: Center

NHL TEAMS: New York Rangers, 1960-75; Boston Bruins, 1975-81

AWARDS/HONORS: Lady Byng Memorial Trophy, 1972, 1976; Bill Masterton Memorial Trophy, 1971; Lester B. Pearson Award, 1972; NHL Second Team All-Star, 1972; NHL All-Star Game, 1970-73, 1980; Hockey Hall of Fame, 1985

debit with the Blueshirts during the 1960-61 season.

Though Ratelle was never able to top the magic he had performed in the 1971-72 season when he finished just short of the 50-goal mark, he remained one of the NHL's best centers, piling up more than 90 points in two of the next three seasons.

Despite his diffident demeanor, Ratelle was extremely popular with the Blueshirts faithful and seemed a fixture in New York as long as he could play.

But on November 5, 1975, Ratelle was involved in a landmark trade. Along with Brad Park, he was sent to the Boston Bruins in exchange for Phil Esposito and Carol Vadnais. Originally, the deal was labeled a steal for the Rangers; Ratelle, whom management considered "over the hill," was regarded as a "throw-in," while Park and Esposito were the prime components of the package.

However, it didn't take long for Gentleman Jean to prove his critics wrong. At the end of the 1975-76 season, Ratelle was at the top of the Bruins' scoring list with an impressive 90 points.

A year later, Jean regained his starry form and proved the Bruins had received the better of the deal. Once again, he led the team in scoring with 94 points (33 goals and 61 assists), which was quite an achievement for an "over-the-hill" hockey player.

Ratelle went on to play five and a half more seasons in Boston, finishing his 20-year career with an average of nearly a point a game and retiring as the NHL's sixth all-time leading scorer at the time. As a Ranger he compiled 336 goals and 817 points.

He completed his playing career in 1981 and was elected into hockey's Hall of Fame four years later in 1985.

CHUCK RAYNER

1 9 4 5 - 1 9 5 3

It's a pity that Charlie Rayner never played for a Stanley Cup–winner. But he certainly spilled enough blood and broke enough bones en route to an illustrious career in Rangers livery. And, as an added fillip, it should be recorded that Charlie is the only goaltender ever to have scored a goal by skating the length of the rink in an organized hockey game, though not in the NHL.

He was also among the very first to participate in what was then a revolutionary two-goalie experiment along with his longtime sidekick and pal, James "Sugar Jim" Henry.

The 1949-50 season was in many ways the high point of Rayner's career, as he almost single-handedly led the Rangers to the Stanley Cup finals.

It is a measure of Rayner's ability that he won the Hart Trophy as the NHL's most valuable player in the 1949-50 season. He was only the second goaltender in history to have done so at that time.

LEFT: Jean Ratelle leads a rush. *From the Stan Fischler Collection*

Playing for a mediocre Rangers team that never finished higher than fourth, "Bonnie Prince Charlie" led the Rangers to a first-round upset of the Canadiens in the 1950 playoffs. The Blueshirts went on to the final round against the Detroit Red Wings. Never playing a single home game, the Blueshirts surprised the entire NHL with their strong bid, only to lose the seventh game in an electrifying, double overtime affair.

Rayner was the first goaltender ever to score a goal on an end-to-end rush. While he was playing for the all-star Royal Canadian Army team during World War II, Chuck was guarding his net when a 10-man scramble occurred behind it and the puck squirted free. No one was between Charlie and the enemy net. The temptation was too much for him to resist.

He left his net and charged down the ice. His opponents were so surprised that they simply stopped in their tracks. Rayner skated within a few feet of the opponent's

goal and shot. The opposing goaltender was dumbfounded and lunged, but the puck sailed right into the net.

When he won the Hart Trophy in 1950, it was one of the most popular announcements in the annals of the game, as Rayner was one of the nicest guys in his sport. Oddly enough, the year he won the Hart Trophy, he placed only fourth in the standings for the Vezina Trophy.

It was his remarkable and sensational performance in the 1950 playoffs that compensated for this. He was incredible during the series as he stopped virtually impossible shots.

Although the Rangers' quest for the Stanley Cup was stopped, the Hart Trophy voting results were a credit to hockey's sportsmanship when the tall goaltender's name was announced.

Rayner received 36 out of a possible 54 points for a 13-point lead over Ted Kennedy of the Toronto Maple Leafs. The great Maurice Richard of the Montreal Canadiens finished third in the balloting with 18 points.

Chuck made the Second All-Star Team three times, in 1948-49, 1949-50, and 1950-51. In his eight seasons with the New York Rangers, which encompassed 424 games, he had 24 shutouts plus one shutout in the playoffs.

Rayner won the West Side Association Trophy as the Rangers' most valuable player during the years 1945-46 and 1946-47 and shared it in 1948-49 with Edgar Laprade.

In August 1973, "Bonnie Prince Charlie" was inducted into hockey's Hall of Fame in honor of his contributions to the sport.

CHUCK RAYNER

BORN: Sutherland, Saskatchewan, Canada; August 11, 1920

DIED: October 5, 2002

POSITION: Goaltender

NHL TEAMS: New York/ Brooklyn Americans, 1940-42; New York Rangers, 1945-53

AWARDS/HONORS: Hart Memorial Trophy, 1950; NHL Second Team All-Star, 1949-51; Hockey Hall of Fame, 1973

ABOVE: Rangers goalie Charlie Rayner lunges for the puck. *From the Stan Fischler Collection*

Claude Earl Rayner was born in the small town of Sutherland, Saskatchewan, on August 11, 1920. Like all of the youngsters of that locale, he went down to the local skating rinks to play the national pastime. Chuck always wanted to be a goaltender. As a 16-year-old in 1936, Chuck played goalie when the Saskatoon Wesleys reached the Junior playoffs against the Winnipeg Monarchs. He then went into the goal for the Kenora Thistles in 1936.

At the end of the 1939-40 season, Chuck was assigned to the New York

Americans' farm club, the Springfield Indians. Rayner had only played seven games for the Indians when Earl Robertson of the Americans suffered a head injury, leaving open a berth in the nets.

Rayner was called up to take Robertson's place, and so, in 1940, the young man from Sutherland was playing in the NHL.

Rayner played for the Americans throughout the 1941-42 season. He then went home and joined the Royal Canadian

Armed Forces. Discharged from the service in 1945, Chuck returned to the NHL to discover that the Americans had disbanded and that all members of the team were distributed among the other NHL teams.

Lester Patrick of the New York Rangers pulled out Chuck Rayner's name. Patrick had already hired a goalie, "Sugar Jim" Henry, but Chuck finally won the Rangers' goalkeeping job permanently.

Rayner had to retire after the 1952-53 season. He had damaged the cartilage in his knee. Although an operation had temporarily saved the knee, it was weakened to the point that he felt he could no longer play.

After his retirement, Rayner returned to Western Canada, where he coached the Nelson Leafs. After two years, he then went to Alberta and coached the Edmonton Flyers. He next did some work for the Rangers, followed by the Detroit Red Wings organization with his friend, Sid Abel.

By the mid-'60s, he had been coaching nine years, but he didn't enjoy it. Chuck didn't like having to tell a kid that he was traded. As a result, "Bonnie Prince Charlie" left the sport completely.

Chuck was a courageous man who often played hurt. He was the kind of athlete who played despite debilitating injuries. It was unfortunate that Rayner never played on a Stanley Cup championship team. However, no one will ever forget Rayner's heroics with the Cinderella Rangers during the exciting 1950 playoffs.

MIKE RICHTER

1988 - 2003

In the long history of Rangers goaltenders, no one was more unique than Mike Richter. For starters, he was a native of Philadelphia. Who could imagine someone from Flyers country becoming one of the foremost netminders in New York history?

On top of that, Mike belied the traditional image of the goofy goalie.

Richter was a scholar—attending Columbia University in the off-season—who indulged in areas foreign to most stickhandlers. Politics fascinated him as a player, and he has pursued that interest to this day.

But most of all, Richter was a master of the puck-stopping art and a primary reason that the Rangers won the 1994 Stanley Cup. Just watch a video clip of Richter stopping Pavel Bure on a penalty shot, and you will understand why he can be favorably compared to Davey Kerr, who guarded the New York nets in 1939-40 when the Blueshirts defeated Toronto for the third Stanley Cup in Rangers history.

Kerr led the Blueshirts to the top of the NHL. Before him, Lorne Chabot was present for the first Cup. Charlie Rayner, Lorne Worsley, and Ed Giacomin also helped the Rangers maintain their status. But none of these goaltenders could compare to the brilliance and success both on and off the ice achieved by the inimitable Richter.

Mike was remarkable in many ways. He could handle the media pressure that athletes face in the world's largest television market, achieve win after win for a team striving for the Stanley Cup, and captivate fans with his sparkling and solid performances. He represented the power and prestige of New York City along with Patrick Ewing, Don Mattingly, and other athletic giants.

Richter was raised in Abington, Pennsylvania, a suburb of Philadelphia. He grew up playing hockey and often competed at high levels. After finishing high school, he had to choose between Harvard and a good hockey school at Wisconsin. He chose the latter and played well enough to be selected 28th overall by the Rangers in the 1985 NHL entry draft.

In the first round of the 1989 playoffs, the Rangers faced a powerful Pittsburgh Penguins club led by Mario Lemieux.

New York's starting goalie had failed to stop the Penguins' tide, so Blueshirts coach Phil Esposito—with his club's back to the wall—chose to take an enormous gamble; he thrust a peach-faced, untried rookie into the breach.

MIKE RICHTER

BORN: Abington, Pennsylvania; September 22, 1966

POSITION: Goaltender

NHL TEAMS: New York Rangers, 1988-2003

AWARDS/HONORS: NHL All-Star Game, 1992, 1994, 2000; NHL All-Star Game MVP, 1994; World Cup MVP, 1996

Few knew anything about Mike Richter at the time, and truth be known, he looked like a sitting duck when the game began.

Although Pittsburgh's offense overwhelmed the Rangers, Richter performed expertly in goal, foiling Lemieux on at least two occasions.

True, the Rangers lost the game—and the series—but Richter had made his mark.

He became a regular for the 1993-94 season, in which the Rangers were awarded the Presidents' Trophy for most points in the NHL. They went on to sweep the New York Islanders in the first round of the playoffs and annihilated the Washington Capitals in the second round four games to one. In the Eastern Conference championship, the Rangers, with a seventh-game hat trick by Messier and a wraparound goal by Stephane Matteau in a clutch Game 6 performance, defeated the New Jersey Devils.

The Blueshirts advanced to the Stanley Cup finals against the Vancouver Canucks, and it was then that Mike lifted his game a notch higher. One of Richter's finest moments came in the fourth game of the series. The Canucks forced a turnover in the neutral zone and the "Russian Rocket," Pavel Bure, was pulled down on a breakaway and awarded a penalty shot. "Here comes Bure against Mike Richter. SAVE BY RICHTER! WHAT A SAVE BY MIKE RICHTER!" shouted MSG announcer Sam Rosen when it happened. Richter made the most amazing save of the game, if not his career.

Despite the save, Vancouver was leading the game 2-0. However, the Rangers were able to take control of the contest and the series as they won two games in Vancouver. They won the Stanley Cup in the seventh game of the series with Richter making exceptional saves, sprawling on his back, using the butterfly on the ground, and gloving the high shots.

Richter had taken New York hockey fans—and the NHL—by storm. He had gained elite status in the hockey world. The United States team soon designated him as its starting goaltender for the World Cup of Hockey in 1996. The team was victorious in the tournament. With typical low-key humor, Richter jokingly admitted that he focused too much on hockey and not enough on other chores such as doing laundry.

Richter and his teammates had defeated a Canadian team featuring Joe Sakic, Rob Blake, Eric Lindros, Mario Lemieux, Rob Francis, Patrick Roy, and Martin Brodeur. Not only did his team win the gold medal, but former New York Ranger and star of the Canadian team Theo Fleury noted that Mike Richter was responsible for the team's accomplishment.

"The guy should never have to buy another drink for the rest of his life," said Fleury. In retrospect, the win was almost as incredible as the Americans' Olympic win over the Soviet Union in 1980.

The years following his Stanley Cup and World Cup glory were not as rosy. Richter's Rangers turned south and missed the playoffs every year after the 1996-97 season, consistently posting records below .500. Some attribute it to Mark Messier's departure from the team, but a knee injury and post-concussion syndrome plagued Richter, and the Rangers and eventually forced him to retire.

Despite lagging at the end of his career, Mike finished with franchise

records in wins (301), appearances (666), minutes played (38,185), victories in post-season play (41), and shutouts in postseason play (nine). In his astonishing 1993-94 campaign, Richter posted commendable numbers: 42 wins, a .910 save percentage, and a 2.57 goals-against average.

Since he had only completed two years of studies at the University of Wisconsin, Richter wanted to finish his degree and launch a new career. He attended Yale and served as an assistant coach for their hockey team.

Richter also offered his assistance to poor and sick children through a charitable program run by the Rangers.

In retrospect, Richter proved to be one of the best goalies in Rangers history and a true warrior who battled every game to the end, even when injuries plagued him late in his career. From the time he stepped on to an NHL rink to Mike Richter Night, when his jersey was lifted up to the rafters of Madison Square Garden, Richter demonstrated the true spirit of hockey.

ALLAN STANLEY

1 9 4 8 - 1 9 5 4

One would be hard pressed to find a more unfortunate tale of an unappreciated Ranger than the saga of Allan Stanley. Here was a defenseman with exceptional but unobtrusive talent who arrived on Broadway with an enormous build-up and departed with an exhausted letdown for himself, management, and fans.

So one might wonder why Allan Stanley is mentioned here in the first place. The answer is simple; although fans failed to appreciate Stanley's qualities, his teammates and management did, and "Big Allan" was a major contributor to his club's ascent to the 1950 Stanley Cup finals. He also happens to be in the Hall of Fame.

Looking back, it can be said that Allan's career began on a high note. The Rangers were desperate for defensemen in the years immediately following World War II and decided to dip into the vast American Hockey League pool for talent. Stanley had become property of Lou Pieri, owner of the American League's Providence Reds, so Rangers boss Frank Boucher negotiated a deal for Stanley through the AHL boss.

To obtain Stanley, New York dispatched three pro players, cash, and the rights held by the Rangers to the services of an amateur. At the time, the value was estimated to be about $70,000. By today's

fiscal standards, it would be worth more than a million dollars.

"One night," said Stan Saplin, who had been the Rangers' creative press agent, "Allan was a minor-leaguer in Providence, enjoying a postgame glass of beer with a few teammates at midnight. The next noon, he was in Leone's Restaurant in Manhattan and being acclaimed, in effect, as 'The Savior' of the downtrodden Rangers."

At first glance, Stanley lived up to his buildup, playing with a poise and confidence rarely seen in rookies. Despite a late start and an injury that hampered him later in the season, Stanley was runner-up to teammate Pentti Lund for the Calder Trophy as the league's top rookie.

One of Stanley's biggest attributes, his endless patience, was also his biggest liability with Rangers fans; he wasn't flashy, and as a result, his skating, passing, and shooting skills were sometimes lost on the gatherings at the Garden.

In no time at all, the "$70,000 Rookie" was being chided as the "$70,000 Beauty," and then the "$70,000 Lemon." None of this would have happened had the Blueshirts been winners, but they hovered between mediocrity and melancholy.

Boucher, who had brought Stanley to New York, appreciated Allan's talents more than most and was upset by the fans' reaction. Every so often, Boucher decided to spare Stanley any more hurt by playing him only in away games, but that just left the Rangers with a rusty defenseman and further increased the fans' hostility.

"They'd boo every time I touched the puck," Stanley recalled. "Then they began to boo every time I got on the ice.

ALLAN STANLEY

BORN: Timmins, Ontario, Canada; March 1, 1926

DIED: October 18, 2013

POSITION: Defense

NHL TEAMS: New York Rangers, 1948-54; Chicago Blackhawks, 1954-56; Boston Bruins, 1956-58; Toronto Maple Leafs, 1958-68; Philadelphia Flyers, 1968-69

AWARDS/HONORS: Hockey Hall of Fame, 1981

Why, even the few games when I sat on the bench, they'd yell at me."

The agony went on for six years, but for one brief break when the Blueshirts took the Detroit Red Wings to the seventh game of the 1950 Stanley Cup finals before losing. Lynn Patrick was the New York coach at the time and called Stanley his most valuable Ranger. Although he played defense, Stanley had seven points in 12 games.

"Every summer," Stanley once recalled, "I'd think about improving my play the next year and winning the fans over to my side. I was always hoping that I'd play like Superman."

He was even chosen as captain in December 1951 when Frank Eddolls stepped down. But the Rangers' continued struggles and Stanley's lack of flash began to grate even more on the Garden faithful.

And so Stanley's agony went on, seemingly interminably, until a cool Wednesday in 1954, when an unexpected but not necessarily welcome light was visible at the end of the tunnel.

Boucher raced into the Rangers' press office and announced with a mixture of anger and relief that he had traded Stanley and forward Nick Mickoski to the Chicago Blackhawks for Bill Gadsby, a high-quality defenseman, and Pete Conacher, a forward.

The trade was as sensational as the original deal for Stanley, since Gadsby was also considered a potential star. (As it happened, Gadsby played 20 years in the NHL—though he never skated for a Cup-winner—and was named to the Hall of Fame in 1970.)

With little hint of martyrdom, "Big Allan" played two unpleasant seasons in Chicago for a feeble team. In the fall of 1956, the Blackhawks gave up, and general manager Tommy Ivan prepared to send him to the Hawks' minor-league affiliate in Buffalo.

The Bruins, in need of an extra defenseman, bought him from Chicago for something less than the waiver price of $15,000. It was one of the best buys since the creation of the NHL.

Stanley's impact with the Bruins was immediate and powerful. A season earlier, Boston was a fifth-place team in the six-team NHL. With Stanley starting as a Bruins blue-liner one year later, the club had climbed into first place. Bruins general manager Lynn Patrick claimed that "Big Allan" was "one of the main reasons" for the resurgence.

"Stanley was playing a calculating brand of hockey," said Stan Saplin, who had covered the defenseman when he played in New York. "Almost every move was sound. His deliberate pace was deceptive, giving him an appearance of being slower and less effective than he actually was. His easy skating style made tough plays look simple, coupled with the fact that, by style, he was not a rushing defenseman but rather one who stayed back."

Needless to say, Stanley played some of his best games against the Rangers at Madison Square Garden. He played two seasons in Boston, and when the Bruins figured "Big Allan" had had it, they traded him to Toronto for Jim Morrison. Although they were looking for a younger backliner, the Bruins had made an awful move. Allan was far from finished. Skating for Punch Imlach in Toronto, Stanley was just as good as he'd been in his Boston prime. It was the kind of move that helped brand Imlach a genius.

Stanley skated just as deliberately in Toronto as he had with the Rangers. The difference was that he was now playing before a sophisticated Maple Leaf Gardens audience who appreciated his defensive gifts as much as his boss, Imlach, did.

It was no coincidence that the Leafs annexed four Stanley Cups with the big guy snowshoeing behind the blue line. Stanley's play had a blend of majesty and intelligence that was both hard and clean. He played textbook defense, you might say, the kind that is as rare today as a nickel cup of coffee.

Allan Stanley was born on March 1, 1926, in Timmins, Ontario. He began his career in professional hockey in 1943 with the Boston Olympics of the Eastern Hockey League. In 1946, he joined the Providence Reds, where he remained until he was dealt to the Rangers.

Could "Big Allan" have achieved the same distinction as a Ranger? Under the circumstances, it would have been a 50-1 shot.

The inescapable problem in New York was frustrated fans who would not, or could not, get off his back.

"There is always a nucleus of fans," Saplin once said, "who pay their way in whether their team is winning or not. They need an outlet, though, for the bitterness that grows within them as failure piles upon failure."

In the eyes of the Rangers faithful, Stanley was an abject failure, a skater who never fulfilled his notices, would never cut it on Broadway, and needless to say, would never make it to hockey's Hall of Fame.

But "Big Allan" did, and part of his endorsement was his excellent, albeit short, career as a Bruin as well as his Cup-winning seasons in Toronto.

It was a strange and very painful counterpoint for Rangers fans who had wanted so much from the defenseman. It was even harder to digest when Stanley played so well against his former team at Madison Square Garden.

One night, the Rangers were playing host to Boston at the Garden. Stanley played brilliantly for the Bruins, who defeated New York in that contest. Many Rangers fans had difficulty understanding how well the player they once had booed out of the Big Apple was playing for the New Englanders.

As Stanley left the dressing room and walked out onto Manhattan's 49th Street after the match, a Rangers fan approached him. The New York rooter had a quizzical look on his face as he admonished the defenseman.

'You didn't play that way when you were with us," the fan said accusingly.

"Yes, I did," Stanley replied, a bit sadly. " Yes, I did!"

Stanley wound up with exactly 100 career goals, 433 points, and four Stanley Cup rings. In 1980, he was inducted into the Hockey Hall of Fame.

Had Rangers fans been as patient with Allan as he was with the puck, the big fellow might have graced the Garden as a Ranger through his entire career.

But to that conjecture, the studious Stanley might have responded with a line from William Shakespeare: "There's much virtue in IF."

JOHN VANBIESBROUCK

1 9 8 3 - 1 9 9 3

Over the years, top Rangers goaltenders have emerged from diverse locations. Hall of Famer Charlie Rayner learned his hockey in the remote hamlet of Sutherland, Saskatchewan, while Mike Richter began his career playing street hockey in Philadelphia.

Then there is the saga of John Vanbiesbrouck, who probably should have been a Red Wing since he originally started his netminding career in Detroit.

Considered by some scouts to be "too small" to be a goalie, Vanbiesbrouck caught the attention of Rangers birddogs during his Junior hockey stint with the Sault Ste. Marie (Ontario) Greyhounds of the Ontario Hockey Association.

The "Beezer," as he became known to the Garden crowd, impressed the Blueshirts' brass on a one-game call-up in 1981-82. He received another invitation to the big club in 1983-84 and continued to impress. But it wasn't until the 1983-84 playoffs in the old Central Hockey League that John convinced the Rangers' management that he belonged at the top.

Although his Tulsa Oilers were forced out of their home rink in the playoffs, Vanbiesbrouck nevertheless paced them with four wins in four games and a 2.50 goals-against average, outstanding numbers for the CHL at that time.

His performance in Tulsa won him a promotion to New York in 1984-85, and

John remained a Ranger through the 1992-93 season.

His size never was a detriment and in some ways was actually an asset. Vanbiesbrouck boasted excellent lateral speed, and his competitive drive was equaled by few. Not surprisingly, that drive helped his improvement every year.

By the 1985-86 campaign, "Beezer" had reached his prime.

Winning the Vezina Trophy as the league's top netminder as well as being selected to the First All-Star Team, John became the goalie the Rangers had been looking for ever since the departure of Eddie Giacomin 10 years earlier.

Vanbiesbrouck remained the Blueshirts' number-one netminder until 1989, when another smallish goalie, Mike Richter, showed up and battled "Beezer" for his job. While it quickly became

---

JOHN VANBIESBROUCK

BORN: Detroit, Michigan; September 4, 1963

POSITION: Goalie

NHL TEAMS: New York Rangers, 1983-1993; Florida Panthers, 1993-98; Philadelphia Flyers, 1998-2000; New York Islanders, 2000-01; New Jersey Devils, 2001-02

AWARDS/HONORS: Vezina Trophy, 1986; NHL First Team All-Star, 1986; NHL All-Star Game, 1996-97

apparent that Richter was something special, the Rangers were still unwilling to forsake their franchise goalie.

As a result, Vanbiesbrouck and Richter were platooned, creating the best one-two goaltending punch in the league. For four years, the pair would remain a dynamic duo and one of the best in the game. Even during this tough competition, John found time to represent his country, starting in goal for Uncle Sam in the 1987 and 1991 Canada Cups.

Ultimately, the New York brass had to make a decision about the two netminders.

Choosing youth over experience, the high command decided to leave Vanbiesbrouck unprotected in the 1993 expansion draft.

The newly minted Florida Panthers, desperate to launch their inaugural campaign with a name goaltender, selected "Beezer" first in the draft. Within three seasons, Vanbiesbrouck had almost single-handedly legitimized a mediocre expansion team with his wizardry in goal.

In 1996, the aging but dynamic goalie led the underdog Panthers on an improbable run all the way to the Stanley Cup finals. Though Florida lost to a loaded Colorado Avalanche team in four games, hockey savants recognized the improbability of the Panthers' run and attributed it in large part to Vanbiesbrouck.

John Vanbiesbrouck was born in Detroit, Michigan, on September 4, 1962. At 15, he had yet to be claimed in the "midget draft," so he chose to visit Sault Ste. Marie, Ontario, for a tryout with the local Greyhounds of the Ontario Hockey League. John made the team and spent three years sharply honing his netminding

talents. By the time he was 18 and eligible for the entry draft, no one doubted he would be chosen.

Vanbiesbrouck became a free agent for the first time in his career in the summer of 1998, but finding work wasn't a problem. The Philadelphia Flyers won the sweepstakes and signed "Beezer" to a three-year contract worth approximately $11.25 million. His results were less than expected.

In his first year as a Flyer, the Maple Leafs eliminated Philadelphia in the opening playoff round. The year 1998 wasn't all bad for John, though; he teamed with his old rival, Mike Richter, for the U.S. team in the 1998 Nagano Olympics.

Vanbiesbrouck's last full NHL season split between the other two New York Metro-area teams, the Devils and Islanders, came in 2000-01. He would play five more games with the Devils before calling it quits for good in 2002, becoming only the second American-born goalie to win 300 NHL games. (Tom Barrasso had accomplished the feat a month earlier.)

After retiring, "Beezer" bought a share in the OHL's Sault Ste. Marie Greyhounds, with whom he served as general manager and coach. He then moved into the television realm as an analyst.

From a historic perspective, John ranks among the best goalies in Rangers history. One of the few bright spots of the 1980s New York team, Vanbiesbrouck made hockey eminently watchable for Rangers fans in that decade.

GUMP WORSLEY

1952 - 1963

"The Gumper." What a man. What a goaltender. What character! From his rookie-of-the-year season in 1952-53 to his last year on Broadway, Worsley crafted a niche as one of the game's most colorful characters. He was also among the last of a dying breed: the maskless goalie. In fact, it took 24 years for Gump to give in and agree to wear a mask while tending goal.

He thus became the last outstanding NHL goalie to do so, yet ironically, he never overcame his intense fear of flying.

Few first-rate netminders have been more durable than Worsley. He turned pro in 1952, when the National Hockey League embraced but six teams, and retired more than two decades later, when more than twice that number existed.

He was the premier goalie on the Montreal Canadiens with whom he won four Stanley Cups, yet he is best known for his escapades as a member of the Rangers between 1952 and 1963.

Throughout some of those seasons, the Rangers often seemed mired in a subterranean section of the NHL. Worsley always seemed to perform like Horatio at the bridge.

New York fans appreciated the roly-poly goalie, but his coach, the volatile Phil Watson, was less enthused.

Watson constantly singled out Worsley for criticism in one form or another. "The Gumper" didn't exactly

GUMP WORSLEY

BORN: Montreal, Quebec, Canada; May 14, 1929

DIED: January 26, 2007

POSITION: Goaltender

NHL TEAMS: New York Rangers, 1952-53, 1954-63; Montreal Canadiens, 1963-70; Minnesota North Stars, 1970-74

AWARDS/HONORS: Calder Memorial Trophy, 1953; Vezina Trophy, 1966 (shared with Charlie Hodge), 1968 (shared with Rogatien Vachon); NHL First Team All-Star, 1968; NHL Second Team All-Star, 1966; NHL All-Star Game, 1961-62, 1965, 1972; Hockey Hall of Fame, 1980

help matters, baiting Watson at every possible opportunity.

When asked his opinion of the fiery Rangers coach, Worsley replied, "As a coach, he was a good waiter." Despite Watson's harangues, Worsley played splendid goal for the Rangers in the late 1950s, leading them to the playoffs in 1956, 1957, and 1958.

In his autobiography, *They Call Me Gump,* Worsley admitted that he turned to alcohol to ease his anguish. "I was using the bottle to chase all of those bad games and bad goals. I used to feel like a duck in a shooting gallery."

RIGHT: Gump Worsley prepares to thwart a Gordie Howe attack. *From the Stan Fischler Collection*

When asked by a reporter which NHL team gave him the most trouble in goal, Gump deadpanned, "The Rangers."

Worsley's Manhattan miseries ended on June 4, 1963, when he was traded to the Montreal Canadiens. As Gump succinctly put it, "That was the day I got out of the Rangers' jailhouse!"

"I WAS USING THE BOTTLE TO CHASE ALL OF THOSE BAD GAMES AND BAD GOALS. I USED TO FEEL LIKE A DUCK IN A SHOOTING GALLERY."

Playing for the Canadiens was not exactly Utopia for Worsley, at least not at first. But he was unquestionably an asset to the Montrealers. He proved it in the spring of 1965 during the Stanley Cup finals against the Chicago Blackhawks.

After playing the first two games of the series, Gump tore a thigh muscle in Game 3 and had to be replaced. The series went down to a seventh and final game with the teams tied at three games apiece. Gump had been taking injections for his injury and was improving, but doubted that he would play in the seventh match.

Prior to the game, Worsley was sitting in the Montreal Forum's lounge when Larry Aubut, the Canadiens' trainer, walked in and told him he was playing.

"I glanced at my wife, Doreen, as she ordered a rye and ginger ale—for herself. I could have used one too, but instead I headed for our dressing room to get ready for the game." Worsley recalled. "Was I nervous? Here I'd been playing pro hockey for 15 years and finally was getting the big opportunity. This was it, the final game of the Stanley Cup championship. You bet your ass I was nervous."

Almost immediately, Camille Henry of the Blackhawks—once Gump's teammate on the Rangers—skated in alone against Worsley. "My legs were knocking," Worsley admitted. But he made the save, and the team went on to blank the Blackhawks 4-0.

"Nothing," said Worsley, "has ever matched that thrill. The first Cup victory is always the biggest moment in a hockey player's life. I was the luckiest guy in the world."

Lorne Worsley was born on May 14, 1929, in Montreal. As a kid, Worsley admired goaltender Davey Kerr, hero of the Rangers' 1940 Stanley Cup championship team. Gump received his first break after winning a tryout with the Verdon Cyclones, a Junior team from a Montreal suburb, while playing for a second commercial-league club. It was then that he was given his nickname. A teammate noticed that Lorne bore a striking resemblance to comic book character Andy Gump, and he began calling him Gump. Soon after, all his teammates followed suit.

In 1949 Worsley was invited to the Rangers' training camp and was assigned to the Blueshirts' farm team, the New

York Rovers of the old Eastern League. He played well and drank well.

"We ran from bar to bar in those days," Worsley confessed, "and you know how many bars there are in New York: about 10,000. After most games, we'd go out drinking and stay out until the joints closed at four o'clock in the morning. We were always there for the last call."

Nevertheless, Worsley continued the upward climb from the Rovers to the New Haven Ramblers of the American League, with stopovers at other New York farm clubs in St. Paul and Saskatoon before reaching the Rangers.

Then came an ironic twist.

> "NOTHING HAS EVER MATCHED THAT THRILL. THE FIRST CUP VICTORY IS ALWAYS THE BIGGEST MOMENT IN A HOCKEY PLAYER'S LIFE. I WAS THE LUCKIEST GUY IN THE WORLD."

Although he won the NHL's Calder Trophy as the rookie of the year in 1953 while amassing 13 wins, a 3.06 goals-against average, and two shutouts, his job was by no means secure. The Rangers had purchased Johnny Bower, a highly regarded minor-league goalie, and installed him in the net ahead of Gump the following season. But Worsley returned to stay the following year and remained a New Yorker until he was dealt to the Canadiens. After a squabble with the Habs' management in 1970, he was picked up by the Minnesota North Stars and concluded his career in April 1974.

Worsley played his 860th regular-season NHL game against the Philadelphia Flyers on April 2, 1974. The final goal—he allowed 2,432 in his NHL career—was scored by Dave Schultz, who had been born the year Worsley played his first pro game in 1949.

"That made me feel old," Worsley said. "Too old to consider another comeback."

He retired and became a scout for the Minnesota North Stars. In 1980 Worsley was inducted into the Hockey Hall of Fame. "The Gumper" never did look like much of a goalie, but he did know how to stop the puck, and his longevity and championship rings attest to the fact that he did his job better than most.

Worsley died January 27, 2007.

When all is said and done, Gump will go down in hockey annals as one of the most colorful, boisterous, and best in his profession.

Even though he never delivered a Stanley Cup to Rangerville, Worsley will always be fondly remembered by fans who had the pleasure of watching—and listening—to him in the 1950s and 1960s.

RANGERS

The Rangers perform their postgame victory celebration.
Photo by David Perlmutter

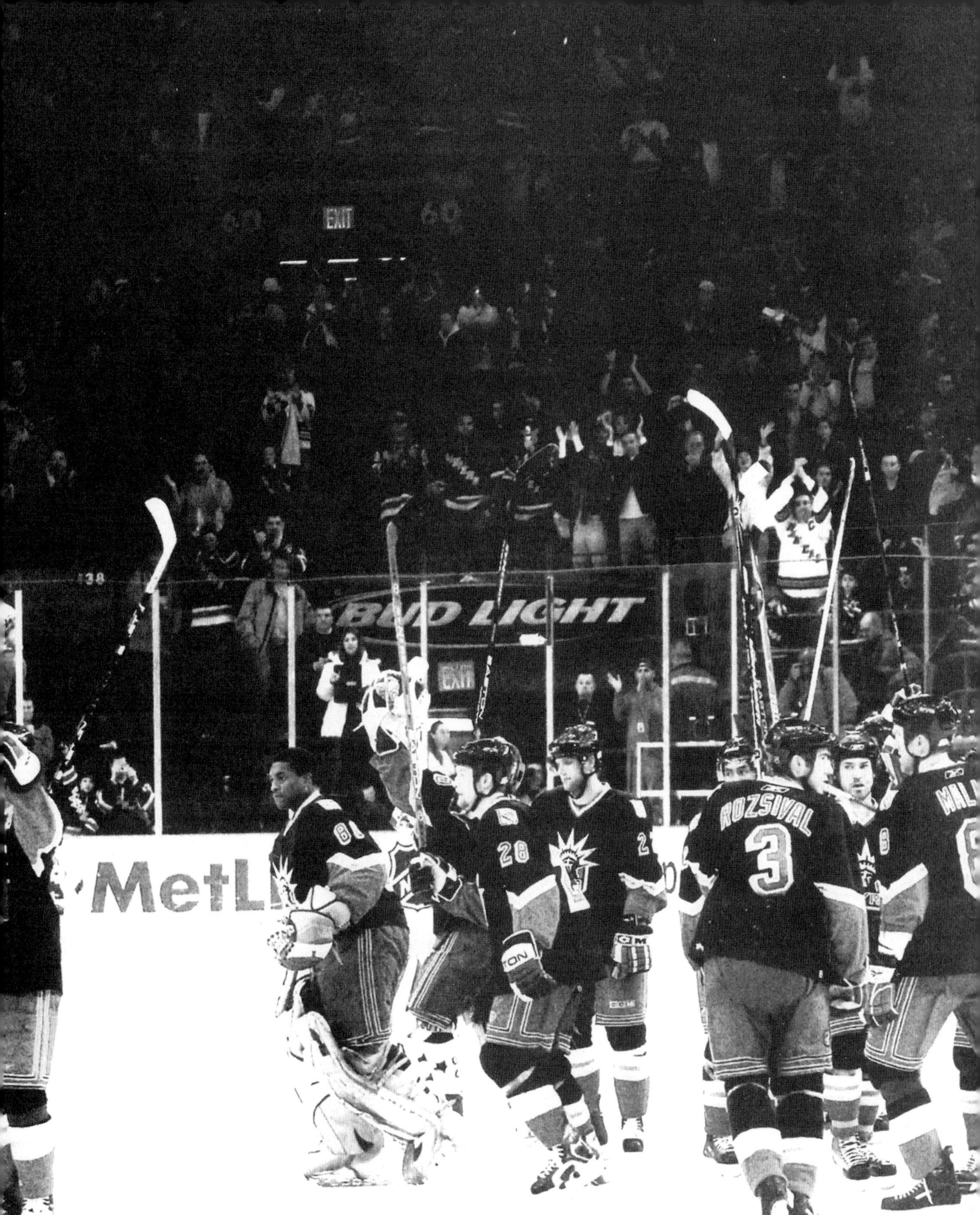
EXIT
BUD LIGHT
EXIT
ROZSIVAL
3
28

HENRIK LUNDQVIST

2005 - PRESENT

To some, it may seem like a stretch to compare a hockey player to his baseball counterpart. But in special cases, exceptions can be made.

Just as the former NY Yankees captain, Derek Jeter, became the idol of New York diamond fans, so too has Henrik Lundqvist blossomed into one of the most popular performers in the Big Apple's athletic history.

Lundqvist joined the Rangers as the 205th pick in the 7th round of the 2000 NHL Draft. With Kevin Weekes suffering a series of leg injuries, the young Swede seized the number-one job and it became clear he was here to stay.

In 53 appearances as an NHL rookie in 2005-06, he earned 30 wins and a .922 SV%. While he struggled in his first trip to the playoffs, during which he only appeared three times, Lundqvist still earned a nomination for the Vezina Trophy and a place on the NHL All-Rookie team. Despite this splendid first-year display, Lundqvist was still not considered for the Calder Trophy as rookie of the year.

"I know it is hard to excel in this league, and I know how hard it is to be at the top of your game every night," Lundqvist said. "I try to do my best every time I go out there."

Henrik's 30 wins made him the first Rangers rookie since Mike Richter to top the 20-win plateau, and two of his seasonal mile-stone victories came against the Rangers' closest rivals. His 20th victory came in the form of a 3-1 win over the New Jersey Devils, and his 30th was a 5-1 victory against the New York Islanders.

With his first North American season under his belt, Lundqvist continued to improve during his sophomore season. His starts climbed to 70, while his wins escalated to 37 en route to his second consecutive Vezina nomination. It was at this time that he earned the nickname "King Henrik," due to his spectacular ability, refusal to lose, and propensity for including Sweden's *krona* (or "crown" in Swedish) on his mask.

In the spring of 2007, the newly crowned Lundqvist also became the first

HENRIK LUNDQVIST

BORN: Arc, Sweden; March 2, 1982

POSITION: Goaltender

NHL TEAMS: New York Rangers, 2005-Present

AWARDS/HONORS: Vezina Trophy, 2012; NHL First Team All-Star, 2012; NHL All-Star Game, 2009, 2011, 2012; John Halligan Good Guy Award (Rangers), 2008; Victoria Cup (IIHF), 2008; Team MVP, 2007-2013; Steven McDonald Extra Effort Award (Rangers), 2006; **NHL All-Rookie Team, 2006; World Championships - Best Goaltender (IIHF), 2004**

NEW YORK RANGERS

Rangers netminder to win a home playoff game since Mike Richter in 1997, and he did it in style by blanking the Thrashers.

Lundqvist's observers could cite many examples of his sparkling play, but few appearances had more impact than a 7-0 shellacking applied to Atlanta in Game 3 of the 2007 opening playoff round.

Despite an ultimately unsuccessful playoff run, the goalie elicited quite a bit of praise, especially from coach Tom Renney, who did not often rave about his players.

"That was a triple A-plus," Renney said. "That was All-Star goaltending. That's MVP goaltending. That's Stanley Cup goaltending. That's everything."

As expectations grew, so too did Lundqvist, making quite a splash and shattering records. In February 2008, he became the first Ranger since Eddie Giacomin, in his 1970 campaign, to record eight shutouts in one season. He earned his 30th win in his next game, making him the only goalie other than Ron Hextall to notch 30 wins in each of his first three NHL seasons. Before the season ended, Lundqvist would record a ninth shutout, which a Blueshirt had not done since Giacomin in 1966. Each season Lundqvist's play followed a similar blueprint: you could pencil him in for between 30 and 40 wins, and a save percentage around .920 without ever being too far off the mark.

Following the lockout-shortened 2012-13 season, Lundqvist finally won the Vezina Trophy, behind a stat line of 24 wins, a 2.05 goals against average, and a .926 save percentage.

After another dominant performance in the 2013-14 run to the Stanley Cup, Lundqvist was off and running for the 2014-15 season with Cam Talbot as a competent back-up in goal.

"Nobody will feel right if you don't talk to each other," Lundqvist said. "It's important that you have a good relationship."

And since pain and progress are inseparable, Lundqvist unequivocally will tell you about his medical migraines.

While the Rangers were climbing the NHL ladder toward first place in the league, Henrik suffered a potentially career-threatening injury.

During a game at the Garden against the Carolina Hurricanes, a flying puck hit the Blueshirts netminder in the throat. At first the injury seemed rudimentary, but upon further medical review, it was deemed serious enough to place Hank on long-term injured reserve.

As it happened, Lundqvist was sidelined for nearly two months before returning to action late in the regular season. King Henrik was back on his throne in time for the 2015 Stanley Cup Playoffs.

In the first round against the Penguins, Lundqvist only allowed one goal in each of the Rangers wins in the five-game series. In the second round against the Capitals, the netminder led the Rangers back from a 3-1 series deficit to beat Washington in seven games. In the Game Seven clincher, Lundqvist made 35 saves to lead the Rangers to a 2-1 overtime victory.

The King's 14-3 record in elimination bouts—8-1 in the last two seasons—was not enough, however, to overcome the last hurdle—the Tampa Bay Lightning. The Rangers were eliminated in the Eastern Conference Final in another tight seven-game series.

As the Rangers' all-time leader in regular season wins, shutouts, and playoff wins, and as the only NHL goalie to win 30 games in each of his first seven seasons—and at least 20 wins in each of his first 10 seasons—his pedigree is certainly the pride of the Blueshirt blue paint.

DAN GIRARDI

2005-PRESENT

He's a throwback.

The manner in which Dan Girardi plays defense is virtually identical to battling backliners of years past.

Bygone Rangers such as Bucko McDonald, Harry Howell, and Lou Fontinato come to mind. Their primary focus was to keep their defensive zone clean, yet when opportunity knocked they'd go on the offensive as well.

Call him a horse of a player, indefatigable, dedicated, and fearless—that's what this Welland, Ontario, native is all about.

Perhaps the most amazing aspect of the 6-foot-1, 205-pound defender is that he was never drafted, although all 30 teams could have plucked him in the 2005 Entry Draft.

This was surprising, considering that Girardi had starred for two Major Junior teams—the Barrie Colts and the Guelph Storm.

After being traded to the London Knights, Girardi did one better, leading the club to the Memorial Cup, emblematic of the continent's Major Junior Championship. It was Girardi who shut down an explosive young scorer named Sidney Crosby. London won its first Memorial Cup with a 4-0 shutout.

While that feat was impressive, Girardi's true character was revealed after the celebrations concluded. Early in the playoffs, he had complained that his hand was sore after blocking a shot; without seeking medical attention, young Girardi instead chose to play through the pain. Once the season was over, an X-ray was finally taken. Girardi had been playing—and excelling—with a broken hand.

That same brand of perseverance was evident after Dan signed a two-way American Hockey League contract with the Rangers' affiliate, the Hartford Wolf Pack.

He made his Rangers debut in January 2007, and recorded 6 points in his first half-season in Manhattan.

The blue-collar blueliner excelled under head coach John Tortorella's

---

DAN GIRARDI

BORN: Welland, Ontario, Canada; April 29, 1984

POSITION: Defenseman

NHL TEAMS: New York Rangers, 2005-Present

AWARDS/HONORS: NHL All-Star Game, 2012

conservative defensive system. While the Rangers sat back protecting their own net, Girardi never wilted under pressure. During the 2010-11 season, he led all NHL players in blocked shots, and racked up 31 points, his highest scoring mark since reaching The Show.

During the 2011-12 season, Girardi became one of the club's alternate captains. He skated nearly 30 minutes per game and was tasked with stifling the other team's first line and power play unit. The Herculean effort earned him a role in the 2012 All-Star Game.

After Tortorella was replaced by Alain Vigneault, management showed its confidence in him by signing him through the year 2020. Dan repaid the club by leading the team in average time on ice. Partnered with captain Ryan McDonagh, Girardi starred as one half of one of the league's best shutdown pairs.

Girardi's big-time play continued into the 2015 playoffs. During the Rangers' run to the Conference Finals, the blueliner played some of his best hockey against some of the best offensive stars in the game. Tasked with defending against the likes of Sidney Crosby and Evgeni Malkin, then Alex Ovechkin and Nicklas Backstrom, Girardi rose to the challenge, shutting them all down beautifully.

Earning the nickname "Iron Man" for his steel-like bones and superhuman ability to sacrifice his body, Girardi blocked shot after shot—even once with his face. After taking a Chris Kunitz shot to the face in Game One of the first round, Iron Man missed the remainder of the night but was back on the ice for the next tilt.

Girardi valiantly remained standing in the line of fire until the Rangers' eventual demise in Game Seven of the Eastern Conference Final.

It was later revealed that Iron Man had in fact been playing the last three games of the series with a sprained Medial Collateral Ligament (MCL) in his knee. He still managed to finish second on the team in ice time with an average of 21:37 minutes per game—another superhuman effort to cap off the season.

RYAN MCDONAGH
2010-PRESENT

Sometimes miracles do happen when it comes to hockey trades.

Certainly, lightning struck the Rangers in an exquisite way in June of 2009.

That's when Rangers' President-General Manager Glen Sather delivered Scott Gomez to the Montreal Canadiens primarily to shed cap space, and bring Long Island native Chris Higgins closer to home.

When the dust had cleared on the trading front, Sather also had obtained a little-mentioned defenseman named Ryan McDonagh. Surely, the name should have been shouted to the hills based on eventual performances. McDonagh became a five-star captain of the Blueshirts, and one of the league's best two-way backliners. On the other hand, Gomez was a bust in Montreal, Florida, and San Jose.

Based on Ryan's past performance, perhaps nobody should be astonished at what developed.

After all, the Broadway-bound pick, had been selected 12th overall in the 2007 Draft (which also featured Patrick Kane, James van Riemsdyk, and Jakub Voracek). The University of Wisconsin product showed his mettle long before he reached the NHL. In his first year with the Badgers, McDonagh was named to the WCHA All-Rookie team, finishing 12th among freshman with 12 points. Then, in his junior season, he earned All-WCHA Second Team honors.

Clearly, this was a very special hockey player—a fact that somehow eluded the Canadiens' brain trust. Once he donned a Rangers jersey, McDonagh's excellence became apparent.

He ranked sixth among New York rookies in plus-minus, and netted his first career NHL goal against Hudson River rival New Jersey Devils, on April 9, 2011.

The following season, McDonagh continued to impress the Garden faithful

by scoring seven goals and recording 25 assists, leading the Rangers to an Atlantic Division title and the top seed in the playoffs. That spring, he anchored the Rangers defensive corps that lifted the club to the Eastern Conference Finals, their first trip to the Conference Final since 1997.

Opening the 2013-14 season under new head coach Alain Vigneault, McDonagh improved his offensive game without compromising his defensive prowess. He recorded career highs in goals (14), assists (29), and points (43), en route to the Rangers' first Stanley Cup Final in 20 years. In the playoffs, McDonagh scored four goals and recorded 13 assists for 17 points, before the Rangers ultimately fell to Los Angeles, 4-1 in the series.

McDonagh was named team captain in 2014 for a very good reason.

"He embodies the core values that we feel a captain has to have," Vigneault said. "Probably the most important thing is the respect he has in our dressing room from all the coaches and from management."

The captain's efforts guided the Rangers back to the Conference Final in the 2014-15 season. Leading by example with not just his impressive two-way play but his resilience, it was later revealed that the Blueshirt chief played the final few games of the Conference Final with a broken foot.

McDonagh's ability to shut down the league's offensive juggernauts, such as Sidney Crosby, Alex Ovechkin, and Steven Stamkos, propelled his rise to NHL stardom. With defensive partner Dan Girardi

RYAN MCDONAGH

BORN: St. Paul, Minnesota; June 13, 1989

POSITION: Defenseman

NHL TEAMS: New York Rangers, 2010-Present

AWARDS/HONORS: Player's Player Award (Rangers), 2014; Team MVP (Rangers), 2014; All-Rookie Team (WCHA), 2008

NEW YORK RANGERS

in tow since the beginning, McDonagh helped to form one of the league's most formidable defensive tandems.

KEVIN KLEIN

2014 - PRESENT

When Edward Heyman (song) and Johnny Green (music) wrote their classic tune called "You Came To Me From Out of Nowhere" in 1931, there was no Kevin Klein around, but their theme still holds up on the ice more than eight decades later.

As far as Rangers defensemen are concerned, few have ever surfaced from out of nowhere more emphatically than Kevin Klein has (that is, if you consider the good city of Nashville "Nowhere").

Still, the manner in which Klein became a Ranger seemed to have eluded everyone but general manager Glen Sather, who swung this almost inconspicuous trade in 2014.

Sather made the move that sent Michael Del Zotto packing in exchange for Kevin Klein, a rugged stay-at-home defenseman of which the Rangers were in need. Additionally, Klein was a smart crease-clearing veteran who knew his way around the backend; plus he could score—and score—and score.

The 6-foot-1, 200 pounder added an element that was missing with Del Zotto, and that is gritty play in front of his net, not to mention the ability to be

in the right place at the right time. Klein further established his presence during the Rangers' four-series expedition to the Stanley Cup Final in June 2014. He appeared in 25 postseason games, scoring a goal along with three assists. Better still, his plus/minus record was a commendable +7.

Anyone who thought that his opening season in New York was a fluke had another thing coming during the 2014-15 campaign.

Exhibit A: October 21, 2014 saw the Rangers trailing the Devils 3-1 in New Jersey. After a late Rangers comeback in the final 12 minutes, Klein put the icing on the cake in overtime and beat Corey Schneider with a helpful set-up from Chris Kreider.

Exhibit B: December 8, 2014, when Kevin netted his third overtime winner of the season against the Penguins—after earlier in the night, a high stick from Zach Sill had forced Klein off the ice with a partially torn ear. After 13 stitches and a blown lead by the Rangers, Klein returned to the game and unleashed a slapshot that blew past Marc-Andre Fleury to win the game in overtime.

KEVIN KLEIN

BORN: Kitchner, Ontario, Canada; December 13, 1984

POSITION: Defenseman

NHL TEAMS: Nashville Predators, 2004-2014; New York Rangers, 2014-Present

Klein showed his heroics again in a contest against the Islanders at the Nassau Coliseum. With the Blueshirts trailing 5-3 early in the third period, the visitors made a furious comeback in front of the passionate Long Island fans. With the score tied at 5-5, Klein received a pass from Martin St. Louis and streaked down the right side, beating Jaroslav Halak with a quick wrist shot. This proved to be the game-winner and helped the Rangers, who had been trailing in the standings, pass the Islanders and eventually annex first place in the Metropolitan Division.

"By far he has the best shot on the team, no question," attested Rangers goalie Henrik Lundqvist, who knows all about hard shots. "He always gets it through. It's hard. It's not a great thing in practice—it hurts—but I appreciate it in games."

Klein's perseverance and grim determination made him a strong addition to a defensive unit that's already one of the deepest in the league.

RICK NASH

2012 - PRESENT

"Your reach should exceed your grasp, or what's a heaven for," said poet Robert Browning.

The dark side of show business is "the build-up to a letdown." The same usually holds true for young prospects who are drafted high.

Rick Nash was one such highly anticipated prospect. In the 2002 NHL Entry Draft held in Toronto, the Columbus Blue Jackets plucked Nash first overall. For a prospective NHL player, that was the highest possible compliment one could receive.

Next came achieving the major goals that lay ahead. Act One in the Rick Nash melodrama was all about continuing the prodigious scoring that he produced in the Ontario Hockey League, with his Major Junior team, the London Knights.

During his first season in London, Rick was named the Rookie of the Year on the strength of 66 points. In the following season, he upped his total to 72 points.

Upon entering the National Hockey League, pundits anxiously awaited Rick's debut to determine how well he could make the adjustment to major league hockey. The answer would be in the affirmative.

The Ontario native played admirably over nine seasons with the Columbus Blue Jackets, as both a scorer and a leader.

Not surprisingly, in March 2008, Nash received the C following the departure of Adam Foote. He led by example with 40 goals and 39 assists, leading Columbus to its first playoff appearance in franchise history against the Detroit Red Wings in 2009. Although Columbus was prematurely knocked out of the race, after being swept 4-0 in the series, Nash had passed his first test of leadership.

But all was not peaches and cream in Columbus. Nash developed a sour taste as his club launched the 2009-10 season with an abysmal 2-12-1 record. From that point on, rumors circulated that he would be expendable. Finally, on July 23, 2013, the rumors turned into reality. In a blockbuster deal involving New York and Columbus, the Rangers delivered a package that included Brandon Dubinsky, Artem Anisimov, and Tim Erixon. In return, the Rangers received Nash, who was expected to build on the Blueshirts' offensive arsenal.

Whether it was because he was making a traumatic adjustment, or because 2012-13 was a lockout-shortened season, Nash was less than the scoring machine that had been advertised in 2013-14. While he produced 42 points in 44 regular season games, he virtually disappeared in the playoffs with just one tally in a dozen contests.

His second season on Seventh Avenue started well enough, as Rick recorded three assists in his first two games. But then adversity hit, and hit hard. In an early-October visit to San Jose, the Rangers' pricey winger suffered a concussion. Although he eventually returned to the lineup, it was patently clear that Rick was suffering post-concussion symptoms.

Among other things, he appeared hesitant to leave the perimeter of the offensive zone, and finished the season with—for him—a paltry 39 points, the lowest total since his rookie year.

By playoff time, Nash had an opportunity to redeem himself over a period of two months, as the Rangers paraded through four playoff rounds to the Stanley Cup Final. Throughout the glorious run, Nash's performances were under a continuous critical X-ray. The verdict was bittersweet. On the one hand, he collected a mere 10 points in 25 playoff contests, yet on the other hand, he was regularly lauded for his defensive excellence. The problem there was that the citizens of Rangerville wanted more red lights, rather than raves about Rick's backchecking.

Without a doubt, the onus was on Nash to prove his worth to the demanding Gotham crowd in 2014-15, and from the get-go the goals came—in droves. Slimmer and supremely motivated, Rick looked like—and played like—a new man, even better than the previous-known Nash at his best.

RICK NASH

BORN: Brampton, Ontario, Canada; June 16, 1984

POSITION: Forward (Left/Right Wing)

NHL TEAMS: Columbus Blue Jackets, 2002-2012 (minus the 2004-05 lockout); New York Rangers, 2012-Present

AWARDS/HONORS: Player's Player Award (Rangers), 2015; Team MVP (Rangers), 2015; NHL Foundation Player Award, 2009; NHL All-Star Game, 2004, 2007, 2008, 2009, 2011, 2015; Maurice "Rocket" Richard Trophy, 2004 ; NHL All-Rookie Team, 2003 Olympic Gold Medal, 2010, 2014; World Championships Gold Medal, 2007; World Championships Silver Medal, 2005, 2008

GREATEST MOMENTS AND PLAYERS

One episode, which came early in the season, symbolizes Nash's massive turnaround. The Rangers had scored a goal and from the next faceoff at center ice, Nash leaped after the loose puck as if he was shot from a catapult. Seizing the six-ounce hunk of vulcanized rubber, he broke through the enemy defenses and scored another remarkable goal. *This* is what Ranger fans were longing for and finally got.

That display of excellence was merely a portent of bountiful things to come. On December 23, 2014, Nash notched his first Rangers hat trick, as he lit the lamp three times against the Washington Capitals. On Valentine's Day, February 14, 2015, Ranger fans felt the love from Rick as he scored early in the third period to give the Rangers the lead for good en route to 5-1 victory. This win also happened to be the 500th in Coach Alain Vigneault's career. On March 10, 2015, Nash scored the game-winning goal against the Islanders in a game that helped the Blueshirts eventually surpass their Long Island rival in the Metropolitan Division standings.

Nash's two-way play also continued to excel. With the goals finally coming in bunches, many onlookers tended to overlook his defensive contributions, including continuous excellence on the penalty kill. Those attributes marked him as one of the best two-way forwards in the league. With his reliable play as a constant presence on the Rangers' top line, the Blueshirts found themselves near the top of the Eastern Conference standings throughout the entire season.

Nash's 2014-15 season was his best with the Blueshirts. The left winger scored a career-high 42 goals and added 27 assists to help the Rangers finish with the best regular season record in the NHL.

The 30-year-old's playoff performance was a tad shy of his regular season feats, but when it comes to timely clutch goals, Nash shone.

New York's 2015 playoff run may have been shorter than anticipated but rather exciting. By the end of three series—two of which extended into Game Seven decisions—the team had collected 13 one-goal games and repeatedly bounced back from the brink of elimination.

When one goal can be the difference between finishing the playoffs on the ice and spending it on the greens, Nash proved his worth.

His most momentous tally of the postseason came 54 seconds into the final frame in Game Six against the Capitals, after a rough second period that saw the Blueshirts trailing 18-4 in shots. Although the club had managed to skate off the ice, leading 2-1 after the middle set, Nash's third period goal to extend the lead to 3-1 was monumental in shattering Washington's momentum.

Capitalizing on the fallout, teammate Dan Boyle added another for a seemingly safe 4-1 lead.

However, the Rangers know better than anyone—nothing and no one's safe in the playoffs. The Capitals came back furiously to add two more to the board, to give the Rangers an unnerving 4-3 victory to keep the season alive and force a Game Seven.

CAM TALBOT

2010 - PRESENT

If this didn't actually happen, one might have thought that a Hollywood scriptwriter had created a novel about a fictional hockey player.

Chapter one would zero in on a boy from Caledonia, Ontario.

Instead of going the traditional route via Major Junior hockey, Cam Talbot opted for the most unlikely state in which to hone his goaltending skills—Alabama.

After enrolling in the program at the University of Alabama-Huntsville, he easily smoothed into action with the varsity squad, for an unlikely start to a spectacular career.

"For a Canadian kid like me," says Talbot, "playing in the Deep South gave me a culture shock, but I got over it. And the best thing was that the college didn't have a junior or senior goaltender and I got to play right away.

"Danton Cole, who had played in the NHL, was my head coach at Huntsville," Talbot recalled. "Cole was there for the three years I was. And when I arrived, he saw that I was out of shape and pushed me. I needed that. He was generous with my games played and really helped with my development."

While playing hockey, Talbot worked on a Corporate Finance degree and still has three courses left in order to earn his diploma. Meanwhile, a number of hockey agents contacted him, realizing he had professional potential.

Nevertheless, Talbot remained undrafted, although the Rangers signed him as a free agent on March 30, 2010. By that time, he had altered his style and had become more methodical and less of a reactionary goalie.

"What happened," Talbot explains, "is that I used to rely on desperation saves. But unless your name is Jonathan Quick, you can only rely on reactionary goals for so long. What followed is that I started playing a smarter game—more methodical."

Former NHL assistant Kurt Kleinendorst had coached at Huntsville and explained that Talbot's improvement was linked to the excessive number of shots he faced in every game.

"I definitely thrive on that," says Cam. "I'd rather have 40 shots because it keeps my head in the game as opposed to only 20 shots. When I have so few shots, I have to stay focused and I get cold once in a while, if I'm not getting at least a shot every five minutes."

CAM TALBOT

BORN: Caledonia, Ontario, Canada; July 5, 1987

POSITION: Goaltender

NHL TEAMS: New York Rangers, 2010-Present

AWARDS/HONORS: Steven McDonald Extra Effort Award (Rangers), 2015

After signing with the Rangers, he was sent to their American Hockey League team in Hartford. But it wasn't till the 2013-14 season that it became clear that there might be a more permanent place for Talbot in the NHL. Starting the season with Hartford, the goalie posted a 4-0-1 record, with a 2.49 GAA and a .924 SV%. Five games was enough of a trial for the Rangers brass to make the call to bring the 25-year-old up to replace an injured Henrik Lundqvist. An October 24, 2013 matchup at Philadelphia marked both Talbot's first NHL appearance and loss. Despite a solid performance by the netkeeper, who stopped 25 of 27 shots, the Rangers dropped the game 2-1, losing their sixth in eight games to start the season.

Nevertheless, Cam rebounded two nights later, stopping 32 of 34 Detroit shots. He would eventually get his first NHL shutout in Montreal. It turned out to be the Blueshirts' first shutout on the road against the Canadiens since Feb 25, 1967, the year before the first NHL expansion after World War II.

He finished the 2013-14 regular season leading all first-year goalies with a 1.64 Goals Against Average and .941 Save Percentage. And in his first NHL playoff appearance, on April 29, 2014, he stopped all five shots he faced in Game Six of the Metropolitan Division Semifinals at Philadelphia.

"Cam gave us a chance to win every game," said Coach Alain Vigneault. "He did what a goaltender is supposed to do."

Despite Talbot's instant success, skeptics wondered whether he could continue to succeed over the long haul. Some argued that he was a flash in the pan.

Talbot began his sophomore season with three straight losses but soon rebounded with four wins, including three shutouts, in his next five starts.

Not once did Cam complain about being the understudy to the all-popular Henrik Lundqvist. His philosophy was quite simple—it relied on appreciating the opportunity he was given.

Sure enough, opportunity knocked even louder shortly after the All-Star Game in January of 2015, when Lundqvist was sidelined with a rare injury against the Carolina Hurricanes. The King was struck in the neck under his protective guard, causing a serious vascular injury.

When it seemed Lundqvist would be sidelined for a long period of time, a black cloud of uncertainty hovered over Rangerville. And the most prominent questions was this: could Talbot hold down the fort till the main man returned?

Over a period of 25 games, Cam answered that emphatically affirmative, compiling a record of 18-4-3, despite a first-start loss to the Nashville Predators.

Cam then earned points in all of his next nine starts (7-0-2), becoming the first Rangers netminder to accomplish the feat, since the 1996-97 season when Mike Richter went 14-0-2.

Considering this remarkable goaltending melodrama, it was hardly surprising that by the end of the 2014-15 season, the media was touting Talbot as perhaps being a number-one goalie for another

NHL team, rather than serving as an understudy to The King.

After all, it would seem the Prince saved more than just pucks for the Rangers—he saved them the season.

****

GREATEST
MOMENTS AND PLAYERS

CONTEMPORARY UNSUNG HEROS

Unsung: adj. 1.not acclaimed or honoured – Collins English Dictionary

There are heroes who inspire banner headlines, and there are others who slip between the journalistic cracks.

The fact that the latter often outwork the former happens to be a simple fact of hockey life.

A trio who fit into this category includes Carl Hagelin, Kevin Hayes, and Mats Zuccarello.

Each has contributed significantly to the Rangers renaissance and figure to impact the Blueshirts for seasons to come.

CARL HAGELIN—THE SWEDISH SWIFTY

Born and raised in Södertälje, Sweden, Carl Hagelin didn't have to look far to get involved in hockey. Beginning his career in the Swedish juniors in 2005-06, Hagelin played for two seasons for Södertälje SK, his hometown team in the J20 SuperElit league. In his second season with Södertälje SK, he was named team captain, while also tying for the team lead in scoring.

During his two-year run in Södertälje, Hagelin netted 44 goals and 51 assists, good for fifth all-time in points and goals in his team's history.

Despite Hagelin's strong numbers in Sweden, the 5'11" winger was seen by some as too small for the NHL game. However, his speed and ability were enough to get the Rangers to come calling, as they made Hagelin the 168th overall pick, in the sixth round of the 2007 NHL Entry Draft. Before beginning a professional career, though, Hagelin had another option available, as the University of Michigan offered him a scholarship, making him the first Swedish-born player to suit up for the Wolverines.

Hagelin made an immediate impact, scoring in his first ever game as a collegiate and helping lead Michigan to the NCAA Frozen Four in his freshman year. By his junior season, he had developed a reputation as a two-way winger. The lefty netted collegiate career-bests in goals (19) and points (50) during his third year at Michigan and helped lead his squad to another NCAA tournament appearance. As a senior, Hagelin won the Central Collegiate Hockey Association (CCHA) Best Defensive Forward Award and was also named All-CCHA first team. He notched 49 points in 44 games that season, as the Wolverines reached the NCAA National Championship before his collegiate career came to an end.

After his time at Michigan, the Rangers, still owning Hagelin's rights, signed the left winger to a professional contract. The 2011-12 season marked his first as a pro, beginning with the Rangers' affiliate in the American Hockey League, the Connecticut Whale. Aided by his time spent in the NCAA, Hagelin quickly adapted to the professional game. The winger notched 13 points in only 17 games before getting the call to join the big club.

On November 25, 2011, just over seven months after his NCAA career came to an end, Hagelin laced up his skates for the first time as a member of the Rangers. Continuing his trend of fitting in quickly, Hagelin notched an assist in his first NHL game before scoring his first goal the next night against the Philadelphia Flyers. Hagelin totaled 14 goals and 24 assists in his first season as a Blueshirt. This was enough to get him invited to the 2012 NHL All-Star weekend, where he competed in the Rookie Showcase. Hagelin demonstrated the burst of energy that has become his trademark, as he won the fastest skater challenge.

Hagelin has become a good fit in Head Coach Alain Vigneault's system, which emphasizes team speed and strong two-way play. He became a fixture on the Rangers' penalty-killing team while also providing a reliable scoring touch. More importantly, the team has made the playoffs in each season since Hagelin first donned a Rangers jersey.

Still, Hagelin commands few headlines but is valued by management as one of the Blueshirts' unsung heroes.

KEVIN HAYES—THE FLYING GOLDEN EAGLE

The odd part of Kevin Hayes's Rangers experience is that he was never supposed to be a Blueshirt in the first place.

Although the Chicago Blackhawks had drafted him, the Windy City sextet failed to lock him up to a contract. As a result he wound up in Gotham as an unrestricted free agent without ever having played a game in The Show. The big-bodied center made an instant impact on the Garden Faithful.

Hockey has always played a large role in Hayes's life. As a child, he had the unique experience of having two family members that played professionally, as his cousins Keith Tkachuk and Tom Fitzgerald were NHL mainstays throughout the 1990s and into the 2000s. Hayes played locally in Dedham, Massachusetts, where his skills began to flourish. Playing for his hometown Noble and Greenough School, Hayes earned Prep Player of the Year and All-New England East honors in 2009-10.

Hayes's local dominance earned him some serious hype within the American hockey landscape. While considering his collegiate hockey options, Chicago made him the 24th overall pick in the first round of the 2010 NHL Entry Draft. Hayes almost immediately joined the Blackhawks to participate in their development camp, but continued forward with plans to play NCAA hockey in order to better develop his game.

When deciding where to play college hockey, Hayes didn't have to look far. Boston College was a powerhouse in the NCAA and undoubtedly the most consistent title contender on the East Coast. Even better, his brother

Jimmy was already an established star for the Eagles, and Kevin jumped at the chance to play for a local team with his brother. The two played alongside one another during Kevin's freshman and Jimmy's junior campaign.

Success was not easily attainable for Kevin at first, however. Jimmy was clearly the more experienced player and left BC after his junior season in order to sign a professional contract with the Blackhawks. Meanwhile, Kevin struggled with injuries in both his freshman and junior seasons, missing several games in each campaign. Hayes put together a strong sophomore season however, as he appeared in all 44 games for the Eagles. While his scoring output wasn't substantial (7 goals, 21 assists), many of his points were timely, as he notched three game-winning goals throughout the year. More importantly, Hayes helped lead his squad to a National Championship that season, as he was featured on a team with several future NHL-ers, including soon-to-be Rangers teammate Chris Kreider.

By his senior season, Hayes had championship experience on his resume, but had yet to take the big step most were expecting from him. That all changed in his final collegiate season however, as he spent the year on the Eagles top line, alongside Hobey Baker Award winner Johnny Gaudreau. Hayes broke out by scoring 28 goals and 39 assists in 40 games played—nearly tripling his point total from his junior season. While the Hobey Baker trophy went to his linemate, Hayes himself was named a Top 10 Finalist for the award given to collegiate hockey's best player. In total, he notched at least one point in 31 out of 40 contests, and was second in the country in scoring.

Hayes arrived in New York with a reputation of being a solid two-way player, with a heavy right-handed shot that can be particularly helpful on the power play. In his rookie year in 2014-15, he had posted 17 goals and 45 points through 79 games. Despite this, he remained considerably less publicized than many of his more prominent teammates.

MATS ZUCCARELLO—FROM NORWAY TO BROADWAY

While Carl Hagelin and Kevin Hayes came to the Rangers from hockey hotbeds—Sweden and New England, respectively—Mats Zuccarello's path to Seventh Avenue was paved down a much more unlikely track. Zuccarello was born in 1987 in Oslo, Norway, a place where hockey and other winter sports thrive, but NHL talent isn't abundant. He began skating by age three and was learning the basics of the sport less than two years later. Zuccarello joined his first team when skating for Valerenga, a local children's club team.

In order to continue his development, Mats enrolled into the Norwegian College of Elite Sports (NTG), in 2004. After graduating NTG in 2006, Zuccarello became a regular starter for Frisk Asker in the GET-ligaen, Norway's premier league. He continued to excel, and by his second full season in the league, he was named Most Valuable Player after posting 64 points (24 goals, 40 assists) in 33 games. Mats' leadership skills also became evident, as he helped Frisk Asker win its first championship in 30 years.

After three seasons in GET-ligaen, Zuccarello attracted attention from top European teams. In 2008, he signed with Modo Hockey of the Elitserien, Sweden's premier league. He recorded a league-leading 64 points in his second season and was voted the league's MVP by his fellow Elitserien players.

Despite Zuccarello's European success, he was unable to generate enough interest to get noticed in the NHL Draft. Following his MVP season for Modo in 2009-10 however, one team finally found a diamond in the rough. Zuccarello was signed as an undrafted free agent to a two-year, entry-level contract by the Rangers in the summer of 2010.

After a stint with the Connecticut Whale, the Rangers' American Hockey League (AHL) affiliate, Zuccy made his NHL debut on December 23, 2010. This was no small feat, as he became only the seventh Norwegian to

play in the NHL, and the second that entered the league as an undrafted free agent.

Mats didn't wait long to make an impact on Seventh Avenue. He assisted on a goal during his second NHL game, and lit the lamp for the first time a week later. His first NHL goal was a dramatic one, as he corralled a rebound and beat Carolina's Cam Ward from a near-impossible angle to propel the Rangers to an overtime victory.

Zuccarello went on to appear in 42 games that season, notching 23 points along the way. However, Lady Luck was not smiling on him for the next two years, as he spent the majority of this time in the AHL.

This negative experience inspired him to return to Europe, as Zuccarello spent a year playing in the Kontinental Hockey League. Zuccarello's NHL departure wasn't a long one, as he returned to New York following the lockout that began the 2012-13 season.

Mats played well enough to be signed to another one-year deal with the Rangers for the 2013-14 season. It was clear that Zuccy's career would soar once Alain Vigneault became Rangers head coach and began using him in a variety of roles. Despite being one of the league's smallest players, Mats proved totally fearless, taking on some of the biggest, toughest opponents in the league. His assets to the team were apparent over the course of 77 games, as he registered career-highs in goals (19), assists (40), and points (59). Not only did Mats become the first Norwegian to ever play in the Cup Final, but he was also the only NHL player to represent his country in the 2014 Winter Olympics.

Zuccarello earned another one-year contract with the Rangers for 2014-15, but also found himself at a career crossroads. He was seeking more long-term security than he was getting on his year-to-year deals. As the trade deadline neared and contract negotiations stalled, the winger was subject to trade rumors brought on by his pending free agency. Just prior to the deadline however, the two sides reached an agreement and Zuccarello signed the Lightning in the Eastern Conference Final, Zuccarello addressed the media during break-up day. It was revealed that the injury was more terrifying than anticipated.

The shot he took had caused a skull fracture and a brain contusion. It had caused enough damage that he had temporarily lost the ability to speak and move his arm for four days. Even during his address, he struggled through his words and divulged that there was still a bit of speech therapy and rehab in his future.

As tough as hockey players come, Zuccarello answered the next few questions regarding his return with a confirmation that he would be back on the ice for the start of the next season.

THE HIGH
COMMAND

The 2006-07 New York Rangers.
Photo by David Perlmutter

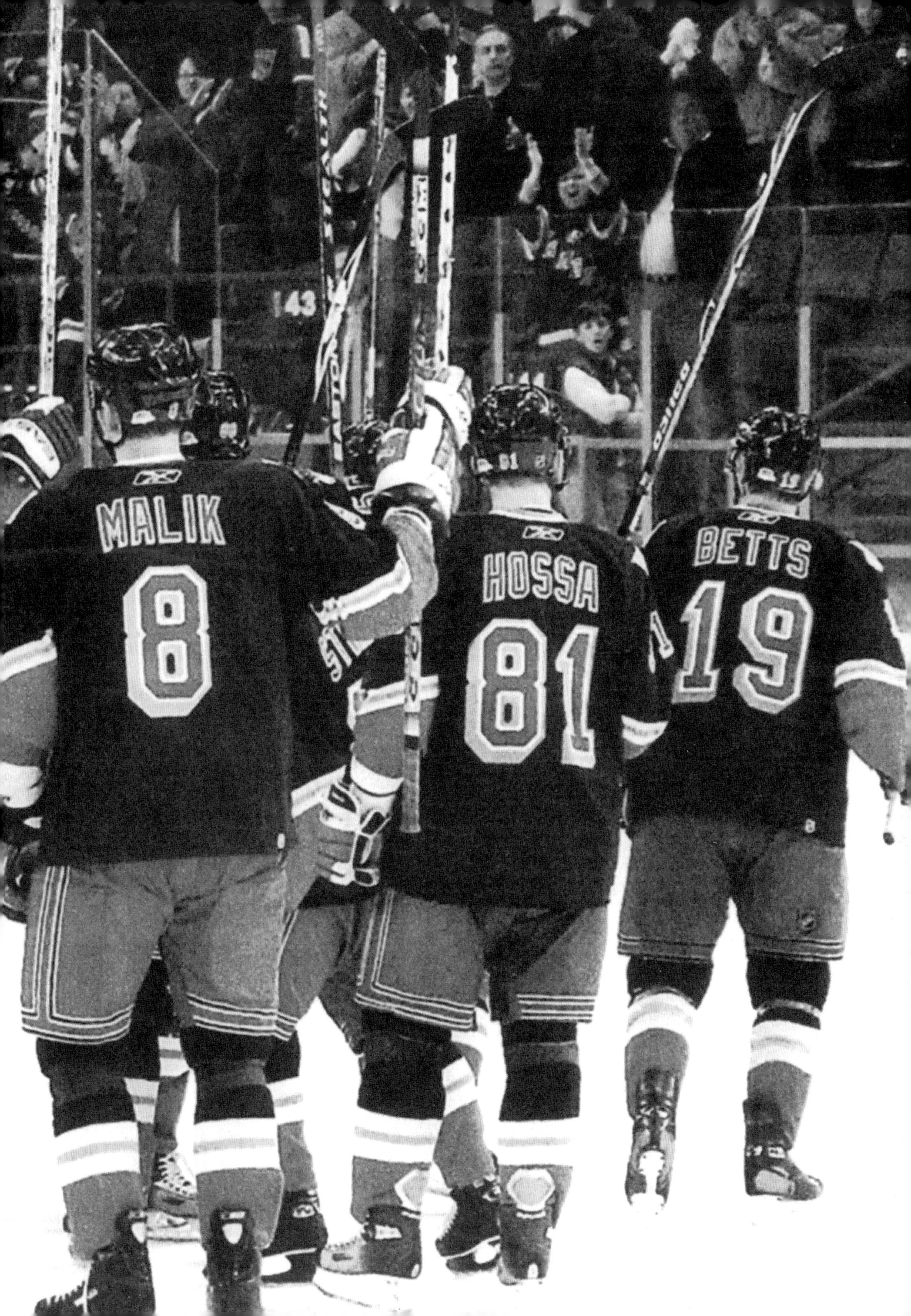
MALIK
8
HOSSA
81
BETTS
19
143

ALAIN VIGNEAULT

2013 - PRESENT

On his very first day after being anointed the 35th coach of the New York Rangers, Alain Vigneault took the stage at Radio City Music Hall and in a trice won the hearts of the hard-nosed New York media in attendance. He looked around at the throng, smiled, and said, "From now on just call me A.V."

The aforementioned initials could have been equated with *Advantage Vigneault* because, from that point on, the feedback about the 54-year-old head coach was nothing less than A-OK.

Calm, cool, and collected, Vigneault came to Seventh Avenue with a splendid résumé that was developed as a player and later refined at an assortment of stops along the way to the National Hockey League.

His move onto center stage developed in the wings as a veritably unknown stickhandler. During the 1981-82 season, the 167th overall pick in the 1981 Draft made his NHL debut with the St. Louis Blues. The defenseman scored one goal and two assists in 14 games.

In time it became clear to Vigneault that he was going to reach the top as a major leaguer, and after three seasons playing at several levels, he chose to retire and pursue a career as a coach. Vigneault began with his first stint behind the bench with the Trois Rivieries of the Quebec Major Junior Hockey League (QMJHL). The Rivieries went 28-40-2 and failed to make the play-offs with AV behind the bench.

The following season, the Quebec City native received his second job at the Junior level with the Hull Olympiques. In his first season, AV led the team to the QMJHL Championship. He spent the next three seasons in Hull, leading the Olympiques to the postseason in all three seasons.

Alain's big break occurred in 1992 when he entered the NHL as an assistant with the Ottawa Senators under Coach Rick Bowness. Vigneault spent three-plus seasons with Ottawa, and received raves for his insights.

"Alain is one of the smartest coaches I've ever encountered," said former NHL goalie and Madison Square Garden Network analyst Glenn "Chico" Resch. "Right from the moment he went to Ottawa he showed that he belonged in The Show."

After three seasons with Ottawa, Vigneault was let go after Bowness was fired 19 games into the 1995-96 season. AV returned to the QMJHL in the 1995-96

ALAIN VIGNEAULT

BORN: Quebec City, Quebec, Canada; May 14, 1961

POSITION: Defenseman

NHL TEAMS:

PLAYING YEARS: St. Louis Blues, 1981-83

COACHING YEARS: Montreal Canadiens, 1997-2001; Vancouver Canucks, 2006-13; New York Rangers, 2010-Present

AWARDS/HONORS: Jack Adams Award, 2007

season, coaching the Beauport Harfangs. In two seasons with the Harfangs, he led the team to two playoff appearances, including a trip to the finals in 1995-96.

It wasn't until 1997 that Vigneault hit the jackpot, being named head coach of the Montreal Canadiens. The Habs made the playoffs in their first season under AV but missed the next two years. However, after his third season with Montreal, he was fired and returned to the QMJHL, this time with the Prince Edward Island Rocket. Two seasons later, he was back coaching professional hockey, this time for the Manitoba Moose, the American Hockey League (AHL) affiliate of the Vancouver Canucks. The Moose earned 100 points and reached the second round of the playoffs in his lone season coaching the club.

Vigneault was named head coach of the Canucks the next season. He led the squad to a franchise-high 49 wins and won the Jack Adams Award as NHL Coach of the Year.

The Canucks thrived under AV, making the playoffs every season, including a President's Trophy in 2010 and berth in the NHL Final, losing to the Boston Bruins in seven games. That should have ensured a long term in Vancouver, but after a first-round playoff exit in 2013, AV was released.

Shortly after John Tortorella was fired as Rangers coach in the summer of 2013, Glen Sather immediately tabbed Vigneault for the challenging head coaching job in Manhattan.

After a rough start to the first half of the 2013-14 season, the Rangers picked up their game and made a late run, finishing second in the Metropolitan Division. The team continued their stellar play into the playoffs, as Vigneault led the squad to its first Eastern Conference Championship and Stanley Cup Final since 1994.

His sophomore season with the club saw another formidable regular season as the Rangers finished the 82-game spread with a franchise record-setting 113 points, winning the President's Trophy—another first since the 1994 season. After two seven-game series, however, the Blueshirts' keen ability to pull out all the stops in elimination bouts came to a heartbreaking end just short of the Prince of Wales Trophy for the Eastern Conference Championship.

Rangers President/General Manager Glen Sather had seen from the beginning that Vigneault had the coaching style and attitude to the take the Rangers to the top of the NHL.

"He's certainly been everything we thought he was: well-organized, very good at his job, gets along well with players and media." Sather added: "I like his up-tempo practices and games; I like the way we play."

The head coach's style has brought the Blueshirts to new realms of success, and his quiet yet friendly nature has certainly won the hearts of the Rangers staff and media.

GLEN SATHER

1 9 7 1 - 1 9 7 4

In 2010, the World Hockey Association bestowed the honor of being inducted into the Hockey Hall of Fame's "Legends of the Game" category upon someone who's touched all bases in hockey—and then some!

No question, Glen Sather has done it all, most recently as the 10th president and 12th general manager of the Rangers and the club's titular leader since arriving on Seventh Avenue in 2000.

"Slats," as he is known in the hockey community, is admired for his confidence, leadership ability, and managerial common sense.

Sather's legacy in hockey dates back to his Junior days in his native Alberta. He proved good enough to make it to the professional ranks and starred for Memphis of the Central Professional

---

GLEN SATHER

BORN: High River, Alberta, Canada; September 2, 1943

POSITION: Left Wing

NHL TEAMS:

PLAYING YEARS: Boston Bruins, 1966-69; Pittsburgh Penguins, 1969- 71; New York Rangers, 1971-73, 1973-74 (2 GP); St. Louis Blues, 1973-74 (69 GP); Montreal Canadiens, 1974-75; Minnesota North Stars, 1975-76

COACHING YEARS: Edmonton Oilers, 1976-89, 1993-94; New York Rangers (interim), 2002-04

MANAGEMENT YEARS: New York Rangers, 2000-present

AWARDS/HONORS: World Hockey Association Hall of Fame, 2010; Hockey Hall of Fame, 1997; Stanley Cups (GM), 1990; Jack Adams Award, 1986; Stanley Cups (head coach), 1984, 1985, 1987, 1988

Hockey League before eventually signing with the Boston Bruins in 1966. He would later emerge as a loyal foot soldier and an asset to many major-league teams.

Once a member of Boston's big bad Bruins, Sather danced through his playing career with a gung-ho style that compensated for any of his deficiencies.

In 658 NHL games, he tallied 80 goals, 113 assists, and 724 penalty minutes.

"When we scouted Glen, we saw that he was tough to play against," remembers former Bruins general manager Harry Sinden. "So we figured that we should draft him so we wouldn't have to play against him."

Sather was an agitator who tried to rile his opponents by talking trash, not unlike former Ranger Sean Avery.

"When Glen was with the Bruins, he would always yell that he was going to get me from the bench," recalls ex-Ranger Rod Gilbert. "One time I scored a goal, and he was still on the bench yelling that he was going to get me, so I asked him, 'When?'"

According to former Boston teammate Ed Westfall, Sather enjoyed staying up late most nights.

"When I first roomed with 'Slats,' I thought that the curfew was eleven o'clock," says Westfall. "For him, the earliest he would get back to the room was eleven o'clock. I didn't know I had a roommate for a while."

Despite the fact that Glen was relatively small among NHL performers, he proved to be a ready, willing, and most able fighter when it was necessary to drop the gloves.

"He was an agitator, but he would also stand up, and he would fight when he was challenged," said ex-Rangers forward Pete Stemkowski.

When the Penguins traded Sather for Syl Apps on January 26, 1971, Pittsburgh fans were mystified.

"We were forced into trading him," recalls ex-Penguins general manager Red Kelly. "The game after that, fans put up banners asking why I traded him. But later in that game, Apps scored on a breakaway, and fans put away their signs."

Sather's pro playing career ended in 1976 with the Minnesota North Stars, but those who knew him well predicted that he eventually would become a big-league executive.

In 1977, he became coach of the Edmonton Oilers of the World Hockey Association. Sather was the first member of the Oilers to be inducted into the Hall of Fame.

The Oilers entered the NHL in 1979, and Sather was appointed president and general manager. Building around a core of young breakthrough talent—which included Kevin Lowe, Grant Fuhr, Jari Kurri, Paul Coffey, Mark Messier, and a free-agent phenom named Wayne Gretzky—"Slats" schooled his team in the ways of winning.

Edmonton became an NHL power-house with Sather as the mastermind behind five Stanley Cup championships between 1984 and 1990, numerous division titles, and team scoring records, not to mention the career of the record-shattering Gretzky.

"I knew that Edmonton was going to knock off somebody and win a couple of Cups," said ex-Islanders general manager Bill Torrey. "Unfortunately, the Oilers beat our team and began a dynasty of their own."

Sather's .706 winning percentage in the Stanley Cup playoffs is one of the highest in league history. Undaunted, he stepped down as Edmonton coach in 1989 to concentrate on general management duties.

"A lot of Oilers wouldn't be where they are today if it wasn't for Sather," says former Oilers forward Glen Anderson.

The cigar-chomping Sather became an astute executive and one of the league's shrewdest, especially once Edmonton's dynastic days ended. The Oilers struggled to stay afloat as a Canadian small-market team in the expanding NHL. Among the moves he made to strengthen the organization was the 1993 trade of an aging Esa Tikkanen for center Doug Weight, the preeminent playmaking Oilers star of the 1990s. It was generally acknowledged as one of hockey's all-time steals.

Glen's keen sense of team building also led him to stints as Team Canada's general manager and coach of the 1994 Canada Cup and 1996 World Cup of Hockey.

In 1997 Sather was inducted into the Hockey Hall of Fame, but his tenure took another turn shortly afterward.

After 24 years with the Oilers organization, Glen stepped down in 2000 to become the 10th president and 12th general manager of the New York Rangers, for whom he had played in the mid-1970s. As a forward with the Blueshirts, Sather played in 188 regular-season contests and was a member of the 1971-72 club that made a run to the Stanley Cup finals, losing to Boston in six games. Now, however, his job was to redefine the Rangers franchise.

One of Sather's first and by far most popular moves as one of the most influential power brokers in the game was bringing back reliable former Oiler and ex-Ranger and Stanley Cup–winning captain Messier to lead the Blueshirts. But the 2000-01 Rangers could not make the playoffs.

During the summer of 2001, Glen acquired controversial, oft-concussed superstar Eric Lindros and a conditional first-round pick for Jan Halvac, Kim Johnsson, Pavel Brendl, and a third-round pick. When the team struggled down the stretch of the 2001-02 season, Sather went to work again. In March 2002, he sent two prospects and little-used defenseman Igor Ulanov plus picks to Florida for goal-scoring machine Pavel Bure. But for the fifth straight year, the Rangers did not make it into the postseason.

The Rangers required more revamping.

In 2004 Sather engineered a heads-up trade with the Washington Capitals, who received Anson Carter in return for 600-goal scorer Jaromir Jagr. The Rangers missed the playoffs for the seventh straight year; however, the wheels were in motion to bring the Rangers back to the playoffs.

After the NHL lockout during 2004-05, Sather brought up a player he had selected during his first NHL entry draft with the Rangers in 2000—net-minder Henrik Lundqvist.

Behind Jagr and Lundqvist, the Rangers made it to the playoffs in 2005-06 but were swept by the New Jersey Devils in the opening round.

More moves were needed. Through free agency, "Slats" signed another 600-goal scorer, Brendan Shanahan.

During the 2006-07 campaign, the Rangers began to flounder, and Sather stepped up again. This time, he acquired Sean Avery and John Seymour from Los Angeles for Jason Ward, Marc-Andre Cliché, and Jan Marek and called up two young talents in the form of defenseman Daniel Girardi and forward Ryan Callahan.

It turned out to be one of the most one-sided deals in memory. Ward floundered in Los Angeles and was later dealt to Tampa Bay. Meanwhile, Avery literally ignited the Rangers both on the ice and off.

"Sean Avery is the reincarnation of Glen Sather," explained Rangers coach Tom Renney.

The Rangers again made the playoffs, sweeping the Thrashers in the first round before losing in the conference semifinals to the Buffalo Sabres in six games.

Some have suggested that at some point in the future, Sather will retire and return to his native Alberta. But after multiple fruitful seasons on Seventh Avenue, Glen has made it clear that he loves what he's doing and loves where he lives.

"I try not to dwell on the past," said Sather. "Winning all of those Stanley Cups with the Oilers was great, but it is in the past, and I'm looking forward to my future with the Rangers."

NEW YORK RANGERS

"I TRY NOT TO DWELL ON THE PAST. WINNING ALL OF THOSE STANLEY CUPS WITH THE OILERS WAS GREAT, BUT IT IS IN THE PAST, AND I'M LOOKING FORWARD TO MY FUTURE WITH THE RANGERS."

SATHER MAGIC

Reaching the Stanley Cup Final as the Rangers did in 2014 and clinching the President's Trophy as they did in 2015 was hardly an accident.

Rather, it was a product of astute management orchestrated by the boss, President/General Manager Glen Sather.

The following examples offer proof positive, from Exhibits A through E:

A) RANGERS ACQUIRE RYAN MCDONAGH FROM MONTREAL FOR SCOTT GOMEZ

McDonagh has been a force on the Rangers' blueline since he was brought over in a multi-trade on June 30, 2009.

His leadership qualities led to Ryan being named captain of the club in 2014. He has since led the team in ice time, and has offered solid defense. As an added bonus, McDonagh provides an offensive presence as well.

The Minnesota-born defenseman helped lead the team to the Eastern Conference Final in 2012 and the Stanley Cup Final in 2014. By the end of the 2014 postseason, Ryan had recorded 17 playoff points in the 25 playoff games.

B) ANTON STRALMAN IS SIGNED AFTER BEING RELEASED BY NEW JERSEY

Although the Swedish defenseman was given a tryout by the Devils in September 2011, New Jersey failed to retain the blueliner.

Sather struck while the iron was hot, and on November 5, 2011, inked Stralman to a contract. Slowly but relentlessly, Anton gained the confidence of the coaching staff and eventually became a top-four defenseman. During the 2014 Stanley Cup run, Stralman saved what appeared to be a sure goal by clearing the puck as it sat on the goal line. That pivotal move led to a Rangers victory in Game Four.

C) RICK NASH ACQUIRED FOR BRANDON DUBINSKY, ARTEM ANISIMOV, AND TIM ERIXON

Ever in search of a superstar, Sather seized yet another opportunity in a blockbuster deal with the Columbus Blue Jackets.

He dispatched Brandon Dubinsky, Artem Anisimov, and Tim Erixon to the Ohio Sextet for the former Columbus captain.

Although it took time before Nash fulfilled his glowing notices, Rick reached his prime during the 2014-15 season. Employing his speed and size to advantage, Rick emerged as one of the NHL's leading scorers. Playing alongside Derick Brassard and Mats Zuccarello, Nash helped orchestrate a Rangers superior symphony as they finished on top of the Eastern Conference.

D) KEVIN KLEIN COMES TO NEW YORK FOR MICHAEL DEL ZOTTO

Kevin Klein surprises after being obtained for Michael Del Zotto. Nobody in the press corps was particularly excited when Michael Del Zotto was dealt to Nashville for a relatively unknown defenseman Kevin Klein.

In no time at all, Klein was welcomed to the regular blueline rotation because of his reliability both defensively and on the attack. Henrik Lundqvist rated Klein's shot as the hardest on the team, and Kevin's many pivotal goals underline that point.

E) THE RANGERS GET MARTIN ST. LOUIS FOR RYAN CALLAHAN

This was Sather's toughest call simply because Callahan had become one of the most popular leaders in Rangers history. Nevertheless, when the deal was completed on March 6, 2014 for St. Louis, fans realized that New York had not only obtained a Cup-winner but also a future Hall of Famer in the miniscule Martin. As it happened, the likable French-Canadian proved his worth throughout the four 2014 Stanley Cup rounds. He helped the Rangers come back from a 3-1 deficit to beat Pittsburgh in seven games in the conference semifinals. He scored the game winner in overtime in Game Four against Montreal to give the Rangers a 3-1 series lead en route to becoming Eastern Conference Champions.

ORAL
HISTORY

The 1930 edition, one of the best of the Rangers squads.
From the Stan Fischler Collection

TOM LOCKHART

THE AMAZINGLY ZANY MAN BEHIND THE RANGERS' SCENE

Throughout Rangers history, there have been individuals whose work with the hockey club has been as mean-

ingful as those who starred on the ice. One of those remarkable individuals was Tom Lockhart, arguably

the most important—and underrated—individual involved with the growth of hockey in New York. In the

following oral history, obtained during a face-to-face interview, Tom Lockhart, father of amateur hockey in

New York and the Rangers' business manager, tells us these fascinating stories from another era.

Before I was asked to take a job in hockey, I was actually running the boxing shows in the old Madison Square Garden on Eighth Avenue and 50th Street. That was right around the corner from where I was born, so you can't consider me a hockey man like those Canadians. I'm New York all the way. My father was born on 27th Street in Manhattan, so that makes me an original Indian.

I remember meeting Teddy Roosevelt as a kid. My dad took me down to police headquarters, and I shook the great man's hand. He told me about the time he rode up one hill and down the other in the Spanish-American War. Teddy was police commissioner when I met him.

Hockey wasn't even on my mind in those days. I got into sports as a bicycle rider in competition, then did some track and field running for the St. John's Club on 56th Street. Out of that, I somehow became

their representative to the Amateur Athletic Union. Then I got into the boxing end of it and eventually wound up running the matches at the Garden.

Then the damnedest thing happened; I became involved with hockey because the bosses at the Garden wanted me to throw it out. In those days, the early '30s, they had Sunday afternoon amateur hockey as well as the Rangers' and Americans' pro games, and the afternoon games weren't doing any business.

The Garden management had just brought in General John Reed Kilpatrick to get rid of things in the building that weren't paying off, and he called me in with some other AAU officers to eliminate the Sunday afternoon hockey. That didn't hit me right, so I told the General he was making a big mistake; I figured amateur hockey could make a go of it if it was run right.

"Look," the General said, "I'll go along and give Sunday hockey another try under one condition: it has to be run by one man, not the way it is now with a big committee."

One of the guys at the meeting was Fred Rubin, chairman of the National AAU. He went in to talk privately with the General after the meeting was over and nothing had been decided. Meantime, I went back to the Garden, and about five o'clock, Rubin came back and walked over to me to say, "The General told me he knows somebody who should take the hockey job; he's talking about you."

I said, "What'd I do now? What the hell do I know about hockey?" We stood there talking for about 20 minutes, when who walks out of the elevator but the General himself. He says, "Tommy, come up and see me at ten o'clock tomorrow morning." I did, and he told me he wanted me to take the hockey job alone. And that was that. Me, Tommy Lockhart, who had never even owned a pair of roller skates—let alone ice skates—had to sell amateur ice hockey at the Garden.

At that time, we had three amateur teams playing: St. Nick's, the Crescent Club, and the New York Athletic Club. My idea to promote hockey was the same I had used for boxing—promotions, cut-rate tickets, and contacts. I had several contacts in the AAU which served as a starter, but we needed a break and got it in a strange way, which connected mayor

Jimmy Walker and Dan Parker, sports editor of the old *Mirror* [newspaper].

A sportsman fellow named Blumenthal decided the winning team should get a trophy in honor of Jimmy Walker, so he went to Cartier's and bought one for $500; it became the Walker Cup. Somehow, after the Cup was first presented, it wound up in a hock shop on Eighth Avenue, and I was tipped off about it and went up to the General with the story. Dan Parker wrote it up in the *Mirror*. Jimmy Walker in exile in Mexico and his cup was exiled in a hock shop on Eighth Avenue. "What do you want to do about it?" I asked the General. "Bail it out!" he said. So I went down and got the hockey cup for $80.

Parker did us a big favor by giving us a whole column about the Walker Cup and also about Sunday afternoon hockey. He had been coming every Sunday to the games with his grandchild, and he loved it. That started the people coming with their kids, but we still needed more than that.

We got another break that summer when some other promoters decided to organize a hockey league up and down the East Coast. I got wind they were having the meeting on the Fourth of July at the Penn Athletic Club in Philadelphia and decided to invite a friend who was also connected with hockey. I was supposed to meet him at Penn Station, but he showed up with a girl, and by the time we reached Philadelphia, they were so drunk I had to get porters to take them off the train.

When I finally arrived at the Athletic Club, the guy at the desk told me the hockey meeting was all over. "They must've gone home," he said. "But take a look, just in case."

TOM LOCKHART

I walked into the room, and sure enough, some people were sitting around the table, and one of them asked what I was doing there. I replied, "I came down here to join the league." What else could I say? They then said, "Look, we're making the schedule. We're all set to go."

At that point, John Carlin, a real Yankee Doodle boy, jumped up and pointed at me, "Did you say you wanted to put a team in this league?" I replied, "Yes, sir."

He asked how many, and I said three teams. Then he wanted to know where, and when I answered Madison Square Garden, he said, "You're in!" The others protested, "But he can't be." Carlin said, "Tear up that schedule. What the hell's the matter with you guys?" You see, they needed the Garden, and I had it—so they needed me.

After much discussion, they concluded, "Well, if he's coming in, he's going to have to make up the schedule." We finally decided to keep the first two weeks the way they had it, and I'd take it from there. The next item was to pick the name for the new league.

Until that time, somebody had been using a rubber stamp for the papers with the name Eastern Amateur Lacrosse League on it, and I had the thing in my pocket. I took it out, looked at it, and said, "Somebody take the 'Lacrosse' out and put in 'Hockey.'" And that's exactly how the Eastern Amateur Hockey League got its name. I don't know who wound up with the rubber stamp.

That first season, we had seven teams: Baltimore, Atlantic City. Hershey, the Bronx, St. Nick's, New York AC, and the Crescents. When I got back to the Garden the next day, I went over to see Jack Filman, who was doing the broadcasting from the Garden's own radio station. He busted the story, and everyone was talking Eastern Amateur Hockey League. But my problems were just beginning.

They had decided to go with a 48-game schedule—24 home games, 24 away—which put me in a hole since I only had 16 Sunday afternoon dates at the Garden. One of the first things I did was to make deals with each of the clubs to play my home games in their rinks for $250 and the cost of getting down there and back. It worked out well. Those fellows got gates they'd never had before, and it helped to encourage interest in hockey and the league.

My problems still weren't over. I couldn't accommodate all of the extra games, so I had to cheat a little. I'd make up phony games, have the Crescents beating New York AC 1-0, and put down somebody's name for scoring the goal and add an assist or two. Then the next week, I'd add two more and a couple of ties. Turned out 21 games were never played, but nobody noticed it—at least no one in the league.

One time, a fellow from the *Times* got interested in the league and started asking about these games. I said, "Well, I'll tell you. You know the Rangers play on Tuesday night, the Americans play on Thursday night, and the next week it's the reverse. I'd have the teams in there playing in the afternoons. We call them 'dark house' games." If you look back at the *Times*, you'll find a story about Lockhart's "dark house" games.

TOM LOCKHART

The seats were standing up and cheering. But it actually happened—21 games never occurred, and the league finished its full schedule of games played in that first year.

By the time the season was over, we were selling out the Garden. Our trick was a little different from today's procedures. As you left the building after seeing a game, you could buy your ticket for next week before they went on general sale. That meant we sold out a week in advance.

By the middle of the summer, we began getting letters about tickets for the new schedule. We struck it good because we were catering to the little fellow, the working man. The first year, we sold tickets at 25 cents for any seat in the house. Then it went up to 50 and 75 cents, but that wasn't bad because the little fellow knew that every Sunday, if he had 75 cents or half a dollar, he'd have the same seat as when he bought his first ticket. A man could bring three kids for less than three dollars. The father was happy and so were the kids. They saw a game or they could run all over the place; we didn't chase the kids like they do today.

Another thing people liked was our program. It had no ads, just all kinds of columns—a gossip column, a league column—in short, plenty of reading material. We used to sell more programs in one day than the Rangers would in two games. And nobody left their program in the building; there was so much in it to take home and read. That was all part of my principle: you give them something they have to take home, and when a friend comes into the house, sees it, and asks what that's all about,

the fan tells him, and we have another customer.

All the fuss over the Sunday afternoon amateur hockey ultimately seeped down to the Rangers' office, and pretty soon, I got a call from manager Lester Patrick. He thought we had a good thing going and felt he could help.

I said, "Great, what can you do?"

"Well," he offered, "Next season, I could bring you some good hockey players from Canada." One word led to another, and we decided to ice only one team instead of the three and spent half a day trying to name it. We had the Rangers and the Ramblers, so we "roved" between and called it the Rovers.

Before our season began, Lester went up to Winnipeg for the start of his training camp and picked out some good, young players for us. We eventually wound up with Mac and Neil Colville, Alex Shibicky, Murray Patrick, Joe Cooper, and Bert Gardiner— two defensemen, three forwards, and a goaltender. We started with about 10 men and never had more than 11, and we played and won the league championship with 11.

The trouble with hockey now is that they have too many men. They sit on the bench too long and don't get ice. That way, they don't develop the way they used to when we had the Eastern League. And we also had a lot more interesting things for the customers. A lot more.

I used to have figure skaters come in and skate between periods. Did you know I was the one to bring the Shipstad and Johnson ice show into the Garden for the first time? They had come off the outdoor rinks in

TOM LOCKHART

Minnesota, then played Colonies Club in Chicago. We saw their act and booked them into the Garden, even though they had never skated on arena ice before. Well, that was something. There was a big difference between our Garden ice and the night club stuff. Maybe that's what made them.

I'll never forget their first appearance. It was between periods of our hockey game, and Shipstad and Johnson were in the dressing room, very nervous. Then they got the call to go out, and they ran for the entrance both at once. The second they hit the ice, both of them fell right on their behinds. The house went bananas. They got up, did their act, and came off moaning, "Well, I guess we're finished as an act."

A minute later, one of the Garden big shots walked into their dressing room to say, "That was a helluva act!"

"What?" they asked. And he said, "The next time you go out there, do it again."

The boys asked, "Do what?" And he said, "Fall!" That fall put the Shipstad and Johnson show on the road and led to their Ice Follies—made a fortune for them both.

That wasn't all; we also gave [the great figure skater] Sonja Henie her debut. She had just won the Olympics and was coming to New York for a visit, so the General contacted me to say she was turning pro and that we should get her to skate at the Garden.

We had a Rovers game scheduled in the afternoon and an all-star event in the evening, so we figured we'd put Sonja on in between. Some Swedish organization was in charge of selling tickets and sold the

place out, but everyone had to come to the Rovers game first since they didn't know exactly when she'd go on.

What a sight. A terrific game was going on, but for the 30-odd minutes, you could've heard a pin drop. Nobody made a sound whether the guy scored or not. Nothing. At the end of the period, the teams went back to their dressing rooms completely disgusted. They had played fantastically, but nobody reacted. Then Sonja came out, and the roof fell in. Everyone in the stands was Swedish, you see.

It was some show, and we decided to have Sonja skate everywhere we had an Eastern League game—Hershey, Baltimore, Atlantic City—and the Rovers were the supporting cast. Still, she was a funny duck and never my cup of tea.

No doubt about it, Sonja Henie was a tough act to follow, but we managed to top her with a live bear, and believe it or not, we even flew airplanes in the Garden. Whenever somebody came in with a suggestion, I'd try it. If you said you wanted to come to the hockey game and walk the length of the ice on your head, Tom Lockhart would bill you.

The airplanes were an example. When I tell you we flew airplanes in the Garden, I'm not kidding. It started with this big toymaker in the city. He walked into the Garden one afternoon with an idea: airplane races. He was putting out toy airplanes—the ones we had as kids that you'd run with and they'd go up in the air, their wheels turning—and he wanted us to race them on the ice. So we took a couple of the

TOM LOCKHART

players in the Metropolitan League, lined them up at one end of the rink before the Rovers game, and had them skate three or four laps around the Garden and then pick a winner. That's how we flew airplanes in the building.

Another guy wanted to have bicycle races on the ice. Since I was an experienced bike racer, I knew it wouldn't be easy to make those turns and told the guy, "I'll prove you can't." I got on the bike and peddled up a head of steam, but when I got near the end boards, I damn near plowed through them and killed myself. I told him if the frame could be altered it might work, but I'm glad I dropped the idea because we might have killed somebody. Working with live bears was a lot easier, believe me.

The bear was Jack Filman's idea. He was doing publicity for the Garden at the time and told me he'd seen this great act at a roller skating rink. I asked what the act was like, and he replied, "There's a bear that skates." I said, "How can he skate? And if he does, he's skating on a roller floor." Filman said, "Well, we can put him on ice skates, couldn't we?"

One discussion led to another, and we decided that maybe we could do something with it. So we went up to take a look at the bear. The bear's owner was a foreigner, and it must have taken us eight hours to explain to him what we were trying to do and for him to say what his bear could do. He'd tell me the bear roller skates, and I'd tell him I'm not interested in roller skates. I want him to ice skate. If we'd say skates, he

would say he's got skates. Finally, he got the message.

We then asked him how much he wanted, but before he could answer, I said, "I'll give you 20 dollars," and he agreed.

With that settled, the next trick was to get the bear into the Garden before our Sunday afternoon doubleheader. I didn't want anybody at the Garden to know that there was a bear coming in because there'd be hell to pay if they heard about it. It might start a riot, and there'd be 18 guys wanting to know who's going to hold the bear.

After a while, I figured out the best technique. Early that Sunday morning, I went down to the employees' entrance on 49th Street and talked to the guy at the door. I said, "There's a cab coming here with Jack Filman and a bear."

He said, "Wha'?"

"I want you to let him in, open room 29, and get the bear in there. And don't talk about it!"

Sure enough, Filman brought the bear, we locked him in room 29, and then he and I put our heads together because we had a big problem—where were we going to get skates for the bear? I mean, now we're dealing with a size 40 shoe. We went to the Rangers' equipment room, and the biggest skate we could find would only go as far as the bear's instep. Meantime, Harry Westerby, the Rangers' trainer, is screaming at us for taking his equipment for a bear. After we explained the act to him, he suddenly got enthusiastic and finally came up with the longest skates on the hockey team.

TOM LOCKHART

The next question was how to put the skates on the bear. By then, it was past noon, and everybody in the back of the Garden was getting into the act. The Met League game was starting and people were in the building, so we had to be sure the cops didn't let anybody through to the back to disturb the bear. We had decided to attach the skates to the bear's feet with rope, which we did, making it pretty secure.

All of a sudden, the bear's owner chimes in that the bear can't go skating on ice unless he goes out with him, and he's got to have skates, too. The search is on again; we find skates, put them on the foreigner, and then learn he's never been on ice skates in his life. He's even having trouble staying up in one place just in the room. While all this is going on, the bear is using the room as a toilet, and the cleanup crew has to come in with a pail and mop several times. It got so bad that the next day, the sanitation department had to come in and disinfect the room.

Anyway, once we got a cord for the trainer to attach to the bear, we were about ready. I said, "Wait a minute, we ought to tell the two teams what we're up to." It was the Rovers versus the Hershey Bears. I mentioned that the bear would come out and the trainer would be with him on skates, even though he couldn't skate. We had the thing perfectly timed out, and the electrician had the spotlights ready; I had the countdown: "Four, three, two, one!"

We brought the bear out with the guy holding the cord. He let five feet, then 10 feet out—and fell flat on his stomach. But he wouldn't let go of that cord; he just hung on as the bear skated all over the ice, pulling him around the rink.

By this time, the people were up on their seats. I looked around and saw the General sitting there and enjoying it; everybody was having a great time. They were all howling. But now I knew we had another problem: how were we going to get the bear off the ice? That big fella was just skating all over the place with no intentions of leaving, and we had a hockey game to play. Already, I had all kinds of advisors since the whole back-of-the-Garden crowd was in on this, but nobody could do a thing that worked. Finally, some woman walked up to me right out of the blue and said, "You want the bear off the ice?" I replied, "Yeah, of course I want the bear off the ice!"

Next thing I know, she walks out on the ice—no skates, no nothin'—puts her two fingers into her mouth, whistles, and sure enough, the bear comes over, pulling the Italian guy behind him like a car pulling a trailer. We took the bear back to his dressing room and along came the General, who said he thought we had a helluva act. It was so good we took it down to Hershey, and it was a hit there, too.

Boy, did we have fun in those days. I can tell you a good one about when I once told a group of intelligent people how ice hockey started. The first time I told this story was in the 23rd Street YMCA in the late '30s. That was when Murray Patrick, Lester's big son, was playing for the Rangers.

One day, Murray walked into my office and said, "My father wants me to go down and play in New Haven." So I answered, "Well, what the hell do you want me to do, argue with your father?" He said, "No, no that ain't it. There's a friend of mine down at the Y, and I promised to go there Saturday night and talk about ice hockey. I also sent a film down."

I told Murray not to worry about it; I'd get one of the Met League guys to go to the Y instead. But I forgot all about it until that Saturday night, when a friend of mine from the Met League, Al Such, walked in. I said, "Hey, what're you doin' tonight? I'll buy you a dinner, and we'll go down to the Y and give a hockey talk."

We arrived, and they showed the film. When it was over, a fellow came on stage and announced, "Tonight, we have one of the greatest hockey players in the world to tell you about ice hockey—Mr. Tom Lockhart!" With that, I scrambled up on the stage and got a hand.

"I'll tell you my experience in playing ice hockey," I began. "As a kid, I lived on the East Side, and in the winter, we'd go up to Central Park. I went there one day with a pair of skates and sat down by the side of the lake and tied the skates on. Finally, I stood up and wet my pants! That's my experience with ice hockey." When they heard that, they whistled and cheered like mad.

You never knew what you were going to come up with in that Eastern League. I remember the time John Handwerg, a dirt farmer from River Vale, New Jersey, got the bug to get in hockey and had an arena built

out there in the sticks—at least, it was the sticks then—and Lester Patrick and I went out to see the guy.

We got him into the league the following year, and in a strange sort of way, he was responsible for making Bill Chadwick the great referee he turned out to be later on. I already had Chadwick working in the Eastern League, and one night, he refereed in River Vale. The next day, he came into my office to say he was quitting.

"I ain't never goin' back to River Vale," he fumed. "This guy Handwerg abused me too much."

That infuriated me. I told him, "You get back there next Sunday, Bill, with your skates." He did, and I took him to the dressing room and we walked right past Handwerg without a peep. After Chadwick put his skates on, I said, "Bill, when you go out on the ice, I'll be sitting there right on the bench, and I'll be at this gate when you come off. In other words, I'll be backing you all the way."

And that's exactly what happened. The game was over, and Bill and I went back to the referee's room. After about a minute, there was a rap at the door; it was Handwerg. He asked if he could come in and walked over to Chadwick and said, "I'm sorry, Bill. I'll never abuse you again."

To me, that was the turning point in Chadwick's career. Bill then went on to become one of the best referees in NHL history. But he wasn't the only good one. There was a little referee called Mickey Slowik who nearly got killed by a player named Joe Desson; this was in a playoff game in New Haven against Johnstown. Desson was a big defenseman with New Haven, and at one point, Slowik blew his whistle and pointed his finger at Desson to go to the penalty box. Slowik then turned to the penalty timekeeper along the boards to give him the details of the penalty.

But Mickey had made the mistake of not waiting for Desson to go to the penalty box. Suddenly, Desson came up behind with his stick, banged Slowik pretty hard, and knocked him clear into the stands. All hell broke loose. Finally, a cop stepped right out onto the ice and arrested Desson, and another cop came and they took him to court for inciting a riot. Everybody wondered what I would do as president of the league. I suspended him for life.

A lot of people were really against Joe, but to me, he was all right. It's all in how you look at things: some people whisper; some people shout. You look for trouble when you think a guy is going to give it to you, but the principle is that everybody in his own environment is a king and dies just like I do. So there's no difference. Desson was a hard player, but he wasn't alone.

I saw some dillies in my day, and I can remember one time when the craziest thing happened to a quiet guy, Art Coulter, who played defense for Lester on the Rangers.

Lester and I were sitting together in the seats next to the penalty box when Coulter got a penalty; I don't recall what it was for,

but I do know Lester was wearing a new hat and was very proud of it. So Coulter, known for being a very reserved guy with not much of a temper, came into the box about to sit down, and what do you think happens? He goes berserk. First, he grabbed Lester's new hat and started beating me over the head with it. Lester's yelling, "Gimme my hat back," and I'm covering my head, wondering what I ever did to deserve that beating. This took all of five or 10 seconds, and then just as quickly as it started, it ended. Coulter sat down, Lester grabbed his hat, I straightened out, and everything returned to normal.

Like I said, lots of interesting things happen. When I was running the Eastern League in the mid-'40s, we worked out a deal one year where we played teams from the Quebec Senior League—Montreal, Sherbrooke, Shawinigan Falls, Quebec City, and Valleyfield. Not too many people remember, but I was the first one with the first all-black line playing at Madison Square Garden when we had the tie-up with the Quebec League. The line played for Sherbrooke and was composed of the Carnegie Brothers, Herbie and Ossie, and Manny McIntyre. They were terrific. Then I had a Chinese player, Larry Kwong, on the Rovers for quite a while and several other characters. Hank D'Amore was one. Now, there's a story for you.

During World War II, I was sitting in my office one day when this short, chubby fellow walked in. Bear in mind that many of the players were in the Army then, and it was very hard to get enough men to fill out a team. This guy looked just like the comedian Lou Costello from Abbott and Costello, and he said, "I want to play hockey for you."

"Sure," I answered, "I'll give you 10 dollars a week, and you're on." Naturally, I was kidding about the pay, but in the same breath, he came back and replied, "I'll take it!"

By now I wondered what I was getting into, so I told him I better see what he could do on the ice. He went to the dressing room, got fitted out, and then attended a Rovers practice. It turned out he not only could skate and shoot; he was one of the best men on the ice, if not the best. "C'mon down to my office," I told him.

D'Amore changed into his regular clothes and walked in. "Well," he asked, "Was I all right? Can I play for you?"

"You can not only play for me," I answered, "But I'm going to make you coach!" And I meant it. At that time, we also had a team called the Crescents from the old Brooklyn Ice Palace, so I made D'Amore the playing coach and gave him a heck of a lot more money than he ever bargained for. Later, we switched him over to the Rovers, and he became one of the most popular players we ever had.

Along with the Rovers, we also ran the Met League, which was composed of players young and old from the New York area. Chadwick came up from that league, and so did a lot of other good ones. Dom Baolto, later an NHL linesman, Mike Nardello, Mickey Slowik—they were just a few.

The Met Leaguers would play their game of three 15-minute periods at 1:30, and then the Rovers would come on at 3:30 on Sunday afternoons. The Rovers had the usual 20-minute periods. Even though the Met Leaguers weren't as good, they played exciting hockey, and the fans loved them. One night, they managed to save the Rangers a great deal of embarrassment.

It was in the [early] '50s, and we were having our usual Sunday doubleheader; the Met Leaguers had finished, and the Rovers game was on. That night, the Rangers were supposed to play the Red Wings, but both teams were coming in from out of town, and there had been a fierce blizzard all up and down the Eastern Seaboard. We were in the first period of the Rovers game when a phone call came in from [someone with the Rangers]. "We're stuck in Buffalo," he tells me, "and there's no way we can get to New York in time for the game." He said they'd probably make it to the Garden eventually, but he had no idea when the train would be able to pull out of Buffalo.

The Garden was in big trouble. They had 15,000 people in the building for the night game and no teams to play hockey, and I was the guy who they asked to save the whole shebang for them. Well, I got on the phone and called the Met League coaches—Harold Heinz, Al Such, the whole bunch—and told them to get their players and be at the Garden promptly at 7:30.

In those days, Rangers games started at 8:30, so we had a little time to prepare. The question was whether we'd be able to scrape up enough of them to make a game of it, since many of the kids had already

TOM LOCKHART

gone home after playing their game and we didn't know where they'd be now.

By seven o'clock that night, I couldn't believe it. A swamp of them showed up— enough for two full teams. We called them the Met League All-Stars and promptly at 8:30 put two teams on the ice. Everybody in the place was skeptical, including me, but then some magic happened. Those Met Leaguers played like they never did before; they must've thought that they were in the NHL the way they went at it, and soon the entire crowd was roaring as though it was the Stanley Cup final. They played two periods of the greatest hockey anybody ever saw. The only thing that annoyed the people was that we were about to start the third period when the Rangers and Red Wings showed up, and we couldn't finish the game.

The Met Leaguers were a tough act to follow, but the Rangers came through that night, too. They put on a terrific show against an equally great Detroit team which ended early in the morning. Everybody went home happy.

That Met League exhibition proved something to me: an American kid can play the game as well as any Canadian young-ster as long as the American has enough ice. In those days, our trouble was that you couldn't find enough places where the kids could play. In the whole city of New York, maybe a handful of rinks existed; that really burned Lester Patrick because he wanted an American player on the Rangers in the worst way.

Incidents like the night the Met Leaguers wowed the Rangers fans are good for hockey; they created a new interest. People who had never read about hockey are suddenly hearing about the American kids. These are the stories. The normal game stuff is nothing. It's the same hash every week. So when you get a situation like that or have a bear skate at the Garden or hold airplane races, you get people say-ing, "Gee, They've got quite an act. You've never seen anything like it." That's fun, and it was good for hockey.

TOM LOCKHART

BABE PRATT

THE RAMBUNCTIOUS—AND VERY FUNNY—DEFENSEMAN

For years I had heard about Babe Pratt, the gregarious, storytelling defenseman. I finally got to meet him in August 1968 at Pratt's executive office of a New Westminster, British Columbia, lumber company. Babe was 52 at the time and was just as I pictured him, jolly and full of yarns about the Rangers' years of Phil Watson and Bryan Hextall as well as Conn Smythe's Toronto Maple Leafs. His office window overlooked a river blanketed with logs. Two years later, Pratt returned to hockey as assistant to the vice president of the Vancouver Canucks, the NHL entry from British Columbia.

Winnipeg, which is where I grew up, was a terrific hockey town; they had great teams there going back to the 19th century and always seemed to be winning the Allan Cup for supremacy in senior amateur hockey. There were also several Winnipeg teams who received the Memorial Cup for the Canadian Junior Championship.

In those early days of pro hockey, I think Winnipeg Amphitheater had the only artificial ice plant outside of Toronto. In fact, the city was such a hotbed of hockey that, when I was a kid, they had a saying: no matter where you were in the world, you could find a Swedish match, an English sailor, a German whore, and a hockey player from Winnipeg.

I wasn't the first hockey player in my family; my older brother was pretty good, but he was even better as a soccer player.

And in those days, a fellow could make more money in soccer than hockey, so he went to England and played there. But then he found out he could get paid even more money in Scotland for playing hockey, so he wound up in that country. He might have made it as an NHL player, but he never cared about hockey as much as I did.

Naturally, we had a lot of hockey heroes in Winnipeg; mine was Frank Frederickson, who came from Iceland and lived near us. I watched Frank play and felt I wanted to be just like him. Luckily, it was easy to practice in Winnipeg since we had something like 64 rinks for kids 12 years old and under.

We always played outdoors on natural ice, and there was no problem getting the ice because it would get as cold as 30 or 40 below zero. Our games were held every Saturday morning, and I can remember some of them vividly. In fact, I recall how we won the championship even though we got beat 8-0 in the final game. We had found out that there were six guys on the other team who were overage, so they forfeited to us. The following year, we played in the playground league and got beat legitimately.

When I reached the age of 15, I began to play for real winners. I was one of the Junior champions of Manitoba, and even though I played defense, I led the league in scoring. As a puck carrier, I was pretty good; anytime I had the puck, I'd go down the ice with it—something like Bobby Orr [did].

There wasn't enough hockey around for me to play. That's how much I loved it. Once, I played four games in one day. Between noon and 1:00 p.m., I played for the high school; then at 4:30, I had a game at another high school; at 7:00 that night, I played in the church league; and there was a taxi waiting to take me to an 8:30 game, played in 30 below zero [weather]. I think I won every game that day.

On nights when there weren't regular-league games, we'd have to wait until the public skating sessions were over in the local rinks. Usually, it would be about 10:00 at night before we were able to get on the ice. My father often came down to watch me; he loved hockey. Lester Patrick always said that an athlete's greatest asset is healthy parents; I was lucky enough to have them.

I eventually went to Kenora, a town in Western Ontario not that far from Winnipeg, and played Junior hockey there. There are lots of Indians in that area, and my coach was a full-blooded one named Sandy Sanderson. He was a fine coach with great compassion for youngsters—something that's missing today. All we seem to have in Junior hockey coaches nowadays are a bunch of fellows who want to do nothing but win and send players to the big leagues, completely ignoring character-building in the boys. They're so interested in pushing into the majors that they haven't got the understanding to work with the player who isn't that good.

When I played in Kenora, I was scouted by Al Ritchie, who worked for the New York Rangers. Lester Patrick was then the Rangers' boss, and he was to hockey what John McGraw was to baseball. Lester had friends everywhere in Western Canada; when any of his buddies saw a hockey player he thought might make a good pro, he'd get in touch with Lester, who would send his head scout, Al Ritchie, out to investigate. Well, Al told many people I was the greatest prospect he'd ever scouted and invited me to the New York Rangers' training camp in 1934.

Lester had asked 23 amateurs to that camp, and as things turned out, 16 of them made it to the big leagues. Neil and Mac Colville, Alex Shibicky, Bert Gardiner, Joe Cooper, Lynn and Muzz Patrick, Don Metz, Phil Watson, and Mel Hill were there, among others. At the time, Lester wanted me to turn pro, but I still had two years of Junior hockey left. Then he got stuck because two of his regulars, Ching Johnson and Earl Seibert, were holding out for more dough, and he needed an extra defenseman to work out with the team. He asked me to stay with the club, and I worked out with the Rangers for 10 days.

BABE PRATT

After practicing with Bill and Bun Cook and Frank Boucher, I really felt like I belonged with the big club. However, I decided to go back and play Junior hockey for another year, and it was a fabulous one. Our team finished first, and I led the league in scoring with 20 points.

The next fall, I went back to the New York training camp and turned pro with the Rangers, although Lester farmed me out to Philadelphia for two months along with the Colvilles, Shibicky, and Phil Watson. That was the first year Lester got together a sprinkling of old-timers—Boucher, Johnson, Murray Murdoch, and Butch Keeling—and a bunch of youngsters, and we made the playoffs easily. We reached the Stanley Cup finals only to get beat in the fifth game of a three-out-of-five series.

From that point on, Lester went with youth. He brought up Bryan Hextall, Art Coulter, Clint Smith, and in the following year, Muzz Patrick. When I started playing with the Rangers, Lester alternately teamed me with Ching Johnson, Art Coulter, and Ott Heller.

By the late 1930s, Ching was getting old by hockey standards and on his way out of the NHL, and I would be the one to take his place. Of course, you can never take the place of a great athlete who retires; you simply do the job in your own way. Ching was not what you'd call a "picture player"—he wasn't a beautiful passer or stickhandler— but he was one of the hardest hitters in the history of the game, a great leader, and an absolute bulwark on defense.

He'd hit a man and grin from ear to ear, and he'd be that way in the dressing room, too. There was never a time when Ching didn't have itching powder in his pocket, ready for a practical joke. One time, he gave Lester Patrick a hot foot, and Lester's shoe caught on fire; Lester was half-asleep at the time, and after they put out the fire, he couldn't walk for a week. It took a lot of nerve to do that to Lester Patrick.

Of all the players on the Rangers, Muzz Patrick became my closest friend; he was the flamboyant type, and I was no Little Lord Fauntleroy, either. In fact, Lester classified me as "Peck's Bad Boy" from the time I joined the team. I remember when Lester came to Winnipeg and a little redcap said to him, "God, you kept Pratt in terrific shape; he ain't had a drink all summer." Lester answered, "I think that's marvelous for a 17-year-old boy!"

Lester reacted to Muzz the way he did to me. Once, Muzz's name appeared in Walter Winchell's [*New York Mirror* gossip] column; it was about his being in the company of a beautiful showgirl. Shortly thereafter, we had a meeting, and Lester threw the paper over, asking Muzz if he'd seen the item.

Muzz looked at it for a few seconds, then replied, "Isn't that marvelous, Lester? And very well written." Knowing his father, Muzz anticipated that Lester would harangue him about the article, so he said, "Lester, I just want to ask you something. How many hockey players have ever made Winchell's column?"

"None," Lester answered. Muzz smiled and said, "Well, I'm getting you the greatest

BABE PRATT

publicity you've ever had." At that point, Lester thought about it for a moment, then admitted, "You got me pal; you got me."

Both of Lester's sons, Muzz and Lynn, were with the Rangers at the same time, and in one way, it was quite a handicap to them. People would keep mentioning Lester and Frank Patrick to the young guys and reminisce about how great they were.

On the other hand, Lynn and Muzz got a lot of help from their father. I always look at it this way: if your father isn't going to help you, who is? It's the same in almost any business controlled by a family. It's handed down to the sons; you don't see a Rockefeller digging ditches.

Even though he called me "Peck's Bad Boy," Lester liked me, and I loved playing in New York. It was a great hockey town then and still is. Lester made sure that the new Rangers appreciated the place. He'd tell them, "Where's Helen Hayes? Where's John Barrymore? Where are all the great stage actors, the great singers, and the Metropolitan Opera? Where does anybody go who's any good? What do they do? They go to New York."

But you can't sell a kid a bill of goods like that anymore. He'll just turn around and say, "I'll go where the dollars are"; if they're in Manitoba, that's where he'll play.

After a while, though, I think Lester got a bit disturbed at some of my extracurricular activities. I was having fun, but I got hurt; that was during World War II when talent was scarce, and he had an opportunity to make a deal with Toronto whereby

he'd get two players for me. Since the team wasn't winning, I was expendable. That's how I wound up with the Leafs.

As it turned out, I went from one great character to another: Conn Smythe, the Leafs manager. I guess Conn was the greatest exhorter hockey has ever known, and he had the greatest coach in Hap Day. What made things really unusual was that I was the only player in hockey to room with his coach.

You know, lots of people think that happened because then I'd be under the coach's thumb, but I didn't feel that way. I always thought Hap was a lonely man who needed my company.

In any event, I had some great times with the Leafs. I won the Hart Trophy as the NHL's most valuable player and got 57 points in 50 games as a defenseman; it was 20 years before that record was broken by Pierre Pilote of the Chicago Blackhawks. He scored 59 points in 70 games.

But I guess my greatest thrill was beating Detroit for the Stanley Cup in 1945. You have to remember that in 1942, Toronto had lost three straight games in the Cup finals to Detroit, then bounced back to take the next four—the only time that ever happened in Cup [finals] play. In 1945, the Leafs won the first three and lost the next three to Detroit. I'll always remember the seventh, deciding game.

It was in Detroit, and whenever we played there, we usually left for the rink at about 7:30. I was rooming with Hap Day as usual, snoring away, when Hap came in and kicked me right out of bed. I woke up on the floor, looked up, and said, "What the hell's with you, Hap?"

"How can you sleep when the final Cup game is going to start in less than an hour?" he demanded. "How can you do it?"

"Well, Hap," I said, "It's simple, because the game doesn't start until 8:30. That's when I'll go to work."

He wasn't upset anymore. "Well, Babe," he replied, "I'll tell you one thing, you were never short on building yourself up, so I'll look forward to a good game from you."

The score was tied in the third period when Detroit had a man off with a penalty. I started toward the Red Wings' net and took a pass from Nick Metz, a great but under-rated player. Harry Lumley was the goalie for Detroit, and Earl Siebert and Flash Hollett were on defense. When I got the puck, I skated in from the point, made a double-pass with Metz, and received it back on my stick. I slid a long one into the corner of the net. It turned out to be the winning goal.

I always felt that if any one person could have been given the Stanley Cup to keep for himself that year, Hap Day should have gotten it for the way he handled our club. We had great goaltending from Frank McCool, plus some good players like Wally Stanowski, Elwin Morris, Gus Bodnar, Teeder Kennedy, and Mel Hill. But to me, Hap Day was the man who made it all work.

During the 1946-47 season, the Leafs traded me to the Boston Bruins, a move I considered very fortunate. Winding up with a club like Boston was discouraging; still, I had a chance to play with the "Kraut Line"

of Milt Schmidt, Woody Dumart, and Bobby Bauer and with guys like Bill Cowley, Dit Clapper, and Johnny Crawford. The Bruins' problem was that they never practiced. With a team like Toronto, I could keep my weight down because we worked out every day for two hours; in Boston, I had no control over my weight and was never in the condition I used to be. This hurt me, and I became susceptible to injuries. I always feel that when a player gets hurt, it's usually because he's not in shape.

In my case, Art Ross, the Boston manager, sent me down to the minors for a couple of weeks, thinking I'd come right back. But I arrived in Hershey and got injured again, and when it came time to return to the Bruins, I was in the hospital, so they took somebody else instead.

On the other hand, it was somewhat fortunate that I stayed there because the Bears won the American League championship and we got $1,800 apiece as a playoff check, while Boston got beaten in the first round of the playoffs. I think their players received only $600.

I never did play in the NHL again. In 1947-48, I spent part of the season in Cleveland, then in 1948-49, I went to play three seasons for New Westminster in the Pacific Coast Hockey League. My last year was with Tacoma in 1951-52.

Over the years, I saw a lot of hockey and many good hockey players. Looking back, I'd say that Milt Schmidt of the Boston Bruins had the most drive. Schmidt, Syl Apps of the Maple Leafs, and Neil Colville of the Rangers were the three greatest puck carriers I've ever seen. Of course, the greatest goal scorer was "Rocket" Richard, but he wasn't the greatest player; to me, that was Jean Béliveau. He was a polished performer who did everything—stickhandle, shoot, the works! As for the smaller men, Stan Mikita of the Blackhawks [was] a little guy who [could] shoot the way Doug Bentley used to and make plays like Bill Cowley did for Boston. However, "Little" Stan [was] a hundred percent for himself, whereas these other guys were more team men.

Looking back at the defensemen, Doug Harvey ranks as the greatest along with "Black" Jack Stewart, who played for the Red Wings and Blackhawks. Stewart never was the puck carrier that Harvey was—just a real fine, sound defenseman.

Then you get to Bobby Orr. His roaming up the ice at will [hurt] him and [got] him hurt, too. . . . Defensemen should never rush against five men; they should rush when they get a break.

If you ask me, today's game could be improved with a rule change here and there. I'd love to see them do away with the blueline; I really think this would open up the game.

I'd also like to see the nets put right in the backboard. That would eliminate the habit modern defensemen have of going behind the net and standing there. With everything in front of them, they'd have to go up the ice with the puck, and this would also stop a lot of that body checking behind the nets. The puck would be alive, and there'd be more sustained action.

Let's face it, the game is different today, and so are the players. In my day, you had to be able to stickhandle; some of these fellows I see now couldn't stickhandle past their mothers without losing the puck, and some couldn't pass it to their mothers if they were starving to death and it was a piece of bread they were handing them.

But they do a heck of a job on defense by slamming into guys, going down, and stopping pucks. They earn their money there. But for real hockey—the way the fundamentals were originally taught by people like Lester Patrick and Art Ross—these fellows playing today can't do the job.

When I played, we were taught not to shoot the puck until we saw the whites of the goaltender's eyes. Now they blast them from anywhere, hoping the puck will hit somebody's skates or ankles and bounce into the net. And when they go to sign next year's contract, the manager never asks whether the player stickhandled through the whole team, faked the goaltender, and tucked the puck in the net; all he says is, "How many did you get?"

Another difference is that the modern players don't have the laughs we used to, and that includes the hockey writers, too. Believe it or not, I once wrote a story for Jim Burchard in the *New York World Telegram*. We'd been playing the Maple Leafs in the playoffs, and Toronto had just brought up a rookie named Hank Goldup. After one of the games, Burchard came over to me and said, "Babe, make me my story; c'mon, write it for me."

BABE PRATT

I said, "I was on the ice the same time as Goldup, and it was the first time I played against him. I wanted to see if he could shoot. He did, and he scored the winning goal." The next night, I picked up the paper, and there was the headline: PRATT FINDS OUT ROOKIE CAN SHOOT, POPS IN WINNER, I was only kidding around, and Burchard made me the goof on the play.

One year, I think 1936, the writers were the ones who gave out assists on goals, something like official scorers in baseball today. They were so funny. They once gave three assists on one goal.

It happened when we were playing the New York Americans and little Roy Worters was their goalie. Sweeney Schriner put the puck in for the Americans, and the scorer gave the assists to Art Chapman and Lorne Carr. Carr went over to the scorer and said, "Hey, why don't you give an assist to Worters? He's a nice fellow." So he did—three assists on that one goal.

As I said, things were different then. Even the arenas have changed. They used to be noisy, and the fans were closer to the ice; now they're big and new, but they're not the same. I went to the opening of the new Madison Square Garden, and when I got inside, I looked around and thought, "Jesus, this is a cold-looking joint."

The crowds have changed, too. You don't get the same funny cracks we used to, especially from the gallery gods. I remember once at the [old] Garden, there was a game with the Red Wings, who we were beating 6-1. Jack Adams, Detroit's manager, had just gotten his citizenship papers, and suddenly a fan yelled out, "Hey, Adams, it's a good thing you got citizenship; now you can get home relief!"

Another time, we were leading the Americans by about six goals. A voice from the stands yelled down to me, "Hey, Walter, why don't you turn the net around? Nobody's looking!"

The attitudes have changed; everything is all business. When a hockey player gets on a plane, he's as apt to pick up the *Wall Street Journal* as anything else. And when business gets more important than the sport itself, that's not right.

BABE PRATT

GERRY COSBY

FROM RANGERS FARM HAND TO EQUIPMENT IMPRESARIO

While Lester Patrick's accomplishments on the ice and as a hockey coach and manager have been well chronicled, some of his lesser-known achievements have gone unnoticed. One of Patrick's most interesting moves was the manner in which he persuaded one of the Rangers' farm-team goalies, Gerry Cosby, to become the nation's foremost hockey equipment manufacturer and store owner. In an oral history which he related in person to this author, Gerry Cosby detailed his incredible transformation from professional goaltender to hockey entrepreneur.

There are lots of ways to break into hockey, but mine, I think, was the craziest route of all: I walked out on the ice from a seat behind an office desk. This was in 1928, when I was working as an office boy and switchboard operator in the old Boston Arena.

The Bruins had a farm team [at the time] called the Boston Tigers which played in the old Canadian-American League—now the American League—against Providence, Quebec City, Springfield, and several other teams. As it turned out, the goalie for the Tigers was a character who liked to bend his elbow a bit. One day, he bent it so much the manager told him he was finished. Unfortunately, this left the Tigers without a goalie.

Eddie Powers, the Tigers' manager [at the time], came to me and asked, "How'd you like to get in the other net and be our

goalie for a while?" Well, here I was, a kid who never played goal in his life, and they wanted me to go in against those pros, no less. But Powers kept after me. "Look," he said, "our goalie's already gone. We need some help. All this equipment is in the dressing room." The way he put it, it was impossible for me to resist. So I went down to the dressing room, and that was a joke right there. I first tried on the goalie skates. They were size nine and a half; I wear a six. Everything else was also too big for me, but it was too late. I made my commitment, so I got dressed and went out on the ice as practice goalie for the Boston Tigers.

I really got beat up. I didn't know how to skate, and even so, the skates were way too big, as was everything else, including those guys shooting at me. Somehow, though, I managed to survive the first day and figured that was it; they'd bring in a regular goalie for the next practice. For one reason or another, it didn't work out that way, and Powers told me to try it again. Sure enough, I got creamed the second time, but not quite as bad. The third time was even better, and by the end of the week, I actually started to feel like coming back for more.

The Bruins [of the NHL] also practiced in the arena and had a guy named Tiny Thompson as goalie, one of the best ever. One day not too long after I started working out with the Tigers, Art Ross, manager of the Bruins, asked me to work out with them. The Bruins! So I became the practice goalie for the Bruins and a member of the Boston hockey club. It was a big break because Tiny Thompson was such a great help to me.

His theory was that a good goalie never left his feet or fell down—at least if he could help it. Of course, I can tell you, I saw Tiny fall plenty during regular games, but only when necessary. "Keep working," Tiny kept telling me. "You'll get better if you have the mind for it."

He was right. My goaltending improved steadily because I was a real nut for hockey and worked at it. Even a month or two later, I was still taking a beating, but already I knew it was worth it. Tiny used to keep me supplied with goalie sticks; he must have been telling me something.

Another way I learned was just by standing between those pipes and facing [top Bruins] like Cooney Weiland, Dutch Gainor, Dit Clapper, Eddie Shore, Lionel Hitchman, Marty Barry, and Red Beatty. Shore was the greatest. He was a rushing defenseman, tough and strong. I think if I had to compare him to today's players, he'd fit in perfectly.

And what do you think I was getting paid for all this suicide? Nothing. Not one single penny. But I was learning the kind of hockey science a man couldn't pay for, and eventually, I became pretty good. Then Walter Brown, that great Boston sportsman, decided to take an American team on an exhibition tour of Europe. In those days, that was quite a big thing, and we could thank a guy named Jeff Dixon for that. He was manager of the Palais des Sport, the Madison Square Garden of Paris.

Dixon figured that the Europeans would pay to see good ice hockey, and he imported us, financed our trip, and booked us all over the place. Paris was really something. The Palais des Sport had a capacity of 15,000 or 16,000, but when we skated for warm-ups out on the ice, it looked as if nobody showed up to see us. There were a few people in the second balcony, but that's all. However, when it came time for the opening face-off, suddenly the place was full. Later, we learned the Parisians all made a habit of eating late, and that they all show up at the same time.

That was in 1932. A year later, [Uncle Sam] entered a team in the world championships and traveled across Europe again. I can remember staying at some of those fancy Swiss resorts high up in the Alps—Davos, Arosta. That was really something. One morning, I opened the window in my room, and I swear a cloud came through, floated across the room, and went out the other. Never saw anything like that before in my life.

GERRY COSBY

ABOVE: After his stint as a goalie, Gerry Cosby became a prominent name in the hockey equipment business. *From the Stan Fischler Collection*

We often played on outdoor rinks because that's the way they liked watching ice hockey in Europe—from grandstands, as if it were a soccer game. From my viewpoint, it was difficult to play outdoors because the sun usually was very bright, creating an unbelievable glare off the ice. Someone would take a shot at me from center ice, and I'd lose it in the sun. They scored several goals like that.

I finally ended up wearing a cap—like baseball players use—to shade my eyes from the sun. When you played outdoors

in Europe, you never knew what to expect from one rink to the next. At some places, there were hardly any sideboards; they'd be only five or six inches high, and we'd spend half the time chasing after pucks.

Of course, there were some awfully nice indoor rinks, too. Paris was one, then there was London, Berlin, and Prague. Needless to say, Prague has a warm spot in my heart because we won the world championships there in 1933. I gave up only one goal in five games. I'll never forget it. The left wing came down the ice, faked a shot, and

GERRY COSBY

I made a move too fast. He just slid it along the ice and had me. On a simple little shot like that, I was a dead duck. Anyway, we won the championship and toured Europe for six more weeks.

When I got back to the States, I became a runner on Wall Street. That certainly was the toughest job I ever had; when I got home from doing a day's running down there, I was ready for bed. I couldn't wait for the start of the next hockey season so I could take a "vacation."

Working on Wall Street put me in New York, so the first thing I did when the fall came was to join the New York Athletic Club because it had a hockey team. Then I decided to go a step further.

There were two pro teams in town, the Rangers and the Americans, and I figured they might be able to use a practice goalie.

I called up Lester Patrick, the Rangers' coach, and said, "Mister Patrick, my name is Cosby, Gerry Cosby from Boston. I've been the practice goalie for the Bruins and the Boston Tigers, and I'd like to come out and practice with the Rangers."

He replied, "Fine. Come on down; we need somebody. We're practicing tomorrow morning at 11 a.m."

The next morning, I arrived at the old Garden on Eighth Avenue and 49th Street and walked into the dressing room, where everybody was standing half-dressed. I figured either Patrick had given me the wrong hour or I had forgotten what time to get there, although I didn't think I'd ever forget anything like that. So I went up to Lester and introduced myself.

Well, he saw me standing there—a little guy, a nobody—practically buried in my own equipment, and then he looked around the room and all the major leaguers there. They were the best, the cream of hockey stars—Bill and Bun Cook, Frank Boucher, Murray Murdoch, Butch Keeling, and Ching Johnson. And then he turned back to me and yelled, "Fellows, I want to introduce you to Gerry Cosby. He called me up yesterday, and he wants to try out for our team!"

I couldn't believe my ears. I had no intention of trying out for the Rangers. All I wanted to do was be the practice goalie, as I was in Boston. When I heard Lester say that, I felt like going through the floor. Anyway, he knew what I really meant and let me dress and work out with the club; the next thing I knew, I got the job as practice goalie, where I learned plenty.

But I still had the travel bug from the previous year, and by the time the season was over, I got a letter from Bunny Ahearne, the guy who runs hockey in Europe. He [was] the boss of all the world hockey tournaments and the one who [decided] who [played] who everywhere, except in the pros. At the time, Bunny was nothing more than a little travel agent who had office space in the same building as the British Ice Hockey Association, and since he was close to them, he started booking the passage for teams going to Europe—and that's exactly how he got into hockey. Anyway, Bunny had heard about me and wanted to know whether I'd be interested in going to England the next season to play hockey there.

GERRY COSBY

It seems they had a new rink in Wembley, London, with a seating capacity of 11,000. Wembley was to have two teams, the Canadians and the Lions, and [Ahearne] wanted me to play for the Lions.

I was to be the only American on the team; there were three Englishmen and the rest Canadians. I enjoyed England. It took me a little while to get settled in, but the people there turned out to be very warm and friendly. We also had a pretty good team. One or two boys really could skate, and we wound up winning the last game 2-0 and defeating the previous champions. The English thought that was the greatest thing ever.

The weird thing about England [was] that I managed to go to college there, even though I never finished high school in the United States. One morning, I got a letter from the Minister of Labor, Sir John Simon, informing me that I'd have to leave England because I was taking employment away from a British subject. Well, here I was playing hockey, and right in the middle of the season they wanted to send me home.

I went to Sir Arthur Alvin, the managing director of Wembley Stadium, and showed him the letter. He arranged for an extension, but Sir John wouldn't get off my back. He wanted me out of there, and it looked bad for a while until I figured an out. I enrolled in a business college in London, took a few courses, and then they let me alone because I had become a student.

After that experience, I came home and got my job back as practice goalie for the Rangers. By now it was 1936, and I was notified of my selection as goalie for the United States Olympic team.

I'm probably the only player in the history of hockey to turn down an invitation to play in the Olympics, but that's what I did, and it was one of the biggest mistakes of my life. I had gotten a job in the construction business with Stewart Iglehart, the great polo player, and at that time, business was going well with his firm, and he didn't think I should leave just then to play in the Olympics. He was very persuasive, and I decided to stay home and continue working for him. The Olympic team was going to carry two goalies, myself and a fellow named Tom Moon from Boston. They ended up taking just Moon, who used to be a goal judge in Boston. He went over with them, and they ended up in second place.

While all this was going on, I became more and more interested in the science of hockey and its equipment and was lucky in a couple of ways. I got to be very good friends with Lester Patrick, and whenever I had an idea, I knew I could get a good ear from him. One day, I went up to him and said, "Lester, it's kind of ridiculous to wear elbow pads on the outside of a hockey jersey, isn't it?"

He agreed but wanted to know what I could do about it. "I will tell you what," I suggested, "I could build a jersey that would have elbow pads underneath."

He said, "Do it!" I did, and that's how all the pros started wearing their elbow pads out of sight. But I wasn't even beginning to get into the equipment business yet. After all, I still wanted to play hockey and was gaining so much self-confidence I felt I could do better than just be a practice goalie. By 1939 I figured I was good enough to play for the Rovers, the Rangers' farm team in the Eastern League and a damn good one at that; I mean, guys like the Colville brothers actually went up to the NHL from the Rovers. Tom Lockhart let me be their sub-goalie, and I played a few games for them when their regular, Johnny Fisher, got hurt.

In 1940, the Rovers opened the season with Jack McGill in goal. He was a funny one, always in the nets with a white towel around his neck. But he had a bad knee, and after a while, I was the goalie again. In 1940, that was one of the best Rovers teams they ever had. I remember playing five games in one week and winning all of them. We won the league that year, and I played most of the games. As a goalie, I talked a lot and wouldn't accept anyone out there who wouldn't back-check; if they didn't back check, I let them know right on the ice.

Playing for the Rovers that year changed my whole life, but I didn't realize it at the time. One day, Tommy Lockhart called me into his office to ask a simple question: "Can you get me a gross of hockey sticks?"

If I'd said no, I wouldn't be running the biggest hockey equipment company in the world today. But the answer was yes, and the next thing I knew, I was on the phone with a company in Erie, Pennsylvania, and managed to get Lockhart a gross of sticks at a very good price. It must have been good because he came back to me right away for more; then he wanted some gloves and

pads. That started me in the hockey equipment business in 1940.

By now, I was getting enough orders from Lockhart—also from the Rangers and Americans—to make me think of opening a store. Well, since I had an apartment on York Avenue in Manhattan, I put aside a little room there for equipment and was off and running. Next, I was equipping all the Eastern League teams. I got them sticks, gloves, shin guards, the works. The crazy thing about it was that I didn't have a penny of capital. It was a struggle, but finally, I came up with the money and can gratefully remember when Lockhart once wrote me a check for the merchandise before it even arrived.

Meantime, I was playing hockey for the Rovers and wherever else Lockhart wanted me to go. And, as I said, I was expanding my equipment business. Lockhart was terrific, except for one thing: he liked quality in all kinds of equipment but pucks. I could never understand why he had this thing about buying pucks harder than rocks with edges like razor blades.

He'd pay about seven cents apiece for them, and if a goalie got hit in the face with those edges, it was too bad. I know. Once, in a game against Washington, [the Lions were] taking unbelievable shots on me, and in one rush, my defenseman kept backing up on top of me. Meanwhile, the Washington forward wound up, shot, and the puck deflected off my defenseman's stick and caught me on the side of the face. That sharp edge hit my cheek so hard it actually ripped a hole in my face, and I

GERRY COSBY

can remember coming to and sticking my tongue right out through the hole. They sewed me up in the infirmary, and I went back in and finished the game.

If you think that's crazy, you've got to remember that hockey players are different from other athletes. Take a baseball player: if he gets a hangnail, he's moaning and groaning and probably stays out for three weeks. But hockey players have always been a breed apart, mainly because they're disciplined. Most of them have come from hard-working families, and if they didn't do what they were supposed to, they'd hear about it. To me, they're the greatest people in the world, the most down-to-earth of all athletes.

Well, as I was saying, Lockhart gave me more and more business both on and off the ice. I was handling the two NHL teams, the Eastern league teams, and eventually, the Met League clubs that [once played] out of Madison Square Garden and on the ice. Tom really worked me.

By 1942 the war was on, and lots of players had left for the army. One was Vic Polich, goalie for the Boston Olympics in the Eastern League.

When Vic left the club, Boston was in real trouble because they couldn't come up with a substitute, and that's when I got another distinction. I was the only guy to play on two teams in the same league at the same time, and believe me, it wasn't easy! At that time, we would often play in Washington on, say, Wednesday night and take the train back to New York sometime on Thursday. Then Lockhart would discover that the Olympics

needed me that night—in Washington, of all places. So then Tom would have Frankie Christie, the trainer, meet our train coming in from Washington. "Get back over to track five in five minutes," Christie would say. "You gotta play for Boston tonight." And there I was, returning to Washington again; that happened to me four or five times in one season.

Soon I was playing more hockey than I ever played in my whole life and also doing more business with equipment. The York Avenue apartment wasn't large enough anymore, so I moved to a bigger place opposite Rockefeller Center. Then I got lucky again. At one time, I had arranged an audition for the daughter of Frank O'Shea, a big sporting goods dealer in Chicago. O'Shea remembered that favor, and when he decided to close his business, he called me and sold me 27 cases of equipment. I didn't know it then, but that equipment was a gold mine because after the war broke out, you couldn't buy stuff like that. It kept business going all during the war.

I finally got drafted, and that ended my hockey playing career. I wound up in officers' training school, moved from Miami to Cincinnati, then on to Reno, where my son, Michael, who's running the store now, was born. After the war was over I never gave a thought to playing again, although many of the fellows did. Some were just as good, some had lost it, and some were pathetic cases. Guys who once were great just weren't good anymore.

Frank Brimsek was one. Before the war, they called him "Mr. Zero." He came back to the Bruins but just wasn't the same, and he went on to Chicago, then quit.

But when Brimsek was in his prime, I think he was the best stand-up goalie I've ever seen. When he was hot, he was hot! Any goaltender who can come up with five shutouts in a row has to be fantastic. The thing that I remember most about Brimsek was how well he could handle the puck with his stick; the only goalie I can think of [in later years who was] like that [was] the Rangers' Eddie Giacomin.

Comparing Brimsek with Giacomin is actually contrasting two different eras. Hockey . . . changed completely in the '70s because of expansion and the sport's tremendous growth in the United States. Expansion . . . created such an interest from the squirt to the peewee to the bantam level. I [saw] it up near Sheffield, Massachusetts, where we have a sports shop; I [watched] these peewees shoot a puck and [couldn't] believe my eyes—they [bombed] it just like the pros. Those kids now are playing when they're three and four, wearing pro style skates. They won't settle for any kids' stuff. Our lower levels of hockey in the States have grown so fast that we're ahead of the Canadians on every one short of high school.

Unfortunately, once our kids reach the high school level, they can't get enough competition to develop. They still have to go up to Canada to improve. Inevitably, we'll catch up to the Canadians on all levels. It's all part of the changing scene in hockey. Just one example of the way things evolve is how goal-tenders wear masks today; when I was

playing goal, it was unheard of. I'd certainly wear one now and probably would still have all my teeth and also wouldn't have been scarred from the razor-edge puck. A number of goalies have been badly hurt. Baz Bastien got hit in the eye and lost sight in it while playing for Pittsburgh. With a mask, he'd have come out of it without a nick.

I think all players should wear helmets, too. This stuff about their being heavy, bulky, and hot is a lot of applesauce. They're worn in college games, and nobody seems to mind them.

It's over 30 years since I last put on the pads and played, and hockey has come a long way since then. I honestly think it's a better game today than it ever was. Some old-timers say they don't make the same plays that they used to, but I don't believe it. The game is so much faster, and the players are actually better. I [once] saw a play made by Rod Gilbert, Jean Ratelle, and Vic Hadfield one night that was so fast I was glad I wasn't tending goal. In the old days, Frankie Boucher would take the puck up center ice and would have all the time in the world to make a pass.

Nobody would bother him, and he'd pass through the defenseman's legs, and Bill or Bun Cook would be flying in on the wings, take the pass, and skate in for a shot on goal. To be a goaltender today, you've got to be really super. So many screened shots alone are murder, not to mention the slap shots. A guy has to have great reflexes to be a modern goalie. Personally, I'd like to play now because I always was more alert when the pace was faster.

GERRY COSBY

"IT'S OVER 30 YEARS
SINCE I LAST PUT
ON THE PADS
AND PLAYED, AND
HOCKEY HAS COME
A LONG WAY SINCE
THEN. I HONESTLY
THINK IT'S A BETTER
GAME TODAY THAN
IT EVER WAS."

But I wasn't alert in one respect. I owned some of that Eastern League—in fact, a great deal of it, so much so that I would sell to teams that didn't pay the money they owed for equipment. I have no complaints, though. My store moved to its present location at the new Garden, and it's going very well; so is our manufacturing plant. Not bad for a guy starting out as an office boy who didn't know the first thing about goaltending or equipment or anything about hockey, except that it was played on ice!

FRANK BOUCHER

ARTISTRY IN RHYTHM

I first met Frank Boucher during the 1954-55 season when he hired me to be the Rangers' assistant publicist.

In the spring of 1955, he left Madison Square Garden's employ but frequently returned to New York. On one

such visit in February 1968, Boucher and I spent several hours in the cocktail lounge of the Hotel New Yorker

discussing his years with the Rangers. Frank's eyes twinkled as he told the story of the "stolen" trolley car, and

he laughed that inimitable French-Irish laugh of his as he retold the legendary "Don't wake Lester" anecdote.

Are you kidding? Get a bonus for signing my NHL contract? Not on your life. Back in 1921, that's the way it was—attitudes were different then. We didn't have the agents, attorneys, and what have you that [today's players] have. When the Ottawa Senators asked me to play for them in 1921, I signed a one-year contract for $1,200 and considered myself very lucky and happy to be playing hockey. Nobody cared about images and stuff like that. It's not that way anymore, though; today, hockey players are all business. Why, I've even heard that [one player got] paid for a one-hour speaking engagement what I got paid for a whole season! Imagine that.

And here I won the Lady Byng Trophy seven times and never made more than $8,500 in one season.

Of course, we didn't have a players' association in our day and weren't wrapped up in all those other trappings. Frankly, I don't know whether it was dedication to the sport or if we were just damn fools. But there's one thing I'm sure of: I know we had a heck of a lot more fun than they do today. That's where we had it over them, in the laughs.

I'll never forget that first Rangers training camp. It was the fall of 1926, and Conn Smythe, our [first] manager, had booked us into the Peacock Hotel, which was right on the outskirts of Toronto. Smythe was later replaced by Lester Patrick, but at that time, he was organizing the club, and he was a real stickler for discipline. One of the first things he did was to set an early curfew. That was fine, except that I had been out having a good time with Ching Johnson, and by the time we got back to the hotel that night, the place was completely locked.

No matter how hard we tried, we couldn't get into the place, so we decided to do the next best thing and head for a hotel downtown. Since there were no cabs around, we walked a few blocks to an intersection and discovered a trolley car about to start its first run of the morning. It was about 6 a.m. when we got on the trolley, and the motorman was an awfully friendly chap. We offered him a bit of the applejack we had been drinking, and he proved to be a very congenial host.

After about 10 minutes, he said he had to start the trolley on its run and asked, "Where are you gentlemen going?" I told him we'd like to head for the King Edward Hotel, but at the time, I didn't realize it wasn't exactly on the same route as the trolley normally would go. The motorman said he'd oblige, and before you could say, "Jack Robinson," he turned off all the lights except those up front and started downtown.

We had gone about three blocks when we came to the first trolley station where a half-dozen or so people were waiting to get on, but our man didn't slow down one bit; he just plowed straight ahead as if the only thing that mattered was getting us to the King Edward Hotel. We passed enough passengers in a mile or so that somebody surely must have phoned the Toronto Transit Commission to complain, but as I said, our motorman didn't seem to care—at least, not until we reached a corner where there was a switch. At that point, he must've realized the tracks weren't going to take us to the King Edward even though his route was supposed to go directly ahead.

Suddenly, he gets one of those big steel rods, runs onto the tracks, and pulls the switch, and off we go [off his regular route] toward the hotel. By this time, the three of us made quite a barber shop trio and were singing every good song in the book until we looked up and saw the King Edward ahead. Our friend stopped the trolley directly in front of the hotel, shook our hands, and then took off into the early morning. That was some start for me as a Ranger!

I was associated with the Rangers for 28 years as a player, coach, and manager, and I

FRANK BOUCHER

can say without hesitation that the 1927-28 New York team and the 1939-40 team were . . . among the finest ever seen in the NHL. Naturally, I'm a little partial to the 1927-28 team because I played on it and was in my prime then. What made it so great was its two very strong lines—in those days, we didn't have a three-or four-line system as they do today—plus a defense that no club could equal and good goalkeeping. You knew we were good because we won the Cup in strange circumstances.

We couldn't play any of the final [play-off] games in New York then because Madison Square Garden had other commitments, so all our "home" games had to be played on the road, making it tremendously difficult. We eliminated Pittsburgh and Boston in the opening rounds, then went up against the Montreal Maroons and had to play all the games at the Montreal Forum.

That was the series where our regular goalie, Lorne Chabot, got hurt, and [our manager-coach], old Lester Patrick, went into the nets. From my own standpoint, that was unforgettable because I scored the winning goal at 7:05 of sudden death. Unfortunately, the Maroons were up 2-1 in wins, but I scored the only goal in the fourth game, and we took it 1-0. So it all boiled down to the fifth game since it was a best-of-five series.

After Lester went in as goalie and won, we got Joe Miller to [play goal] for us. He'd been nicknamed "Red Light" Miller because he'd played for the Americans, and they were losers at that time. I personally never thought he was bad, and as things turned out, he was terrific in that last game. Right off the bat, we were behind the eight ball. We got a penalty, and I was sent out to try to kill the clock until our man returned. For quite a few seconds, we did pretty well, and then somebody got the puck to me, and I found myself at center ice, skating in on Red Dutton, a Maroons defenseman. I knew Red's weakness—if you pushed the puck through his legs, he'd give his attention to it instead of watching you. I tried the trick, and sure enough, he looked down. By the time he looked up, I was around him and had picked the puck, skated in on their goalie, Clint Benedict, and flipped it into the right-hand corner.

Not very long after that, we got hit with another penalty. Lester sent me out again. My only concern was to stickhandle the puck as much as possible at center ice; however, I suddenly found myself in a position where my only play was to shoot the puck off the boards and hope to pick up the rebound and keep possession. I miscalculated and shot the puck too far ahead—so far that Dune Munro, the Maroons' defenseman, thought he could intercept it.

The puck was now about midway between Munro and me. As I watched him, I realized he was going to try to beat me to it. He came on for quite a run, and I could almost hear him thinking, "By God, I can't get there in time." He seemed to stop in one motion, then change his mind and go for the puck again. All the while, I was skating madly toward it and, by this time, had reached it. I just swooped over to one side

FRANK BOUCHER

ABOVE: Arguably the greatest line in Rangers history—if not the entire National Hockey League—(from left to right) Bill Cook, Frank Boucher, and Bun Cook paced the Rangers to a pair of Stanley Cups in 1928 and 1933. *From the Stan Fischler Collection*

and let Munro go by; I had the whole ice to myself straight to the goaltender.

I moved directly in on Benedict and landed the goal in almost the exact place as I did earlier. We won the game 2-1 and the Cup. It certainly was a tribute to Lester. If he hadn't gone into the nets when Chabot was hurt, I don't know what we would have done. But that was Lester—a very, very interesting man and a tough taskmaster as well.

One memory of him really stands out in this regard. We had played in Ottawa one night and won the game with some fantastic score like 10-1 and went to a party afterward in Hull, Quebec, the town across the river. I guess we stayed long past our curfew but finally decided it was time to get back to our Pullman, sitting in the Ottawa station. We all knew that Lester must have been asleep, so we tiptoed onto the train and kept passing the word along in whispers, "Don't wake Lester!"

It seemed to us that we managed to sneak in without disturbing him—or so I thought until the next morning, when I walked into the diner for breakfast. Lester, who was sitting there alone, looked up and said, "Good morning, Mr. Boucher." As soon as he called me by my last name, I knew something was wrong. I sat down next to him, and nothing was said for about a minute until Lester offhandedly mentioned to me, "Did you know that Butch Keeling walks in his sleep?"

I said, "No, Lester, I didn't," to which Lester replied, "Y' know, Frank, that's very interesting because at about four in the morning, Butch walked into my compartment, peed on the floor, and whispered something about, 'Don't wake Lester!'"

FRANK BOUCHER

There wasn't much I could say after that, but if you think I was tongue-tied then let me tell you about another situation that really put me on the hot seat for quite some time. That occurred in the 1930-31 season. Cecil Dillon joined the Rangers as a rookie, and it didn't take long for me to discover [that] I was his idol, but not just as a hockey player.

Cecil had been crazy about the Royal Canadian Mounted Police ever since he was a kid, and when he found out that I had once been a Mountie, there was nothing I could do to discourage him. It became embarrassing because I was only a Mountie for a short time, as all the other Rangers knew, and had never served in any of the wild Northwest outposts. Dillon nevertheless began to press me to tell about my experiences. At first, I thought I'd just let him know that nothing really much had happened to me, but I could tell that he was really keen to hear something, so I began with a few honest-to-goodness yarns of incidents that actually did occur. They were my best true stories, and I hoped they'd be sufficient.

I didn't know whether to be happy or sad about it, but Dillon thought my stories were just the greatest things in the world and began begging me to tell some more. Unfortunately, I ran out of true stories and had to make a decision: either let on to Dillon that absolutely nothing else happened that was interesting or start fabricating stories. My mistake was in deciding to do everything possible to make the rookie happy. The next time we sat down, I told him a whole pile of fictitious tales.

You name it, I did it. Boucher battled the Indians; Boucher commanded a dog team in the Arctic; Boucher was all over the Northwest. When my imagination ran dry, I went to the nearest newsstand to pick up a few Western magazines to restore my supply. After a while, I even began to hope that Lester might trade Cecil just to get him off my back. That didn't happen, though; Dillon was an awfully good hockey player and just as nice a guy to boot. His problem was that he kept wanting more Mountie stories, and I had to keep telling them.

Once and only once was I nearly exposed. The Rangers were in Atlantic City for [an exhibition game], and several of us took a stroll on the boardwalk. When we passed a shooting gallery, Dillon asked me to join him in a few rounds, figuring that as a former Mountie, my shooting would be super. Actually, I couldn't shoot the side of a barn.

Cecil started shooting first, and he was deadly accurate. He had done quite a bit of hunting back home in Ontario, so this was second nature to him. When he got through, he handed me the gun, and I couldn't touch a thing—not one bloody target! It reached such a point that I could tell Cecil was wearing a long face because he was horrified at my performance.

I was about to let on to him that I had been telling a pack of fibs when I suddenly thought of something. I took Cecil aside and mentioned that while he was firing at the targets, I had spoken to the fellow running the gallery and had told him to put blanks in my rifle. Cecil fell for it, and as long as he played for the Rangers, he remained convinced of all those Mountie tales.

Maybe that helped me later when I became the Rangers' manager because we needed all the imagination we could get during those bad years. But they didn't come till later; we had some marvelous teams in the '30s. After I retired and was made coach, we had a wonderful bunch of boys in the 1939-40 season. Yes, that was one of the greatest teams in history.

Tops in every position, it started with Davey Kerr in goal, Art Coulter and Murray Patrick as one defense team, and Babe Pratt and Ott Heller on the other. The three forward lines were just fantastic: Phil Watson-Bryan Hextall-Lynn Patrick, Neil and Mac Colville-Alex Shibicky, and Clint Smith-Kilby MacDonald-Alf Pike, with Dutch Hiller as the spare. They were perfect players for a coach because you could encourage suggestions, and they'd always come up with something good that we'd practice and eventually use in a game.

One result was the box defense, where the four players killing a penalty arrange themselves in a box formation in front of the goalkeeper. We had another strategy called offensive penalty killing, which turned out to be the beginning of modern forechecking. In this one, we tried for goals when we were a man short instead of going into a defensive shell. We'd send out three forwards and one defenseman, and we'd forecheck in their own end. Our team was so good, it scored more goals over a season than it had goals scored upon it during penalty killing. Once, though, it backfired on us.

We had perfected this system—or so we thought—and went into Chicago with a 19-game unbeaten streak. In that 20th game, we played rings around the Blackhawks and should have won by a big margin but for some strange reason couldn't score a goal. We were down 1-0 going into the third period.

During intermission, we were battling around ideas in the dressing room when the guys came up with another new one. It was decided that if we were still down by a goal in the final minute of play, we'd pull the goalkeeper and send out an extra skater. Up until that point, the way the system worked, you never put the extra man on the ice until there was a whistle for a face-off. But we thought it'd be better not to make it obvious that we were pulling the goalie—in other words, do it on the fly while the play was still going on. That was the plan.

I made one big mistake; I forgot to tell Lester our plan, and on this particular night, he was sitting on our bench, which he very rarely did in those days. Toward the end of the game, though, he walked over to the Chicago Stadium timekeeper because he didn't trust him and wanted to keep an eye on the clock.

We still were down a goal and had the puck in the opposition's end of the rink. This was the time to try the new plan, and the signal was given for Davey Kerr to come off the ice and for the extra forward to go on. That's exactly what happened, and nobody in the rink knew what was going on except my players and then Lester. But he didn't realize Kerr was removed from the

F R A N K   B O U C H E R

goal. So Lester thought I had made a mistake and put too many men on the ice and started screaming for me to take the extra man off before we got a penalty.

Paul Thompson, the Blackhawks coach, heard him, and when he saw six men in his zone, he started screaming, too. Meanwhile, we had moved the puck into scoring position, and the plan was working perfectly. We were about to put it in the net when the referee blew his whistle to give us a penalty. Then he turned around, saw that Kerr was out, and realized there shouldn't be a penalty at all. But it was too late. The attack was stopped, and we lost the game 1-0.

As things turned out, we won the next five games in a row for an overall record of 24 wins or ties in 25 games and went on to win the Stanley Cup. [World War II had already started], and we lost most of our really good players; when it was over, a lot of them came back, but they had lost a step or two and weren't really the same. That's when we had to start rebuilding, which took quite some time. And naturally, when times were bad, we used to resort to all kinds of tricks to get people into the Garden.

There was one period during the war years when things hit an all-time low. We had lost such fellows as Jim Henry, Murray Patrick, Art Coulter, and Alex Shibicky to the armed forces, and by the time October 1942 came around, more than half of our roster that had finished first the previous spring was gone. It was time for training camp to start, and believe it or not, we didn't have a goalkeeper on hand—not one! Lester was just as worried as I was, and

I told him the only thing we could do was to check out every town in Canada to see if we could find one. We sent telegrams to all our scouts, telling them to wire us if they came across a goalie, and three days later, we got word from our man in Saskatchewan, Al Ritchie. He said he had a chap named Steve Buzinski who'd play goal for us, and so I told Richie to get him to our camp immediately.

Camp was in Winnipeg, as it had been for years, and when we got there and started workouts, I discovered that nobody named Buzinski had arrived. Well, there was nothing much we could do but sit around and hope he'd show up; meanwhile, we sent the boys through the practice skates and light workouts. After a day or so, I really began to get worried, but on this particular afternoon, we were on the ice when I looked over toward the sideboards and got the surprise of my life.

In the Winnipeg Amphitheater, the sideboards were quite a bit higher than in other rinks, and as I looked at them, I saw this tiny fellow walking along, wearing a black helmet over the sideboards. I first thought that it was a "rink rat," one of those lads who'd hang around the rink and clean the ice between workouts. But soon I saw one goalie pad then another climb over the boards, and sure enough, this little chap skated directly to the net. I remember saying to myself when I looked at him, "Oh, my gosh, it can't be him!"

This was Steve Buzinski; he not only was small but was bowlegged, and when he stood in front of the net, you saw nothing

FRANK BOUCHER

but holes. We didn't have much choice since there were no other goalkeepers around, so Steve was our man when the 1942-43 season started. I can't say he was the greatest, but he did try, and he had a strange sense of humor.

One night, we were playing in Detroit, and the Red Wings were scoring on him left and right. Sometime late in the game, one of the Detroit players took a long shot, and Buzinski nabbed it in his glove and casually tossed it aside as though he were a Vezina Trophy winner. Just as he did, one of our boys skated by and heard Steve say, "'Y' know, this is as easy as picking cherries off a tree!"

I can't honestly say our losing was entirely Steve's fault, but when we found out there was another goalie available with more experience—Jimmy Franks—we got him. But we kept Buzinski on the payroll because he was good for his humor, and in those days, we needed all the humor we could get.

Lester finally got rid of him after he refused to attend a practice with our farm team, the Rovers. I believe he told Lester he had some letters to write home, and that's all Lester needed. Buzinski was on the next train to Saskatchewan.

The fun didn't end with Steve. We had some lulus after the war, too. Remember Dr. Tracy, the hypnotist we brought in to help the team win? That was when we were running into tough luck again in the early '50s. Tracy was a big bloke who thought he could give the Rangers a winning complex. The night of a Bruins game, he talked to Buddy

O'Connor and a few of the other players, and then they went out and lost the game in the final minute.

We didn't see much of Dr. Tracy after that, but it wasn't the end of the gimmicks. Gene Leone, the owner of Mama Leone's Restaurant, tried to help us once with what he called "a magic elixir." He concocted some combination of clam juice or broth and a few other items, put it into a big black bottle, and offered it to the boys in the hopes it would get us going.

It worked a lot better than Dr. Tracy had, and we actually started winning after Gene created it. Pretty soon the black bottle became a big thing around town, and Jim Burchard, who was covering hockey for the *World Telegram*, decided we should also take it on our road trips. We had a Saturday night game in Toronto, and Jim took a plane there, bottle in hand.

Damned if we didn't beat the Maple Leafs 4-2. Now everybody's talking about Leone's black bottle and wondering what's in it. I don't think Gene expected it to become so popular, and since he was a busy man, he wasn't able to brew it every time. Once, we didn't have the magic elixir and lost to the Red Wings. Burchard claimed that without the bottle, we were at a psychological disadvantage.

After a while, bottle or not, we got into the old rut and eventually finished in fifth place out of the playoffs. That was the end of the era of the magic elixir. Of course, my hope was to fill the Garden because we had a good hockey team, not a gimmick. At the same time, I was always trying to think

FRANK BOUCHER

of ways to improve the game. One of my ideas was the use of two goaltenders on a team instead of one. I was a good 20 years before my time since it's standard practice today, but in the late '40s, it was somewhat revolutionary.

At that time, I had two good goalkeepers, "Sugar" Jim Henry and Charlie Rayner. Not only were they teammates, but they were also good friends off-ice, and it was always a tough decision whenever I'd have to consider which one to play. I decided to alternate them during the game. So I started to change goaltenders every five minutes, and it worked. Except I ran into an odd thing once again in Toronto when there was only one pair of gloves for them both to use. Every time they passed each other during a change, they'd transfer gloves, which looked kind of funny at the time.

They both lasted with us for a while until we got rid of Henry, though we kept Rayner. Charlie was a good goaltender who helped take us to the Stanley Cup finals in 1950. But then things got rough again.

By 1953-54, we had a horrible hockey team, and I had to figure out how to keep the fans from dropping off; that's when I signed Max Bentley and later talked his older brother, Doug, into coming to New York, even though they both were past their prime.

I got Max at the start of the season, and he still was good, but a funny sort of character. He was a hypochondriac, always carrying boxes of pills around for all his imaginary illnesses. I had a hell of a time just keeping him playing because of some trivial thing that happened to be bothering

him at the time. I felt if I could get Doug to play for us as well, he'd get Max to do things he wouldn't ordinarily do.

Without Doug, I had to pamper Max. We even brought his cousin, Bev, into New York as our spare goalkeeper, just to try to keep Max happy. The Bentleys believed in traveling together, like a tribe. If you invited them over, it was nothing for 12 to 14 Bentleys—the whole shebang—to come along. So I kept after Doug, trying to get him away from Saskatoon, where he was player-coach. Phone calls didn't work, so I finally decided to fly up to Canada and talk directly to him. It took a while—and a lot of money—but I managed to persuade him to take a fling at it with the Rangers.

It was worth every penny of it just to see Doug and Max back together again after all those years with Edgar Laprade on the line with them. I remember Coley Hall of the Vancouver team coming all the way from British Columbia just to see the Bentleys together once more. They scored a whole bunch of goals between them, and we beat the Bruins; after it was over, Hall said, "That was the greatest thing I ever saw."

Personally, I didn't think they'd be sensations right off the bat. But they were fantastic, passing and shooting and skating just like in the old days. Doug was the one who put the desire in Max when Max would lose confidence in himself.

After they teamed up together, we gave the Bruins a good run for fourth place, but Lynn Patrick was coaching Boston at the time and knew what to do to stop them. Realizing that he couldn't make Doug back down, he had his players [check] Max. "As soon as Max goes for the puck," he told them, "you go get him!" They managed to slow Max down, but Doug still played beautifully right down to the end. I wish I could say we made the playoffs, but it didn't happen that way; we finished fifth.

Just watching those Bentleys convinced me of one thing: the biggest mistake ever made in hockey was breaking up that team, Max and Doug, when they played for Chicago. They were a funny pair of brothers.

While all this was going on, I was trying to build up the farm system, especially the Juniors in Guelph, Ontario. A year after the Bentleys, we began to show real progress. Andy Bathgate, Dean Prentice, Harry Howell, and Lou Fontinato all came out of the Guelph Juniors but were still a little green. We missed the playoffs again in 1954-55, my last season as manager of the Rangers. After that, the Guelph kids really developed, and the Rangers had a good run of playoff teams. It sort of did my heart good to see how well they turned out.

MYLES J. LANE

FROM THE ICE RINK TO THE COURTHOUSE

Tall and handsome, Myles Lane still had the carriage of an athlete at age 64 when I interviewed him in December 1969. A former All-America football player as well as hockey star, Lane admitted that he had little time for athletics except long walks.

Lots of places across the United States could qualify as "the hockey capital of the nation," but my choice is Melrose, Massachusetts, my hometown. Even before I grew up, hockey was the number-one sport there, and some really fine players learned the game in our neighborhood.

Many people in the States know the name Hobey Baker since he's one of the few Americans in the Hockey Hall of Fame, but we had a fellow, Melrose "Bags" Wanamaker, who in those days was the next

thing to Baker. He wasn't the only top-notch skater around. Hago Harrington, later a big man in Boston hockey, was also from our area and, like me, played on the big pond in the middle of town whenever it was frozen.

I was about six years old when I got my first pair of skates, and it was something awful trying to learn on them. I attempted to play with the big boys but could hardly stand up on the blades. I was so small, my hockey stick would be taller than I was and ended up around the face of my bigger friends. In other words, I was high sticking at the age of six.

We had hockey little leagues in grammar school then, just as they have in Canada and in parts of the United States now. And don't forget, this was back in the early '20s.

It took a bit of time, but I soon started to improve my skating and, when I reached my teens, was good enough to play defense for our high school team. That was really something. Ours was the best hockey team in the state; we won something like 23 games and lost only one during a single season, and that was because we were physically exhausted.

I'll tell you how good we were. We once scrimmaged with Harvard, the intercollegiate champions, and although they beat us 2-1 in a 60-minute game, it was quite a feather in the cap of Melrose High. That same year, we defeated Boston College.

Even though I was playing defense for the high school team, I liked rushing and did quite a lot of puck carrying; I continued to rush right through my college playing career since nobody said, "Don't do it." Meanwhile, I played against some really first-rate competition. When I was still in high school, I can remember being permitted to play for a team that took on a bunch, passing themselves off as amateurs but who later became the Pittsburgh Yellow Jackets. They were really pros, but nobody said anything about it.

All of this gave me terrific experience. Here I was, only 16 years old, going up against fellows who were professionals. It provided quite a head start for my college tryout, and in retrospect, it made playing college hockey as easy as rolling off a log.

When it came time for me to select a college, I went up to Hanover, New Hampshire, to look over Dartmouth. I had already received three or four football scholarship offers elsewhere but liked the looks of Dartmouth and decided to go there, although they didn't give any hockey scholarships.

College hockey was very big in those days. We played Harvard, Yale, Princeton, Toronto, Boston University, and M.I.T. Whenever we played in Boston against Harvard or Yale, the Garden would be packed, and usually the proceeds for those games went to a charity.

At the time, my heart was set on graduating from Dartmouth and then going to law school. I didn't think I wanted to be a professional athlete for the simple reason that a top-notch hockey player couldn't stay in the NHL for more than eight or 10 years, but one could have a lifetime career by going into law, finance, or some other business.

I also figured only the really big stars made the big money. I knew I was taking something of a gamble, but my target was law school, not the NHL. Then in my senior year, our team went up against the University of Toronto, managed by Conn Smythe, who soon left the university to become the boss of the [Rangers very briefly and then the] Toronto Maple Leafs. Apparently, he liked the way I played because he contacted me to say he'd like me to join the Toronto Maple Leafs.

Naturally, I was flattered but told Smythe I wanted to go to law school, and if I was going to pursue hockey, I would do it with a team in the United States. That way, I could continue my law studies and still play hockey.

MYLES J. LANE

In those days, if a representative of an NHL team talked with you, it meant your name was automatically put on that team's list and no other team could negotiate with you.

So I wound up with my name on the Toronto Maple Leafs' negotiation list. I've since heard that Boston had wanted to sign me, too, because I was a local boy—Melrose is only about seven miles outside Boston—but they couldn't deal with me on account of Smythe. After a while, I convinced Smythe that I didn't want to go to Toronto, so the Leafs swapped my name with the New York Rangers, and Toronto took a player from the New York list.

The Rangers didn't own me; I was still in college and hadn't signed with them. In fact, I didn't talk to anybody connected with the Rangers until after I had made a trip south that spring with the Dartmouth baseball team. We had gone down to Atlanta and were heading home when I got a wire from Colonel Hammond, the Rangers' president. He said he wanted to see me in New York, which was okay with me since we were stopping off at Philadelphia for a game against the University of Pennsylvania.

After the game, I came up to New York and sat down with him. The first thing he said was that he wanted me to sign, but I replied, "Nothing doing." At the time, I just wasn't sure that I wanted to go into hockey. There were other things on my mind—other offers.

One was an opportunity to teach at the Taft School in Connecticut, and I couldn't decide whether I wanted to play one year of hockey or teach one year at Taft, then go to law school. I spoke to Mr. Taft, and he said something to me I've never forgotten: "Mr. Lane, the job is yours if you want it. But don't fool me!"

I asked, "What do you mean?"

He answered, "Don't come here for one year and then leave me. It's a good position if you want to teach the rest of your life, but don't fool with me. Let me know if you intend to stay with me or just want to make it a one-year proposition."

"Mr. Taft," I told him, "I can't fool you, and I can't give you an answer. I have in the back of my head a desire to go into the law business, so I'm not certain whether I'd stay one year or more than one."

Right then and there with that exchange, I decided to accept the Rangers' hockey proposition. In September, I contacted Colonel Hammond and signed with New York, got a bonus, and made a lot more money than any of my college classmates did. When I joined the Rangers, they had four defensemen led by Ching Johnson and Taffy Abel. The third man was Leo Bourgault, a little fellow about 5-foot-8 and 140 pounds. Leo was a rushing defenseman but too small to do much checking. I was the fourth man. Strangely enough, coach Lester Patrick started me with Ching.

I'll never forget my first game at Madison Square Garden. I was thrown off the ice three times with penalties, and Ching finally came over to me and said, "If you don't cut this out, you're going to be the bad man of hockey instead of me."

But my penalties were the result of inexperience more than anything else; after all, I was just a rookie. Then after the game, a funny thing happened.

MYLES J. LANE

A fellow by the name of Eddie O'Neill was covering hockey for the Associated Press at the time, and he came into our dressing room and started interviewing me. His first question was, "How did you feel out there tonight in your first game as a professional?"

I replied, "Well, it wasn't really too bad out there."

Eddie said, "No, give me an angle. Look, I'm like you. I'm a college man. Was there anything different out there from the kind of hockey you experienced at Dartmouth?"

"Look, Eddie," I told him, "that's a silly question because you know as well as I do that there's no comparison between college and professional hockey. It's an entirely different game, like the difference between minor-league baseball and major-league ball."

O'Neill went on. "Let me ask you a couple of questions," he said. "Did you ever play a college game in which you were a lot more tired than you are tonight?"

I said, "Of course I did," and he asked, "Why?"

"When I played college hockey," I replied, "I played as much as 60 minutes without relief. If you're in a daisy chain for 60 minutes, you'll still get tired of walking around. But out there tonight, I'd get relief every three or four minutes, so I wasn't so tired afterwards."

"Wasn't it rough?" O'Neill asked.

"Sure," I said, "it's rougher than the college game, but I wasn't tired because of the relief I got."

When O'Neill was finished, I got dressed, returned to my hotel, and went to bed. The next morning, I went downstairs for breakfast and ran into the desk clerk, a

friend of mine. He asked if I had seen the *Times* that morning, and when I replied, "No," he said, "Here, take a look."

So I picked up the paper and saw a headline across the sports page that read, "LANE SAYS PROFESSIONAL HOCKEY A CINCH COMPARED TO THE COLLEGE BRAND."

That was really something. Worse still, I had to report to the Garden later that day since it was customary to check in with the club on a daily basis. When I walked into the dressing room, there were all those Canadian players—and me just an American collegian—and you could have cut the silence with a knife.

I simply told them the headline was a complete fabrication; I had never made such a claim. And that was that as far as the players themselves were concerned.

Not long after, we took a trip to Montreal to play the Maroons. This was the English team that represented Montreal in the NHL, and they were big, husky, and tough. When we arrived in town, I picked up a paper and read an article exhorting the populace to come down to the game and watch this upstart American collegian get his come-uppance. The paper went on to say how I had told a reporter what a simple game this Canadian hockey was and so forth.

As expected, the people came streaming into the Forum that night looking for blood, and I knew it. On the very first rush I made down the ice, two Maroons came at me and tried to put me right over the side-boards. One of them went off with a penalty.

I rushed down the ice three times, and on those three rushes, three Montreal players went into the cooler. The game got rougher and rougher as it went along. Later on, Ching Johnson skated down the ice and was whacked hard by one of the Maroons. He lost his balance and slid into the backboards. Though he threw both his feet up to break the slide, unfortunately, his skate got caught in the boards, and his ankle twisted around and broke. He was through for the season.

After that happened, Taffy Abel made a rush down the ice, and someone stepped on his foot. He needed 13 stitches to close the wound. That left Leo Bourgault and myself on defense. We got beat 2-1. Then it was on to Pittsburgh and a 0-0 tie, followed by a tie with Detroit. That was my introduction to pro hockey, and the reception was all due to some misinformation.

Naturally, I could handle myself out on the ice. I was about 6-foot-l and 195 pounds, and I remembered what Ching had told me at the start: "The first lesson in the game is to protect yourself. Make sure when you bump somebody that your stick is right up in front of you so they don't give you the stick in the face. When you hit them, hit them hard; hit them clean if you can, but always protect yourself because in this game, there are no medals for bravery."

So whenever I bumped somebody, I remembered Ching's advice and never got into much trouble. I got put off the ice quite a bit but never had to drop my gloves and punch. And after that first incident, I was really never needled about being a collegian. On the whole, the guys were very fair.

When I was with the Rangers, my boss was Lester Patrick, a fine man who treated me fairly. There was no question about it. After a while, he suggested I be sent down to Springfield for some polishing up in the minors, and he was right. If I'd been going to make a career of hockey, I would have said yes and gone to Springfield, but I wasn't in it for life; I was in it to get enough money for law school. Of course, the Rangers didn't know that until Lester suggested I go to Springfield. He wanted me there for a month or two, and I said I'd go, but only on one condition—that I get my full share of money if the club won the Stanley Cup.

He said he couldn't agree to that and maintained I would have to go down to Springfield. It was February, and the season was almost over. "Oh no," I told Lester, "I don't have to go because if you insist that I do, then I'll just quit hockey."

The next thing I knew, I was traded to the Boston Bruins, right there in **my** first year of NHL hockey. That was fine with me because Boston had a strong team; I came from the Boston area and liked players on the club.

Tiny Thompson was the goaltender. Eddie Shore and Lionel Hitchman were the first-string defensemen with George Owen and myself as second-stringers. Up front we had Harry Oliver, Perk Galbraith, Cooney Weiland, and Dutch Gainor.

Dutch was the only man I ever saw in hockey who had a double shift. He'd come at a man, fake it one way, fake it the other, and then walk right through.

Shore was the best of all. He was a lot like [great Boston Red Sox slugger] Ted Williams in that he could help a teammate if you wanted help. Eddie was very fair about

MYLES J. LANE

things; if you asked him how to play this or that man, he'd tell you. He didn't withhold advice. Personally, I liked Shore. He was the greatest hockey player I ever saw. He could skate like . . . Bobby Orr [did], and he could shoot. And he was a great defenseman who could hit. He was a dynamic person who could really lift a team.

One night, we took off for a game in Montreal; it was a wintry night, snowing and all that. What happens? Shore misses the train. The rest of the club was rolling up to Montreal snug on the train while Shore got hold of a Cadillac from a friend of his and drove all night through the mountains in blizzards and then into the next day and arrived in Montreal about an hour before the game. He got into a uniform and beat the Canadiens 2-1. Shore scored both goals.

I know some people have said Shore was a vicious player, but I don't believe they saw him play too much. Let's say he was a tough, rough player who could give it out as well as take it without complaining.

Having players like Shore and Hitchman on defense meant that I didn't play all that much since they kept the stars out there most of the time, and rightly so; after all, it was a money game.

Needless to say, my own personal schedule was different from the other players' since I was going to law school. On Monday, the team would practice that day. I'd study all day long and at six in the evening, I'd have my dinner; then at 7:30 I'd go down to the Garden only a few blocks away, dress, and play the game.

On Wednesday, there'd be a 12:00 to 1:00 practice or maybe 1:00 to 2:00 and the same on Thursday. Occasionally, we'd play in New York on Thursdays. The team would leave in the morning while I was at school, and I'd take the noon or one o'clock train. I'd study all the way down to New York, get off and go to Madison Square Garden, play the game, and come back with the team on the midnight train and get into Boston in the early morning, then go to the classes.

We always had games on weekends, so I'd actually catch the nine o'clock train on Fridays for Montreal, Ottawa, or Toronto, depending on where we happened to be playing that Saturday night. Wherever we were, I'd stay in the hotel all day with the books, then go to the game at night and take the nine o'clock train back to Boston on Sunday morning.

Every so often, there was a conflict between my hockey schedule and law school. Once we had a game in Detroit when I was supposed to be taking my midyear exams. The solution was supplied by the law school, which let me take my exams at the University of Detroit. They sent the exam out ahead, and when the team departed for the next game in Chicago, I was left behind in Detroit. I took the exam on a Friday, and Detroit University sent the papers back to Boston while I got the train to Chicago. They were very cooperative that way.

From time to time, people would ask me whether it was difficult concentrating on the books. Actually, playing was an incentive, and I was doing quite well in the NHL. We knocked off the Canadiens in the first round of the Stanley Cup playoffs, then

MYLES J. LANE

took the Rangers in four straight to win the Cup. I wound up getting that full share of the playoff cut I had demanded of Lester Patrick. But then I had an unfortunate accident that affected my hockey career.

During the summer after my rookie season in the NHL, I was playing baseball in Cape Cod. One day, a bunch of us were in a car driving to a game when the car was forced off the road. I came out of the accident with a broken bone in my knee and three fractured vertebrae in my spine. That kept me out of hockey for a whole year, and I could never again skate as fast as I did before the accident.

To compensate for the loss of speed, I began concentrating more on the defensive play than on rushing with the puck. During my year out of action, a few good things happened to me. I was still going to law school and doing well there and at the same time was coaching football at Harvard.

Meanwhile, I had a good chance to study the Bruins as a team and to think about hockey in general. Art Ross was running the Boston club at the time, and he was a really tough one, although I had no complaints with him. He was a strict taskmaster but a good hockey man. In those days, the club was known as "The Bruising Bruins," and I think the reputation they had as a rough, tough hockey team stemmed from Ross. They hit and hit hard; that's just the way he wanted it.

I realize that I had also learned some of that in New York. In fact, I think Lester Patrick always figured I could stay back to play a little more defense and do a little less rushing. Maybe I did rush too much, and perhaps that's why Lester wanted to send me to Springfield. Looking back, I'd say he was right, but when a guy comes out of college as I did—a star—he thinks he knows a great deal even though he really doesn't know that much. You don't know real hockey until you get into the pro ranks.

I played against a lot of good men, but I think the finest line of all was the one the Rangers had with Frank Boucher centering Bill and Bun Cook. I haven't seen their equal yet. They played together so much and knew each other's moves so perfectly that watching them move the puck around was like observing how a clock works.

Today, the players skate much faster and push the puck a lot, but there isn't the clever stick work we had in my time. Now it's a game of shove and push, hoping to score with blind shots, I think possibly half the goals scored today are because the goalie is screened and doesn't see the puck.

Nels Stewart was another great. He was slow but deadly with the stick and tremendous around the net. Aurel Joliat of the Canadiens was another terrific stickhandler. He must have weighed about 118 pounds soaking wet, but he was a wizard at handling the puck. He had a funny habit of always wearing a black baseball cap when he played, and word around the league was that if you knocked Joliat's black cap off his head, he'd get so mad it'd hurt his play. Well, naturally, the Bruins would try to knock that cap off, and it certainly did upset him. Joliat played on a line with Howie Morenz and Johnny Gagnon, and they were quite a bunch.

Howie Morenz was the fastest thing I ever saw on ice. He'd be in full speed after

MYLES J. LANE

taking only two strides. Offhand, I'd say he was one of the greatest hockey players of all time. Being on the shelf that one year, I really had a good chance to see them all. I'm sure Ross knew I'd eventually quit hockey to go into law, but that didn't matter to him, and he did get some work out of me the year I was out with the injury.

Those were the days when the Bruins had a farm club call the Boston Cubs. They were a good minor-league team in need of a manager, so Ross put me in charge; it turned out to be a very rewarding experience. When I took over, they were in last place, and by season's end, we were on top.

The Cubs consisted of a bunch of young fellows going up to the NHL and a group of veterans who had come down. There was a fellow on the team named Joe Geroux who was a little firecracker, and nobody could handle him, not even Ross. Here I was, the collegian with a broken back, running this club, trying to control Geroux, and attempting to bring them up from last place.

For some reason, I was determined to work with Geroux and help him, even though everybody else had dropped him because he was so wild. I knew he was a great hockey player; all he needed was a little balance. Well, I hadn't been with the Cubs too long when Joe came to me with a problem.

He said, "You know those penalties I get for sometimes losing my head? Well, I don't mind them so much, but the $25 fine is cutting into my income. How can I stay on the ice without getting fined?"

I began thinking to myself, "How am I going to keep him in the game?" I started playing for time and finally inquired, "Joe, why are you asking me that question?"

He replied, "Myles, you're going to law school. You know all the answers!"

I said I wished I did but knew I had to give him some advice, so I said, "Well, Joe, I'll tell you what you have to do: the next time anybody whacks you on that ice, count to 10 before you do anything else."

Joe looked at me and said, "Why 10?"

"Because," I told him, "one of two things will happen. Number one, if the man you hit hasn't broken a leg, he'll skate out of reach, so should you swing that stick at him, you'll miss him. Number two, at the end of the count you'll be all over your mad, so you'll stay on the ice. Right?"

"Well, I'll try it," he said, and for the next month he was the star of the league.

Then it happened.

We went to play a game against New Haven at their rink, and they had a Polish fellow on their team by the name of Dutkowski. As the game moved along, I could see Joe's temper was rising because Dutkowski was bothering him. With only eight or 10 minutes left, we were leading by one goal, however, and I was hopeful everything would be all right.

Dutkowski, a former Chicago Blackhawk, skated near Joe, and suddenly, Joe hit him over the head with his stick with such a clout that it looked as if a geyser of blood was coming out of Dutkowski's head. They carried him off the ice, and there was almost a riot. A special platoon of police was called in, and Joe was put off with a match penalty. Then New Haven scored two goals and beat us.

Later that night, we were on the train back to Boston, and I was sitting and fuming about the incident when in comes Joe, acting like a big St. Bernard. He just sat there watching me and finally asked, "Myles, what's the trouble?"

"Are you kidding?" I said. "Look, Joe, I've been treating you like a brother. I figured to send you back to the major leagues. I've built you up all year long; that's all right, it's part of my job. But you came to me wanting to know all about my law experience. You asked me how to stay on the ice. And what do you do, Joe? You disgraced me out there."

He said, "Myles, I didn't let you down."

"Joe," I asked, "what did I tell you to do?"

"You told me to count to 10, didn't you?" he said.

I said, "Yes."

"And you said I could swing my stick," he told me. I agreed but added, "You didn't count to 10."

"Yes, I did," he insisted.

I said, "Joe, look, when you got into that bumping with Dutkowski, I started to count and got to five, and then you let that stick go."

He replied, "Myles, I forgot to tell you one thing. You know I was born in Poland and came over to Canada when I was seven or eight years old. Whenever I get mad, I forget to count in English, so I count in Polish and counted twice as fast. When I was bumping Dutkowski, I counted to 10 in Polish, let the stick go, and he was in the way!"

What could I say to that?

We had a good team, and after my year of recuperation, I was ready to return to the NHL.

One night I'll never forget was the Eddie Shore-Ace Bailey incident. We were playing Toronto at Boston Garden, and the local papers had more or less played up the game as a grudge match. As far as Ace was concerned, though, he was one of the nicest men ever to play hockey. On this night, Shore had rushed down the length of the ice, and Red Horner of Toronto, no shrinking violet himself, pushed Shore into the boards and really hit him hard. Shore struck his head and went down. Horner got the puck and went up the ice while Bailey dropped back on the Toronto defense. To this day, I really believe Shore was so dizzy getting up that he thought the man in front of him was Horner, not Bailey.

As he went by Ace, Shore just dragged his stick. He didn't bump Ace, he just took the skates out from under him. Not expecting it, Ace fell backwards and struck his head on the ice, and suddenly he started to shudder. Meanwhile, Shore skated back and stood there on defense, dazed. Horner skated up to him, took his gloves off, wound up like a pitcher would before throwing a fastball, and hit Shore on the chin. Shore fell backward, hitting his head on the ice.

Bailey was taken into the Toronto dressing room normally used by the Cubs. The Cubs' trainer, Joe Gilmore, had enough presence of mind to get chopped ice to encase Bailey's head. He looked like a mummy, but I think the ice saved his life; he was bleeding inside, and that ice kept the bleeding down. He had a double fracture of the skull, one on each side.

MYLES J. LANE

In the Bruins' dressing room, they took 18 stitches in Shore's head, and he was out, too, although few people knew that. Bailey was rushed to the hospital, where Dr. Munroe, a famous brain surgeon, operated on him. They put two silver plates in his head. Of course, we didn't know what would happen to him, but we still had the schedule to fulfill and went to New York for a game two nights later.

Shore was suspended for the rest of the year, and as far as the Bruins were concerned, they might as well have quit. They were finished. They couldn't play anymore, but they had to. I remember that night in New York; we were getting regular reports on Bailey's condition, which was quite serious. They didn't think he was going to live, and he remained on the danger list for quite a while. Ace eventually recovered but never played hockey again. Shore came back a season later and was still a great player.

As for me, I finally finished my law studies and quit hockey. I wanted to come to New York, so I said, "Goodbye, NHL, you've helped me a lot. I'm never going to be a star; I've got a broken back. Thanks again for everything."

I got a job with President Roosevelt's old law firm, Roosevelt and O'Connor, and went to the U.S. Attorney's Office as an assistant. During World War II, I spent four years in the navy, then went back to civilian life with a job as chief assistant at the U.S Attorney's Office. I became U.S. Attorney, and after that, chairman of the New York State Crime Commission for 10 years and a partner in the firm of Schwartz and Froelich. Then I was elected to the New York State Supreme Court.

I still enjoy hockey but think the game could be improved a bit. The one thing I don't see enough of is the real bodychecking or the stickhandling we used to have. I feel it's important to keep the speed in the game, and I am a firm believer in the importance of the forward pass.

There could be some changes made in the defensive zone, allowing only lateral passing there offensively. That might bring back the old-time bodychecking and more stickhandling. I'd allow forward passing from the net right up to the red line, but only lateral passing to the second blue line and in the defensive zone. Today, if a defensive man tries to hit an opponent at his blue line, it takes one man out of the play because the offensive player passes up to someone ahead of him. Because they allow forward passing in the defensive zone, there's more emphasis on stickchecking than bodychecking. If a man tries to throw a bodycheck, he winds up out of the play.

Crowds want three things today: scoring, which there is, good stickhandling, which there isn't, and speed, which there certainly is.

But professional hockey has changed since I played. It's now a money game, not a sport—a sales job that consists of giving the public what it wants. Today, hockey is getting the crowds, but if attendance ever drops off, the owners will have to put in more hitting and stick work—and that's when I'll enjoy the game again.

MYLES J. LANE

BERNARD "BOOM BOOM" GEOFFRION

Few players in Rangers history have caused more commotion in fewer games than Hall of Famer Bernard Geoffrion, alias "Boom Boom." A superstar with the Montreal Canadiens when the Habs collected five consecutive Stanley Cups from 1956 to 1960, Geoffrion won the Calder Trophy as well as the Hart and Art Ross prizes. He finished his active playing career in 1964 with Montreal and decided to try his hand at coaching. But in June 1966 Rangers general manager Emile "The Cat" Francis had other ideas. "The Cat" believed that Boomer still had some good hockey years left and claimed him on waivers from Montreal in the spring of 1966. Hockey critics thought Francis was making an egregious error, and even Geoffrion had his doubts. In the following oral history, based on the author's interviews with the "Boomer," Geoffrion details his extraordinary, albeit brief, stint on Broadway.

When Emile Francis offered to sign me, I begged off. "First," I told him, "let me try out for the team, and then if I make it, I'll sign."

But Emile wanted me to sign right away. "What happens," I asked, "if I don't make the club after I've signed?"

Francis laughed. "We'll still have to pay you."

Now I laughed. "OK. Where do I sign?"

You have to understand that on the one hand, I knew that I could play, but on the other hand, I was also worried about looking bad. I survived the training camp, but still I had not made the team. I knew that I had to be ready for the possibility that I no longer was good enough for the NHL. I didn't want pity.

The more I studied them, the more I was convinced this club could be a winner. One guy in particular fascinated me—their young right-winger, Rod Gilbert. I liked him because we had a lot in common. We were both from Montreal. Rod grew up near me, our families knew each other, and I had even met him when he was a tiny, aspiring hockey player who idolized me in my heyday with [the] Canadiens.

Like myself, Rod had come to the NHL directly from Junior hockey, and we were now both Rangers stars. I used to sit next to him in the New York dressing room, and one day I surprised him. "Guess what, Rod?" I mentioned. "I'm going to get more goals this season than you."

He looked at me and laughed. I had said that to him because I knew he could score, but I wanted him to have more incentive. That's what I did with any guy I thought I could help.

Vic Hadfield was a big left winger who had developed a hard shot with his banana-blade stick. The trouble was, he used to shoot the puck into the stands as often as he kept it inside the rink. He had a good sense of humor. "Have you ever seen a stadium that has the nets in the third balcony?" I kidded him. "Are you blind or what?" His eyesight must have improved because in 1971-72, he would score 50 goals!

I still hadn't played my first game for New York, and I was already getting publicity as if I were a local hero. *New York Post* columnist Maury Allen wrote about me, "He is Mickey Mantle and Y.A. Tittle, Bob Cousy, and Stan Musial."

One day I walked into our training camp dressing room, and there was a photographer shoving his camera in my face. "I haven't done anything," I shouted. "Why are you taking my picture? Wait till I do something. Maybe I won't make the team." He backed off, and then I poked my gloved hands into his ribs. "See you downstairs," I said very softly this time. "You want some locker-room pictures?"

The more time I spent with him, the more I wanted to do well for Emile, and the more I analyzed our lineup, the more I realized something good could come out of that roster. I told The Cat, "With the power we have here, there's no doubt in my mind that this team can make the playoffs. You look from the goaltender [Ed Giacomin] to the last guy on the bench, you have quality."

Gradually, I got over the hump in training camp, and part of the reason was motivation. I had it in spades. Not only was the reputation of "Boom Boom" Geoffrion at stake, but there was my family to think about. When there are three kids and a wife to take care of, a man finds more determination than you might think.

When I made the team, I made it on merit, but I was still shaky both in the head and in the legs. In my first period as a Ranger I didn't have all my confidence, but as the game went on I felt better. It took about a dozen games for me to get my playing head screwed on straight. By that time, I had my second wind and confidence back. Fortunately the fans were patient and supported me right from the very start. In my first game at the old Madison Square Garden as a Ranger, I set up a power-play goal from the point, and the fans fell in love with me. So did my teammates.

It's amazing the difference in attitude between a team like [the] Canadiens, which won five straight Stanley Cups, and one like [the] Rangers, which hadn't won since 1940. I found that I had to give the New York guys pep talks all the time, but they knew I was dead serious. In my comeback, I didn't want to play for a loser.

One of my better monologues came after we had finished a practice and were sitting in the room. My eyes went from player

BERNARD "BOOM BOOM" GEOFFRION

to player—Jean Ratelle, Rod Gilbert, Bob Nevin, Red Berenson, Orland Kurtenbach, Camille Henry, Jim Nelson, Rod Seiling, Arnie Brown—and then I got up:

"I can't believe that you guys can't make the playoffs. I understand that after a while you lose and lose and you get that losing feeling in your mind. But I'll tell you this, I didn't come here to play for a losing team. I came here to prove a point: that the Rangers are good enough to make the playoffs."

My speeches meant that I also had to produce. I couldn't be all talk and no action. In road games, I scored for the Rangers throughout October 1966, but I couldn't seem to score at home. On November 6, we had a home game against Toronto. It was about time I did something. Late in the second period, I had finished serving a two-minute penalty. I stepped out of the penalty box, and the puck was on my stick. I had a breakaway from center ice to the goal.

My legs pumped away like in the good old Montreal days. I said to myself, "You've gotta make this one look good."

Bruce Gamble was the Toronto goalie. I had played against him often enough to know what to do, and I did it. I gave him a head feint and he went one way, then another head feint, and he was twisted like a pretzel. With one more deke for good measure, I swept the puck into the net.

What followed is something that I will never forget and never quite understand. I got the greatest ovation that I ever received. The fans got to their feet and cheered and cheered. It was better than when I had scored my 50 goals [for Montreal]. I looked

around the Garden at all the people standing, and still they wouldn't stop. It went on and on and on. After five minutes, I went back onto the ice and took a bow. That just made them cheer harder.

Now, what I'm going to tell you may sound like an exaggeration to make a point, but it isn't. The ovation I got after scoring my first goal as a Ranger in the Garden was the biggest thrill that I ever had. Furthermore, the reception I got from New York fans and the media was better than I could have ever dreamed. It was like I owned the town.

Granted, I didn't have "Big Jean" at center or Bert Olmstead on left wing, but "Cat Francis" put together a pretty good line. My center was veteran Earl Ingarfield, who had worked with Andy Bathgate and Dean Prentice and who knew what he was doing. My left wing was Reggie Fleming of all people, the same guy who terrorized [the] Canadiens in the 1961 playoffs when he was a young whippersnapper with Chicago.

Now, Reggie was a Stanley Cup veteran who could play hard and make a good play, too. Reggie was something like Eddie "Clear the Track" Shack in that you never quite knew what to expect the way he bounced all over the ice.

Once I got into gear, the guys began believing in me and in themselves. Rod Gilbert was one of them. One day he said to me, "'Boom,' if you can give that little extra after all these years, so can I." Rod led the team in goals with 28 in 64 games.

Francis was happy he had talked me into coming to New York, and I was tickled that we agreed. "'Boomer' had that

BERNARD "BOOM BOOM" GEOFFRION

ABOVE: Three of the best (from left to right)—Vic Hadfield, Jean Ratelle, and Bernie Geoffrion. *From the Stan Fischler Collection*

winning attitude," "Cat" told the media. "It's something he could never lose, like his great shot. It's part of him, and it infects everybody."

Whatever it was, my presence was a catalyst. A year earlier, that team had finished dead last with only 47 points. With me in the lineup, they made the playoffs and had 25 more points than the previous season. I played in 58 games and scored 17 goals and 25 assists. Forty-two points in 58 games was not bad for an "old" man.

We wound up in fourth place, but [the] Canadiens, who finished second,

were only five points ahead of us. When I went back to the Forum as a Ranger, the Montreal fans were fair to me. The real fans, the ones who understood the situation, were behind me a hundred percent. But some of them had never forgiven me for 1955, when I won the scoring championship over [their number-one hero] "Rocket" Richard.

Even before I stepped on Forum ice wearing the Rangers uniform, I knew I would get a mixed reaction. I warned (my wife) Marlene, "Fifty to 75 percent of the fans are going to boo me."

BERNARD "BOOM BOOM" GEOFFRION

There was plenty to smile about, especially after our defenseman Jim Nielson gave me a pass and away I went to bang it past Charlie Hodge. If they weren't mad at me before, after I stuck my hand into the net to retrieve the puck, they were livid.

I got two goals that night with John Ferguson checking me. Before a face-off, I razzed Fergie: "'Toe' is making his biggest mistake ever. You can't check me." And I showed him. He was on the ice when I scored both my goals, and he didn't speak to me for the rest of the year.

The best thing was that we beat them 6-3, 4-3, and 5-0, and I scored three goals and eight assists. I led the whole Rangers team with 11 points against [the] Canadiens.

I really liked playing for Emile Francis. He was a ball of fire who really knew the game of hockey, and I give him a lot of credit for our success that year, 1966-67. He knew when to make moves, and he worked hard to turn a losing team into a winner.

As luck would have it, we played [the] Canadiens in the first round of the playoffs. Montreal swept us in four games, but it was not as one-sided as the statistics suggest. We were in every single game, but we couldn't get the breaks.

They beat us 6-4 and 3-1 in Montreal. At Madison Square Garden, it was 3-2 in Game 3, and the killer in Game 4 tells you all about our luck. The score was tied one up, and we went into sudden death. Red Berenson, who was now with the Rangers, came down the left wing and put a beautiful slap shot on the right corner.

It had Rogie Vachon beaten cleanly, but it clanged right off the far post and the rebound went to [the] Canadiens. The next thing I knew, John Ferguson was lumbering around our defenseman, Arnie Brown, and put the puck past Ed Giacomin. The time was 6:28, and after that, I was officially on vacation.

Some holiday! It took me a couple of months to recuperate. My back was sore, my legs were sore, my whole body was sore. Let's face it, my health was not that great. But I told Marlene not to say anything to anybody. I didn't want to complain because if it got out that I wasn't feeling well, management might have an excuse not to invite me back.

My wife and I had a good talk. This was my conclusion: "Marlene, I got a lot of goals. I'm gonna try one more year."

Why did I put my health in jeopardy?

For one thing, you know the heart of a professional athlete. My adrenaline was pumping, and I was loving the adulation I received in New York. I loved everything about the Big Apple, and not just the hockey games.

More than anything, I loved the way the team had come together and the way I felt appreciated. Donnie Marshall said, "If I had to pinpoint one specific thing that turned around the Rangers, it was 'Boom Boom' Geoffrion. He's a champion."

I was enjoying myself. New York was a great city, the Rangers were a great team to play for, and Madison Square Garden was a great arena to play in.

BERNARD "BOOM BOOM" GEOFFRION

MOMENTOUS TIMES
AND PERSONALITIES
IN RANGERS HISTORY

The original Rangers celebrate Lester Patrick Night.
From the Stan Fischler Collection

HOCKEY'S

ROYAL FAMILY:

THE PATRICKS

There is no doubt that one family more than any other connected with the sport—or with any other, for that matter—helped to develop the game of ice hockey and improve it as a salable major-league product. That honor belongs to Lester and Frank Patrick.

Born on December 31, 1883, in Drummondville, Quebec, a short distance from Montreal, Lester was the first of nine children. By the time Frank was born five years later, Lester was already displaying unusual talents in rugby, lacrosse, and cricket as well as hockey. His father, a successful lumberman, moved the family to Montreal when Lester was nine, thereby exposing him to a more stimulating brand of neighborhood hockey. There, the hockey bug attached itself permanently to Lester as he sought games wherever he could find them. When he was 17, Lester enrolled at McGill University but only lasted a year. His all-consuming desire to play hockey persuaded him to work for his father's lumber business in the off-season so he could afford to compete during the winters.

By late in 1902, Lester had earned enough to buy a train ticket to Brandon, Manitoba, where he signed with the local team and proceeded to rewrite the hockey stylebook. A defenseman with a forward's instincts, Lester could never understand why forwards and only forwards were the puck carriers. In those days, just past the turn of the century, the defensemen had only one assignment: to halt the attack.

"Of course, at Brandon, Lester was expected to behave like a defensive player," wrote Elmer Ferguson, the dean of Canadian hockey writers, "but instinct and temperament proved to be too strong."

Rather than resort to the prosaic and boring technique of lifting the puck into the enemy's end of the rink when he captured it, Lester stunned the Brandon spectators by digging his skates into the ice and rushing headlong toward the goal. Although he missed his shot, Lester left both the opposition and his teammates awed by the unorthodox performance, and at the end of the period, he was summoned to the board of directors' room.

"What is the meaning of this?" they demanded of Lester.

He replied with the impeccable logic that was his hallmark in later years: "Why not let defensemen rush if it works—and if the fans like it?"

Unable to cope with Patrick's reply, the directors acknowledged his point and decided to try it again in the next period.

Lester then proceeded to score a goal. In 1903 this was as unheard of as flying to the moon. The crowd loved it, and from that point on, defensemen have become as much a part of an attack as the two wings and center. Conceivably, had Lester not decided to make a rush in Brandon, Bobby Orr might never have been more than a defenseman who hurled the puck from one end of Boston Garden to the other.

But Patrick had just begun to innovate. When he arrived in Brandon, it was traditional for defensemen to stand in front of each other like point and cover-point players in lacrosse. "That doesn't make sense," Lester observed. "It would be a lot more logical to have the defensemen line up abreast." This time, the directors listened without rebuke, and once again, Patrick proved his point. From then on, the tandem defense became the vogue.

After revolutionizing defensive hockey in Brandon, Lester returned to his father's lumber business in Montreal, where he was signed by the strong Montreal Wanderers hockey club. From 1903 through 1905, Canadian hockey was dominated by the Ottawa Silver Seven, a club which won the Stanley Cup three consecutive years. But in March 1906, Ottawa went up against the Montreal Wanderers, led by Lester Patrick, and were defeated 12-10 in the two-game, total-goals series. It was Lester who scored the 11th and 12th goals for Montreal, thereby helping to win the Stanley Cup.

By now, the Patrick name was so renowned in hockey circles that when a wealthy group of businessmen in Renfrew decided to organize a major-league team, they went after Lester. He readily signed with the Renfrew Millionaires at a salary of $3,000 for 12 games. The fee was regarded as astronomical, but it inspired other promoters to grant equally large offers for other stars and set in motion the professional hockey movement.

Meanwhile, Lester's father had decided that his lumbering fortune—and future—was in the Pacific Northwest rather than Montreal, so he moved his family and business to British Columbia. Lester once again helped the Patrick enterprise, this time by scaling, felling, hauling, and sluicing the giant trees of the Fraser Valley. Usually, brother Frank was at his side, and whenever they'd take a break from lumbering, talk would switch to hockey and what they could do about cashing in on the sport's certain eventual boom.

With the aid of a $300,000 note from their father, Lester and Frank poured all their savings into what was to become the Pacific Coast Hockey League. They faced not only the uncertainty of public opinion, but also the dubiousness of hockey players and others who couldn't envision a league embracing Seattle, Victoria, Edmonton, Calgary, Regina, Vancouver, and Saskatoon.

But in 1911, the Pacific Coast Hockey League was born, and for the first time, professional hockey thrived in the United States. A Patrick enclave was established in British Columbia: Lester took the Victoria sextet while Frank ran the Vancouver club.

Any doubts about the wisdom of creating a major hockey league in the West were erased as soon as the schedule began. Starved for evening entertainment, the citizens of Seattle, Vancouver, Victoria, and the other cities in the league welcomed the Patricks' organization, and Lester and Frank responded with a determined effort to improve the brand of hockey being dispensed.

It was the Patricks who introduced the penalty shot to hockey, as well as numbers on the players' jerseys and the new offside rule that enabled a player to pass the puck from behind the opponent's net to a teammate skating in front of it.

The idea for the penalty shot was inspired while the Patricks were visiting England. They had gone to a soccer match and were enthralled by the excitement produced by a penalty shot in the game; consequently, it became part of their ice hockey rules as soon as they returned. Likewise, the scheme for numbering players was the result of a day at a baseball park when the brothers realized that they couldn't identify many of the participants. "If we can't tell who these guys are," said Frank, "it must be the same for our fans watching hockey."

The next season, all Pacific Coast Hockey League players wore numbered jerseys. Fans not only relished the innovation but bought so many souvenir programs that promoters up and down North America picked up on the idea. Soon, "You can't tell the players without a program" became a byword in American sport.

Speeding the flow of a hockey game became an obsession with the Patricks. They were particularly appalled by the way a referee could slow the game down to a virtual halt by an endless series of penalties. At times, each side could be reduced to two men, including the goaltenders, and the games then became a bore. As a result, the Patricks invented the delayed-penalty system that ensures four skaters on the ice no matter how many infractions are called.

They then legalized kicking the puck in certain areas of the rink and also introduced the assist to scoring records. "Practically every forward step taken by professional hockey between 1911 and 1925 can be traced to the keen mind of Frank Patrick and the practical knowledge of Lester, who tried out every rule first to prove its soundness," wrote Arthur Mann. "Between the two, they just about made the game what it was before it hit the big cities below the border."

Thanks to Lester and Frank, the blue lines made their appearance in the Pacific Coast League during the 1914-15 season. To familiarize the fans, Lester informed the local newspapers, and detailed explanations of the purpose of the blue lines were printed in each league city. Needless to say, a bit of confusion resulted, especially in Lester's "home" city of Victoria. He liked to joke about the bafflement and frequently told the story of the day his crack defenseman Ernie "Moose" Johnson was asked by a fan to explain the blueline rules.

Johnson laughed. "What's the blueline all about?" he repeated.

"Don't ask me, bud. As far as I'm concerned, there's only one rule in hockey— you take the puck on your stick and you shoot it in the net!"

RIGHT: Lester Patrick (left) with his sons, Murray (center) and Lynn (right). *From the Stan Fischler Collection*

Although Lester was basically a defenseman and also played rover in the seven-man game, his affection for goaltending would occasion a handful of remarkable exploits between the pipes. The earliest of these occurred in Victoria when Patrick's goalie, Hec Fowler, was ejected from a game. Lester decided to replace him but chose not to wear the traditional pads because he found them too cumbersome. He went into the nets wearing his defenseman's attire and foiled all shots hurled by the Vancouver team. When it was over, Patrick dismissed his feat with typical logic: "I worked on a simple principle—only one puck could come at a time. I stopped each shot and we won!"

After gaining some practical experience in the nets, Lester decided it was ill-advised to retain a rule that forced goaltenders to remain on their feet when making saves. The Patricks promptly changed the regulation, and from that point on, goaltenders began flopping, splitting, and doing everything else possible to keep the puck out of the net.

While all this was occurring, the Patricks were simultaneously engaging in a blood war with the NHL for supremacy in professional hockey. With such cities in Toronto, Montreal, and Ottawa in its fold, the NHL presented an awesome challenge, but Lester and Frank were undaunted. "They fought the National League," wrote Elmer Ferguson, who was covering the game at the time, "raided it, took a whole champion team away on one of their forays, and forced the National League to terms."

The high point of Lester's managerial career at that time was reached in the spring of 1925, when his Victoria team took on the Montreal Canadiens in the Stanley Cup finals at Montreal. Victoria won the opener 5-2 and the second match 3-1 in a best-of-five playoff. Paced by Howie Morenz's three-goal hat trick, the Canadiens topped Victoria 4-2 in the third game, but the visitors, guided by Frank Frederickson's deft passes and his two goals, then routed Montreal 6-1 to take the series.

Flushed with success, Lester sought new worlds to conquer. He didn't have to look far; Boston and the New York Americans had already entered the NHL, and franchises were being sought for Detroit and Chicago as well as for a second team in Manhattan. The demand for players was never greater, and while a paucity of talent still existed in the East, nobody questioned the endless stream of stars in Patrick's Pacific Coast League.

Lester, always the shrewd businessman, fulfilled the demand by selling his Victoria team to a Detroit group while negotiating the sales of other Pacific Coast League players to NHL teams. When Conn Smythe walked out of his organizational job with the Rangers prior to the 1926-27 season, Colonel John Hammond, president of the infant New York team, promptly hired Lester as coach. Frank Patrick turned up as an NHL director and eventually found his way to Boston, where he coached the Bruins.

As Johnny-come-latelys in Manhattan, the Rangers were forced to play catch-up with the New York Americans, who had already captured the imaginations of the city's spectators. It would require some superior hockey dealing in order to ice a representable team. Lester not only made the Rangers but developed them into a club that almost immediately outclassed the rival Amerks. Patrick's background in the Pacific Coast League was his forte; he knew ace players the Easterners had never heard of and made the most of his knowledge.

He remembered a brother act from Saskatoon, Bill and Bun Cook, who had been overlooked by the other franchises, and signed them to Rangers contracts. Then Lester recalled a former member of the Canadian Royal Mounted Police named Frank Boucher, and he, too, was signed. Together with the Cooks, Boucher was to provide some of the most stimulating offensive hockey ever seen.

Bill Cook led the league in scoring with 33 goals in 44 games, and the Rangers—almost unbelievably—finished first place in the American Division, a whopping nine points ahead of the "established" Bruins. On March 20, 1927, Lester made what he thought would be his final appearance as a player, skating on defense for the Rangers. However, on April 12, 1928, he once again took the ice at age 44 when his regular goaltender, Lorne Chabot, was injured in the Stanley Cup series against the Montreal Maroons.

In what has gone down as one of the most spectacular efforts in sports, goalie Lester blunted the drives of such notorious marksmen as Nels Stewart, Hooley Smith,

Babe Siebert, and Jimmy Ward. The following excerpt from the official NHL history as written by Charles L. Coleman concerns what took place on that memorable night in Montreal's Forum:

"Odie Cleghorn, the Pittsburgh manager, was pressed into service to take over from Patrick on the bench when the New York manager took over the spot in goal. From then on, although it was not particularly good hockey, the crowd was entertained by Patrick's antics in the nets and the exhortations of Odie Cleghorn from the bench. Whereas Cleghorn urged the Rangers to prevent the Maroons from shooting, Patrick kept hollering, 'Make 'em shoot.'

"Somehow, these instructions were reconciled, and Patrick did not have too much work, although he spent a lot of time on his hands and knees. Thirty seconds after the start of the third period, Bill Cook put the Rangers one up, and they increased their efforts to protect Patrick. However, Nels Stewart was not to be denied, and he lifted one over the New York manager as he scrambled about on his knees.

"Although the crowd was sympathetic to the veteran's efforts, they were still pulling for the Maroons. Overtime was necessary, and at seven minutes and five seconds, the hard-working Frank Boucher scored the winner on a scrambled pass from Ching Johnson to end Patrick's anguish. His players mobbed him as he left the ice, and it appeared as if nothing could hold the Rangers down."

Except for one game, nothing did. New York defeated Montreal 2-1 in the next game with Chabot protecting in the nets, but Patrick inserted Joe Miller as goalie in the third game, which the Maroons won 2-0. However, Miller then shut out Montreal 1-0 and stopped the Maroons 2-1 in the finale as the Rangers won their first Stanley Cup. It was only their second year in operation.

With the Cook brothers and Boucher leading the attack and such stalwart defensemen as Ching Johnson, Earl Seibert, and Ott Heller, the Rangers won their second Stanley Cup in 1933, routing Toronto in the finals three games to one.

Ever insightful, Lester perceived that some of his more formidable, older players were slowing up and it would soon be time for a change. Once again, his farsightedness paid off handsome dividends. This time, Lester devised the first full-scale farm system in hockey and began developing players in lesser leagues, hopeful that they would eventually feed the big club. In addition, he received help from an unexpected area—his own family.

Grace Patrick had given birth to a pair of extremely agile boys who developed into athletes whose skills rivaled their father. Joseph Lynn and Frederick Murray, or Muzz, could play any sport well—Muzz became heavyweight champion of Canada and was an accomplished six-day bike rider and track star—but ultimately, they loved hockey best.

Sensitive to potential charges of nepotism, Lester tried to avoid those who suggested that the eldest, Lynn, might soon be an NHL star once he became prominent

with the Montreal Royals of 1934. But persuaded by friends that his son deserved a fair chance, Lester invited his boy to the Rangers' training camp in the fall. Twenty-two other young hopefuls arrived at the Winnipeg base, and Lester kept insisting that Lynn was simply mediocre.

Yet Frank Boucher and Bill Cook were especially vocal in pointing out Lynn's assets to Patrick. The verbal bombardment that Lester absorbed was sincere, and the Rangers boss knew it. In time, he relented and signed Lynn to play on the club's third line.

Then Lester's gravest fears were realized; a New York sportswriter condemned the signing as the worst form of favoritism. Lester was furious, and he launched into a tirade against the newspaperman.

"You haven't hurt me," Lester thundered. "You're gnawing at the foundation of the game itself. To us, hockey means playing to win—brother against brother, father against son. It's a sacred precept that a foul mind like yours can't understand. My son made the team on skill alone, as any Ranger would tell you. In my opinion, you're not fit to write about this sport."

Lynn bolstered his father's confidence by pulling his weight with the Blueshirts right away. After two seasons in the NHL, Lynn was hailed by no less a critic than Toronto's manager, Conn Smythe, who offered $20,000 for Lynn's contract. Naturally, Lester refused.

By the late '30s, Lester had rebuilt the Rangers around Lynn, Bryan Hextall, Phil Watson, Babe Pratt, Neil and Mac Colville, and Alex Shibicky. A big defenseman, Pratt emerged as the clown prince of the team and one of Patrick's favorites. Babe saw humor in everything, especially Lester's idiosyncrasies. One of these was Patrick's frugality. Lester would insist that his players buy their sticks only at Alex Taylor's Sporting Goods Store.

"We used to call the stick 'The Lester Patrick Special,'" said Pratt. "It's true that he'd only let us buy it at Taylor's because he had a deal with that store. Those sticks were so hard, you could barely break them. I tried once by jamming the blade into a radiator and jumping on the handle. Why, the damn stick catapulted me, and my head almost hit the ceiling."

Pratt was always fascinated by Lester's curious sense of values, particularly regarding such issues. "We beat Toronto once 5-0 right in Toronto, which was considered incredible because the Leafs never lost at home in those days. And when someone told Lester the boys were skating real good, he said, 'Yeah, but they broke 14 sticks!'"

Patrick won his last Stanley Cup in April 1940, when his Rangers defeated the Toronto Maple Leafs four games to two. The final victory took place on April 11, 1940, in Maple Leaf Gardens after the teams had battled through regulation time and were tied 2-2. Taking a pass from Phil Watson, Bryan Hextall scored the winning goal at 2:07 of the first sudden-death period.

During the postgame ceremony, Lester put one arm around Lynn and the other around Muzz, who starred on defense, then led his victorious crew into the locker room.

"After the game," Pratt recalled, "Lester got us together in the dressing room and said, 'Boys, every piece of equipment in this room belongs to the Rangers, and I don't want to see any of it leaving!'"

The "Silver Fox," as Lester had become known, guided the Rangers to first place in 1941-42, but the Maple Leafs obtained revenge by upsetting the New Yorkers four games to two in the opening round of the playoffs. After that, it was all downhill for Lester. More than any other club, the Rangers were devastated by World War II. Muzz Patrick, Art Coulter, Alex Shibicky, the Colville brothers, and Bill Juzda all joined the armed forces, leaving the Rangers with a skeleton team that finished an abysmal last, 19 points behind fifth-place Chicago. It was the same season after season until the war ended and the veterans returned.

The once nimble legs had stiffened with the passing of time, and neither Lynn nor Muzz nor many of the other pre-war aces could reclaim their glory days. Shortly thereafter, Lester himself retired after 20 years of running the Rangers. At the age of 70, he returned to Victoria and once again operated a team in British Columbia, where he had gotten his start as a promoter.

No individual has had a more profound influence on professional hockey's growth than Lester Patrick. The "Silver Fox" died on June 1, 1960. Lynn eventually became vice president of the St. Louis Blues, and Muzz was coach and general manager of the Rangers. Lester's grandson, Craig (Lynn's son), became a regular forward on the

California Golden Seals in 1971-72 before eventually becoming a successful general manager with the Rangers and, later, the Pittsburgh Penguins.

THE RETURN OF THE BENTLEYS

THE GREATEST FORGOTTEN RANGERS GAME

Over the years, fans have talked with reverence about the time Mark Messier promised a playoff win over the Devils and delivered, not to mention the night the Rangers defeated Vancouver in 1994 to win the Stanley Cup.

Granted, those were memorable moments, but they overshadow one of the greatest games ever played by the Rangers and one that has been completely overlooked with the passing of time.

When it ended that night of January 21, 1954, the 13,463 spectators at Madison Square Garden cried inwardly, if not outwardly. An usher turned to schoolteacher Harvey Bien, who was watching his first professional hockey game, and told him that he needn't bother coming back—there would never be another night like this one, when Doug and Max Bentley came together again and routed the Boston Bruins.

The episode reeked with schmaltz from the start. Thirty-three-year-old Max, the

aging dipsy-doodler, hadn't skated with 37-year-old brother Doug since the pair had been separated seven years earlier after long, star-filled careers as linemates on the Chicago Blackhawks. Doug, who hadn't played in the NHL for more than two years, had spent most of the 1953-54 season as player/coach of the Saskatoon Quakers in the Western League.

What made the scenario even more dramatic was the Rangers' frustration as they desperately tried to clamber ahead of the fourth-place Bruins, Max's chronic depression over his injuries—whether imagined or real—and the prevailing doubt that elderly Doug could reactivate his jackrabbit legs and maintain a big-league pace after such a long layoff.

One man believed he could do it: New York Rangers manager Frank Boucher, the same man who had gambled and first talked Max out of retirement before the 1953-54 season began.

"When I quit hockey in 1955," said Max, "I really was serious about it. . . . Then, Frank Boucher started asking if I'd play just one more season with New York. He kept hiking his offer until I accepted. The money was too good to turn down."

Boucher believed in Max. He remembered how the two brothers had combined for so many beautiful years with the Blackhawks, teaming with Bill Mosienko to make the "Pony Line" perhaps the fastest and most artistic the NHL has ever known. And Boucher also recalled how, after being traded to Toronto for five regulars during the 1947-48 season, Max remained an ace with the Maple Leafs despite his notorious hypochondria. His Toronto boss, Conn Smythe, liked to say, "Maxie felt terrible tonight. Had the chills all day. And all he got was three goals!"

Max signed with Boucher, and a month after the 1953-54 season began, he proved that he hadn't lost his amazing stickhandling touch. "Our town has its biggest hockey hero in years," wrote columnist Jimmy Powers in the *New York Daily News*, "in the frail but ever exciting dipsy-doodler from Delisle, Saskatchewan, Max Bentley. Here is an old pro who brings the Garden crowd to its feet every time he takes the disk in his own zone and starts down the ice with it."

Apart from his unmatched skating agility and sudden feints and swerves, Max's trademark was a galvanic wrist shot that is unknown in contemporary hockey. "He developed that shot milking cows on the farm," said Doug. "Milking made his wrists big and strong."

Max couldn't carry the Rangers alone, and there were many times that he sat, head hung low and a white towel draped over his neck, at the end of the bench, bothered by a bad back or some such ailment. Yet the vintage Max was so impressive that one night, a Garden official approached Boucher about the second Bentley.

"If Max is a sample of what one Bentley can do on that ice," the official told Boucher, "I wish the Rangers had another to go with him. If Doug can stand up, he must be better than most of the kids we've got."

Boucher agreed, in part. He knew that Doug Bentley, in his prime, would have

been a superb catalyst for the Rangers—and Max—but the manager also realized that Doug had only been playing part-time, minor-league hockey while coaching and was too old and out of shape to be considered.

Or was he? The more Frank mulled it over, the more he grew convinced it was worth trying. He phoned the owner of the Saskatoon team, which had a working agreement with the Rangers, and said he wanted Doug in New York; the answer was a resounding "No!"

By now it was December, and the Rangers needed help. Normally mild-mannered, Boucher decided to get tough with the Saskatoon officials and threatened to pull the Rangers-owned players off the team, leaving the Quakers with a skeleton squad. He then tossed in a pacifier: he would replace Doug Bentley with Frankie Eddolls, a former NHL defenseman with positive coaching potential. By mid-January, the Saskatoon officials agreed, and Doug was told to grab the earliest possible flight for New York.

The thermometer read 40 degrees below zero when Doug climbed aboard the plane at Saskatoon Airport on Tuesday, January 20, 1954. From the start, he suffered doubts about the comeback. "I was only doing spot playing with the Quakers," he said. "On top of that, I had been having a bad time with my nerves. I didn't think the NHL would help that condition. That's why I was against the move. But Boucher kept after me, and finally, he offered me the biggest money I ever got in my life, even in my best days with the Blackhawks. The money did it—that, and the fact that I knew I could help Max; I could assist him on the ice and settle him off the ice."

On a Wednesday night, January 21, 1954, the Rangers were scheduled to face the fourth-place Bruins, whom New York trailed by two points. Even under the best of circumstances it would not have been easy for Doug, but plane connections caused additional problems.

"It was late Tuesday night when we left," said Doug, "and just as we were about to take off, I discovered I had left my skates at the Saskatoon Arena. They had to hold the flight while I went back to get them."

Boucher, a former member of the Royal Canadian Mounted Police, had personally flown to Saskatoon to "get his man" and sat alongside Doug as the four-engine propeller craft plied its way east. Neither man slept during the trip, which finally brought them to New York midday Wednesday. There was ice at the Garden that afternoon, so Doug took a practice skate.

By late afternoon, news media carried word that the Bentley brothers would, in fact, be reunited that night against the Bruins. "But," said Doug, "neither Boucher nor Muzz Patrick, the Rangers' coach, said a word about what they were going to do with me. I figured we'd play it all by ear."

Shortly before game time, Patrick and Boucher huddled and eventually decided to place Doug on left wing—his normal position—with Max at center and Edgar Laprade on right wing. Laprade, who was normally a center, had been one of the smoothest, most adroit centers in Rangers history in his prime. But he, too, had aged. At one point, he had even retired, but Boucher persuaded him to skate once more at age 35. Many Rangers fans were skeptical about Laprade's ability to adjust to the right-wing position while skating with the unpredictable Bentleys.

Nobody was as uncertain as Doug Bentley. As he sat nervously twitching his legs in the dressing room before the opening face-off, Doug wondered why he had ever permitted Boucher to talk him into this crazy stunt. "I was afraid I'd make a fool of myself," the elder Bentley recalled. "I was as nervous as a kitten. . . . [I] must have walked up and down the dressing room at least a hundred times."

At last, it was time. Organist Gladys Goodding played "The Star Spangled Banner," and referee Frank Udvari dropped the puck for the opening face-off. Just as quickly, Doug's doubts disappeared. "It seemed," he reflected 15 years later, "that every time we touched the puck, we did the right thing."

Doug scored the first goal at 12:29 of the first period on a pass from defenseman Jack Evans. At 15:44, Max set up Wally Hergesheimer for a power-play score against Bruins goalie Jim Henry. Then Doug fed Paul Ronty, who gave New York a 3-0 lead. The Bentleys were still in low gear, and before the period ended, the Bruins had scored twice to pull within a goal of New York. By this time, though, the crowd knew that they were seeing a re-creation of the Bentley brothers of yesteryear. Only the jerseys were different.

"Once the people started to holler for us," said Doug, "I knew that was it. I knew we'd really go. I knew because right off the bat, I could tell that Max hadn't forgotten any of his tricks—or mine, either."

Just past the six-minute mark in the second period, Patrick sent the Bentleys out again. This time, they combined for the brand of razzle dazzle that later earned them both a niche in the Hockey Hall of Fame. "We crisscrossed a couple of times on our way to their blue line," explained Doug. "Then I fed it to Max, and he put it right in."

Normally nervous, Max was now beside himself with joy, and when he got to the bench after scoring, he draped his arm over his brother's shoulder and said, "Same old Doug. You're skating the same, handing off the same, and fooling 'em the same." Less than two minutes later, they skated out and, with radar-like passes, set up Camille Henry for still another Rangers goal. The middle period ended with New York ahead 6-3.

In the third period, Wally Hergesheimer scored for the Rangers at 9:59, but the fans clamored for the Bentleys, and Patrick acknowledged their cries as the clock reached the 15-minute mark. This time, Edgar Laprade shared in their pattern-passing wizardry, sending veteran hockey writers into fits of gleeful cheering. "To say that the reunion was a success," said Joe Nichols of the *New York Times*, "is a weak understatement. The Bentleys frolicked like a couple of kids out skylarking."

Flanked by the brothers, Laprade swiftly crossed the center red line, then skimmed a pass to Doug on the left, who just as quickly sent it back to Laprade as he crossed the Boston blueline. By now, only one Bruins defenseman was left trying to intercept the anticipated center slot pass from Laprade to Max, who was speeding along the right side. Laprade tantalized the Boston player, almost handing him the puck. When he lunged for it, Edgar flipped it to Max, who was moving on a direct line for the right goalpost.

Meanwhile, Laprade had burst ahead on a direct line for the left goalpost, ready for a return pass. Both goalie Jim Henry and the defenseman—and possibly even Laprade—expected Max to relay the puck back to Edgar, so Henry began edging toward the other side of the net as Max faked and faked and faked the pass. Max continued to move toward the goal until, without even shooting the rubber, he calmly eased it into the right corner while Henry stood there, mesmerized by the Bentleys' magic. The audience went wild. "It was like a dream," Doug recalled. "Everything we did turned out right."

The final score was 8-3 New York. Max and Doug had combined for a total of eight points—Doug had one goal and three assists, and Max two goals and two assists. "They put on a display of smooth, smart stickhandling that brought back memories of a supposedly extinct hockey era," wrote James Burchard of the *World Telegram* and Sun. "It was a joy to behold."

So was the dressing room scene, although at first glance, you couldn't be sure you were witnessing jubilation. There sat the emotional Max, with tears streaking down his face. "He's crying for happiness," said Doug, who was unwinding a few feet away. "He's tickled because we finally played together again . . . and so am I."

Few realized that Doug hadn't slept for nearly two days and had also suffered through a dramatic temperature change, traveling from frigid western Canada to balmy New York. "I'm w⁷ring-ing wet from sweating," Doug commented, "and feel completely bushed. Here, it's 80 degrees warmer than in Saskatoon. I've had no sleep. My nerves are shot, and I had one of the greatest evenings of my life. You explain it."

Explanations flowed as easily as the Bentleys' goals. "I wasn't surprised at Doug's play," said Coach Patrick. "I've seen him play. I know what he can do. I've been sold on Doug Bentley a long, long time."

Boucher, who had dreamed up the scheme, sat beaming on the trainer's bench. "As good as Max is alone," he noted, "he's twice as good with Doug."

It took a while for Max to regain his composure, but when he did, the man who had once been compared to "a scared jackrabbit" on the ice analyzed the extraordinary performance. "I don't think any man ever taps the whole reservoir of his strength," Max mused. "Some go through their entire lives and never get the mileage they should. You can work yourself to a frazzle and fall dead on the floor and swear you can't move a muscle. But if someone sets fire to the house, you'll find yourself

setting a new speed record getting out. This game was like an intoxicating stimulant. As goal after goal whipped in, the whole team worked itself into a frenzy. It was one of those nights—one I won't ever forget."

Only once before had the Bentleys enjoyed such a productive evening. When they were in their prime at Chicago in 1942, Max scored four goals and three assists in one game, while Doug had two goals and four assists. But the Bentleys were 12 years younger then and at their peak. Few of the seasoned observers doubted that this Bentley reunion would I be a very special classic and many were in tears, just as Max.

"I've been covering hockey since 1928," said Jimmy Powers of the *Daily News*, "and this game, to me, was one of the most thrilling of all time. I know because at the end, I was so hoarse from cheering I couldn't talk."

The performance convinced Doug that he should finish the season with New York in hopes of helping the Rangers surpass Boston for a playoff berth. He and Max and tiny Camille Henry gave the New Yorkers an extraordinarily clever power play, but the question troubling Boucher was whether Max and Doug could maintain their brisk pace to the end.

"The opposition started to pound us," said Doug. "The Bruins sent big fellows like Eddie Sandford and Cal Gardner after us. They hit us, leaned on us, and fouled us whenever possible."

When the Rangers played Detroit at Madison Square Garden, Glen Skov of the Red Wings actually speared the "R" off the front of Max's jersey and provoked the younger Bentley into one of his rare fights. But the Bruins' coach, Lynn Patrick, employed the subtlest—and ultimately, the most effective—strategy.

Aware that Max was a hypochondriac, Lynn instructed his players to casually tell Max how terrible he looked. It was to be done nonchalantly but regularly. "Cal Gardner did it best," Lynn recalled. "After a while, Max seemed to get depressed and more depressed, and the quality of his play began slipping."

It was touch and go between the Rangers and Boston until March, when Max's play tapered off and the Bruins pulled ahead, finishing in fourth place by six points. Playoff team or not, the Rangers had nevertheless given their fans enough to cheer about on that unforgettable night in January of 1954, when the Bentleys played together again.

If the episode proved anything, it was that the Chicago Blackhawks should never have split them up during the 1947-48 season when Max was dealt to Toronto. "My father at the time said we shouldn't let them break us up," said Doug, "and he was right. All I could say after that reunion was that I wished we could have turned the clock back 10 years. But we couldn't."

Both Max and Doug retired from active NHL play after the 1953-54 season. Doug was voted into the Hall of Fame in June 1964; two years later, Max was also inducted. From time to time, Max would return to the rink, as he did in April 1968 in an old-timers benefit game at Toronto's Maple Leaf Gardens.

During that game, critics marveled at Max's grace on the ice. "He was as elusive as a jackrabbit," reported Milt Dunnell, sports columnist of the *Toronto Daily Star*, "and the puck appeared magnetized by his stick."

But by then, hockey had changed. The Bobby Hulls and "Boom Boom" Geoffrions had popularized the slap shot, and Max looked on in amazement as well as disgust when he studied the modern game. "Never slapped the puck in my life," he said. "What would make a man do something like that?"

Doug, who coached at Los Angeles in the Western League before returning to Saskatoon to tutor young players, also lamented the change in hockey's style. "Today," Doug observed, "all they do is slap the puck and hope it hits a skate or a stick and goes in the net. They don't know where the puck is going anymore."

Then he paused: "Oh, what I'd give to just turn the clock back once more."

THE
ULTIMATE RIVALRY

The Rangers' rivalries with the New York Islanders and the New Jersey Devils are alive and well. Not to mention white-heat intense.

But back in the dim, distant past, the Rangers faced an opponent that generated every bit as much hatred and fierce emotion as any Blueshirts opponent.

That club was the New York Americans, the city's first National Hockey League team.

The Amerks, as they were known to their followers, opened Madison Square Garden III—prior to the current MSG—in 1925, a year before the Blueshirts were born.

But unlike the immediately successful Rangers, trouble followed the Americans from the moment its bootleg owner, "Big" Bill Dwyer, was imprisoned before his club's opening night.

As a result, the Rangers became New York's aristocratic hockey club, winning Stanley Cups in 1928 and 1933 while the Amerks were winning nothing.

Year after year, the underdog Americans' fans longed for the day when their heroes would vanquish the hated Rangers once and for all.

Then it happened.

Exactly 11 years after the rivalry began, the Amerks and Blueshirts collided in the 1937-38 playoffs.

It was a best-of-three first-round series. Naturally, all games were played at Madison Square Garden.

The Americans had won the opening game by a score of 2-1 in triple overtime, but the Rangers knotted the series with a 4-3 victory in Game 2.

On the day of the finale, March 28, 1938, New York sports fans were aflutter over Game 3.

"By dawn on the 28th, lines had started to form outside the balcony ticket windows on 49th and 50th streets," wrote *Sport Life Magazine* editor Bruce Jacobs. "The gallery was packed long before the teams skated out.

"The sellout crowd cheered lustily when the Rangers and Amerks piled onto the arena surface led by their respective goalies—little Davey Kerr for Lester Patrick's Rangers and massive Earl Robertson for Red Dutton's Amerks."

It should be noted that Americans manager Dutton had crafted the strongest club in franchise history.

Young scoring aces such as Art Chapman, Dave "Sweeney" Schriner, and Lorne Carr were complemented by renowned veterans Hap Day and Nels Stewart, who had previously starred for the Toronto Maple Leafs and Montreal Maroons, respectively.

After a scoreless first period, it appeared as if the Rangers would annihilate their frantic foes. Alex Shibicky and Bryan Hextall staked the Blueshirts to a 2-0 lead before the eight-minute mark.

But the Americans took their time getting on the scoreboard. Carr made it a

2-1 game with only 4:36 gone in the third, and for the next six minutes, Kerr stopped every shot fired his way.

Desperate for the tying goal, Dutton dramatically altered his strategy. The Amerks boss inserted five forwards on the ice, and the plan worked when Stewart, nicknamed "Old Posion," beat Kerr at 10:38.

From that point forward, the teams battled through the third period without a score, setting the stage for the second overtime game in the series.

Jacobs wrote, "Up and down the ice the teams surged in the first overtime period—but no goal was scored. The pressure was terrific. This was sudden-death hockey and any goal was the winning goal—with a trip to Chicago for the Stanley Cup finals in the balance."

The second extra session was no less thrilling as Robertson and Kerr hermetically sealed their respective nets. By the time midnight had arrived, the score was still 2-2.

Enthralled by the spectacle, fans stayed in their seats or rushed to the refreshment stands until the Garden ran out of food as the third overtime period began.

For a moment, it appeared as if the Amerks had won the game. Defenseman Joe Jerwa's shot beat Kerr but hit the post!

Next, it was the Rangers' turn to settle the contest—almost.

Cecil Dillon escaped the Americans' defense for a clean breakaway, but his shot was blunted by Robertson's pad save.

Soon after, Chapman sent Schriner in the clear, but his shot sailed over the net. The third overtime was over.

The Garden clock had passed 1 a.m., and at least one fan had returned from a corner bar.

The gentleman had left the arena when the Rangers were up 2-0. While downing a beer in a Broadway bistro, he asked a newcomer, "How da the game wind up?"

"Wind up?" the other replied. "Why, they're still playin'—the score's 2-2!"

The Amerks fan grabbed his hat and ran back to the Garden in time for the fourth overtime.

It was almost 1:30 a.m. when referee Ag Smith dropped the fourth overtime face-off puck; only this time, the end *was* in sight.

Dutton started his top line, Schriner, Carr, and Chapman, and they took command—tic, tac, toe.

The puck went from defenseman Jerwa to Chapman, who spotted his buddy, Carr, with an opening on the left side.

The man who had put the Amerks on the score sheet hours earlier lit the red light at 40 seconds of the fourth overtime.

"The contest couldn't have been more adaptable to drama had a script been written in advance by Alfred Hitchcock," Jacobs concluded.

And that didn't even account for a curious bit of business.

Had one female spectator had her way, the game may have never reached the extra frames. The woman stormed goal judge Charles Porteous in the first period and pressed the red light buzzer when she thought the Blueshirts had scored a goal. Eventually, the police stepped in to restrain the impulsive female, and referees Bert

McCaffery and Ag Smith restored order to the wrangling players on the ice.

Perhaps the most poignant reaction to the classic game that lasted *more than 120 minutes* came from a passionate young Americans fan named Ben Olan.

Olan, who would later become a Hall of Fame hockey writer with the Associated Press, recalled the longest Rangers game from a child's eyes.

"I loved the Americans passionately," he said, "and listened to that game until about midnight. But I couldn't stay up.

"When I woke up the next morning, I was dying to know who won. I ran downstairs to the corner newsstand, and I timidly looked at the headline. The back sports page of the *Daily News* was partially covered. All I could see was 'AMERKS.' I leaned over and slowly lifted the covering paper to see the rest of the headline: 'BEAT RANGERS.'

"To that point, it was the happiest day of my life."

THE MOST REMARKABLE FANS IN THE WORLD
—————— RANGERS ROOTERS ——————

They come in all shapes, sizes, and professions. White collar, blue collar—you name it. The breed of sports fan known as Rangers rooter is inimitable to say the least. A few samples just begin to tell the story.

There's Ira Gitler, the world-renowned jazz critic for half a century, who was there in 1940 when the Rangers won the Stanley Cup. Gitler once was also a player and hockey author, and is currently manager of his own team, Gitler's Gorillas.

By contrast, another gem would be Dr. Thomas Kolb, a nationally acclaimed radiologist who is just as much at home in the Garden as he is in the operating room. The good doctor has been a longtime season-ticket holder.

Included in the "off the wall" category is "Dancing Larry," who unfailingly does a mambo-cha-cha-cha, whirling-dervish routine in the upper reaches of the Garden during a third period interlude. Larry's routine has become so popular that his dance is regularly featured on the big screen overhanging center ice.

Perhaps the most amazing—and durable—aspect of Rangers fandom is the collective fervor demonstrated for the home team and against the enemy.

ABOVE: The assortment of Rangers rooters is vast. *Photo by David Perlmutter*

One enduring example is a chant directed at Hall of Famer Denis Potvin, who captained the Islanders to four straight Stanley Cups from 1980 to 1983.

"To this day, fans of the archrival Rangers utter his name more frequently and with greater fervor than those who cheered his checks and slap shots," wrote Fred Bierman in the *New York Times*.

The chant "Potvin sucks" is unusual, considering that the defenseman retired in 1968. "It is quite amazing that they're still doing it," recalled Potvin, a television broadcaster for the Florida Panthers. "The whole thing has taken a life of its own."

Sometimes, the chant is heard several times during a game. "As time has passed, the chant has increasingly less to do with Potvin the player or the person. Instead, it has turned into a way for Rangers fans—many of whom never saw Potvin play—to express their general frustrations or to simply have a laugh during a lull in the action," added Bierman.

The late Tom Sarro was very familiar with the Potvin chant. A retired teacher and hockey historian who began going to Rangers games in the 1950s, Sarro and his wife, Angela, were as passionate as any Garden rooters.

Tom once related a wonderful story about "hockey games" he and friends would play en route to the Garden.

"The craziest of all took place in the late '50s," Sarro recalled. "I was with two friends coming back from a Saturday afternoon Rangers game at the old Garden.

"We were on the Fourth Avenue local and feeling a lot of hockey in us on the way back. This was a normal reaction because of the excitement of the game we had just seen. In those days at the Garden, we would crush a paper cup, drop it to the ground, and kick it around the corridor, pretending it was a hockey puck. This was commonplace at the Garden.

"On this day, we took the game a step further and smashed some cups on the floor of the subway car. The three of us were

playing cup hockey in the empty car until two policemen got on board and hauled us into the precinct station house.

"Fortunately for us, my father happened to be a fireman, and my two other friends' fathers were cops, so nothing more came of it. Apparently, to some transit policemen, cup hockey was a bad thing!"

Few Rangers fans were wilder than cowbell-ringing Hilda Chester. A notorious denizen of Ebbets Field during the Brooklyn Dodgers era, Hilda brought her cowbell and voice to the Garden when "Dem Bums" deserted her for Los Angeles.

No one who visited the Garden during the 1940s or 1950s will forget Sally Lark. A buxom blonde, Sally was a season-ticket holder in a unique location.

Lark's pew sat shoulder to shoulder with the penalty bench, which in those days was shared by players of both teams. An interior decorator by trade, Sally could often be seen chatting with the skating sinners, particularly regulars such as "Wild" Bill Ezinicki of the Maple Leafs and Ken Reardon of Les Canadiens.

In the decade before protective glass was installed along the sideboards, it was not uncommon for some rooters to get a "piece" of the action, especially during rough games. One of Sally Lark's female neighbors, sitting in the front row, took umbrage with Ezinicki's behavior.

As the Leafs right wing bent over for a face-off directly in front of her, the lady removed a six-inch hatpin from her chapeau and bayoneted it through Ezzie's hockey pants.

Balcony patrons who sat more than 100 feet above the ice were a breed unto themselves. What better proof is there than the fact that they had their own entrance and stairway at the old Garden?

End arena, side arena, and mezzanine ticket holders would enter through the main entrance on Eighth Avenue. Balconyites were segregated to a portal on 49th Street that led to a tortuous climb up a seemingly endless string of staircases to the arena's top.

Here, another form of segregation took place. Because the old Garden was originally built for boxing, the side balconies overhung the ice at an angle that made it impossible to see the entire playing surface unless you sat in either of the first two rows. From the third row back, a fan could see five-sevenths of the rink. The other two-sevenths—along the near boards—were hidden from view. No message boards existed; thus, the viewer had to "imagine" what was transpiring beneath him when bodies collided and the fans cheered.

In the eyes of many, the end balcony was the best place to watch the game. Seats sharply sloped to the top on a curve, enabling viewers to take in the entire panorama without missing a bodycheck.

A spate of mezzanine seats also had slightly obstructed views, as did a small number on the arena level.

From opening night at the old Garden in 1925 to the mid-1940s, the only protection the fans enjoyed from flying pucks and errant sticks was chicken-wire fencing behind the net and in the corners. The wire was thin enough for players to pop a disagreeable fan or jab sticks through and attack a goal judge. Likewise, fans could easily hit a zebra if they disagreed with a call.

Occasionally, fans wanted to get close and personal with a referee to enlighten the official as to how to call a game the Rangers' way.

The most practical place to do that was a fan-accessible runway that led from the ice along a rubber matting to the officials' dressing room.

One night, after a particularly disturbing Red Storey–handled first period, a fan named Richard Selby headed for that ramp. A passionate Rangers fan, Selby wanted to check on Storey's lineage as directly as possible.

He arrived at the side of the rubber matting just as the tall, striped figure began clomping across the rubber carpet.

Within 10 feet of the referee, the angry Rangers fan opened his barrage: "STOREY, YOU [EXPLETIVE], WHAT THE [EXPLETIVE] DO YOU THINK YOU'RE [EXPLETIVE] DOING OUT THERE?"

As Selby prepared his next salvo, the referee—who had been staring straight ahead—suddenly wheeled in his tracks and took a giant step in the direction of his heckler.

Satisfied that he had delivered his message, Selby exited faster than you can say Roy "Red" Storey.

Such brazen assaults have been rare. Throughout the 18-year-old Rangers-Americans rivalry, a dichotomy of New York rooters was noticed. Those who favored underdogs rooted for the Amerks. The rest pulled for the Blueshirts. After six years, the Rangers had two Stanley Cups, the Americans none—and they would never win one.

Interestingly, the first New York hockey fan club did not belong to the Rangers or the Amerks. In the 1940s, a group of Rovers season ticket holders led by chain-smoking businessman Howard Frank organized the Blue Line Club. By fan club standards, it was a rather sophisticated group of mostly adults which held regular meetings. At season's end, it would stage an organized musical comedy lampooning the Eastern League scene and the Rovers.

Long before the Rangers Fan Club was born, the Blue Line Club embraced some of the most fascinating rooters from all walks of life. One of them was Ella Clifton, an attractive young woman with a gleaming smile who became the Boswell of Rovers teams from the late 1930s through the early 1940s. Clifton amassed voluminous scrapbooks, but more importantly, she developed a photographic history of the Rovers. Because no glass existed along the sideboards in those days, she was able to photograph directly from her front-row seat. At times, she actually got onto the ice.

The Rangers Fan Club came about less spontaneously. After the Blueshirts hit the skids following their 1950 Stanley Cup run, the club's publicist, Herb Goren, laid out a plan to woo fans back to the rink. Noticing the Blue Line Club's success, Goren announced that a Rangers counterpart would be developed with the NHL franchise's support.

Goren presided at a pregame meeting held at the Garden. A college professor named Marino Sabatino was named president, and within a very short time, the RFC boasted its own paper, *The Rangers Review*. Soon, players were appearing at monthly meetings, and a fan club banner, which would hang for years over an end arena barrier, was purchased.

The first major Rangers Fan Club event was an end-of-season dinner and dance held at the Hotel Martinique in March 1954. A fan club skit was followed by manager Frank Boucher and *New York Times* reporter Joe Nichols, who performed a song-and-dance duet to "Are You from Dixie?"

Hollywood comic Gabe Dell and other show business personalities also entertained, as did some Rangers, including Doug Bentley.

Even in its earlier days, the fan club dealt with serious issues. Soon after Bernie Geoffrion, then a Montreal Canadien, clubbed Rangers rookie Ron Murphy, seriously injuring the forward, the fan club dispatched a stern letter to the NHL president, Clarence Campbell, urging severe disciplinary action.

Campbell thanked the fan club for its interest and also told the RFC to mind its own business.

Through the years, unusual fans have managed to emerge distinctly from the crowd. One was Paul Gardella, a tall, handsome former FBI man who occupied a front row mezzanine seat at the old Garden with pal Seymour "Lefty" Adelson, who worked in the Garment Center.

ABOVE: Rangers fans enjoy a game at the Garden. *Photo by David Perlmutter*

Their mezzanine seats placed Gardella and Adelson directly behind the old Garden press box, enabling them to regularly schmooze with the beat reporters. Gardella's razor-sharp wit and Adelson's good nature turned them into media personalities.

Gardella set an unofficial record of sorts, having seen more than 1,000 consecutive games despite blizzards, hurricanes, and any other storms that hit the city.

On one occasion, the Garden entertained thoughts of canceling a Rangers-Red Wings contest because a snowstorm had brought the Big Apple to a halt. The game was played, and the turnout proved a testament to Rangers fans' loyalty. A crowd of 13,040 showed up, including Gardella and Adelson.

A more visible character was a fan who showed up a few minutes before every game wearing a gold *lamé* jacket. The guy would carry a slide trombone in his hand and walk along the arena aisle until he reached the home bench. He would then triumphantly point his slide upward toward the balcony and blow an E-flat loud enough for the whole Garden to hear. That done, he would proceed to his seat to enjoy the game.

Some fans were more militant. Brooklynite George Feeney once organized pickets to protest Muzz Patrick's work as a manager. He also imported "Muzz Must Go" balloons.

High school teacher Marvin Resnick was another colorful personality. During the dog years of Muzz Patrick's managership in the early 1960s, Resnick also organized a "Muzz Must Go" campaign.

According to the story—apocryphal as it may be—Resnick carried his "Muzz Must Go" picket sign along the Eighth Avenue sidewalk near 49th Street. He was urging other fans to boycott the game to protest Patrick's stewardship.

Suddenly, he checked his watch. It was 7:25 p.m. Resnick looked for the nearest trash can, dumped his picket sign, and galloped up to his balcony seat to catch the opening face-off. Following the puck was more important than pursuing the protest.

The Rovers inspired an altogether different breed of fan—youngsters who could not afford NHL tickets or were too young to stay up late for the big-league match.

During World War II, the Rovers donated the entire end balcony seats to the Police Athletic League. The PAL youngsters would arrive as early as 11 a.m. at the 49th Street balcony entrance, although the doors wouldn't open until 1 p.m. They would read newspapers or magazines and discuss the upcoming games. Between noon and 12:30 p.m., Met League players would walk past, heading west to the dressing room entrance on 49th Street near Ninth Avenue. If one of the Met Leaguers such as a top player like

Bob Johnson of the Brooklyn Torpedoes was recognized, some of the PAL kids would hit him up for an autograph.

Nothing proved the early-bird PAL youngsters' devotion more than their durability on subfreezing days. No matter how frigid the weather, the arrival of a grey-uniformed security guard around 12:45 p.m. was a major event. His presence meant that the doors would soon open and "The Big Sprint" would take place.

Shooting for the best seats, a phalanx of kids would burst past the turnstiles as soon as the ushers opened the doors. They would then dash up the stairs, sometimes three steps at a time. Those lucky dozen or so who reached the top first would adroitly tap dance down the steep balcony steps, where they would find their choice seats and await the Met League match at 1:30 p.m.

No matter who the fan was, he paid his money and thus had the privilege to boo players he disliked. From time to time, these would be members of the home team.

Rangers fans were particularly hard on Lynn Patrick when he joined the club in the late 1930s. Blueshirts followers believed that his father, Lester, was showing favoritism. Brother Muzz, who would later become a Ranger, remembered it well.

"They called Lynn everything," Muzz said. "The 'Boss' Son' . . . 'Go Home to Your Mother' . . . 'Sonja.' . . . They called him Sonja because he was a fancy skater, and that's when [figure skater] Sonja Henie was so popular.

"Another reason [fans hassled him] was that he took Art Somers' place at left wing.

Somers was a favorite at the time. So the fans resented Lynn."

In the end, Lynn got the last laugh when he became the first NHL player in 15 years to score 30 goals in a season. (He finished with 32.) Lynn was also named the 1941 All-Star left wing.

"Allan Stanley wasn't as lucky," Muzz recalled. "The Rangers fans rode him right out of town. I remember I was on the Coast when Frank Boucher sent him to Vancouver, and Stanley told me he was glad to get away from the booing. Then he came back, and it was just as bad. When we had a chance to trade him for Bill Gadsby, he went to Chicago."

What drew the fans' ire in Stanley's case, Patrick believed, was his introduction to New York as "the $70,000 investment." That's what Rangers management paid Providence in cash and players to snag the defenseman. It was a huge amount at the time.

"That was another thing," Muzz said. "He was getting his name in the columns and going out with some showgirls. Kay Starr was one, I remember. But I think the thing that annoyed the fans was his slow skating style. It was the same with Harry Howell. Fans seemed to resent the gliders, but they loved the little scrappers. They never booed them."

Another big man who suffered from the fans' indignities was defenseman Gus Kyle, a former Royal Canadian Mounted Policeman.

"But Gus wasn't that tough," Muzz recalled. "He couldn't live up to it. And

he wasn't mobile enough to be a good defenseman."

After the Americans exited the NHL in 1942, Rangers fans could not direct their cheering against any loyal opponent until the Islanders arrived in 1972. However, the void did not prevent Blueshirts rooters from exercising their vocal cords. Rival players such as Ted Lindsay, Milt Schmidt, and Ken Reardon made excellent targets because of their own rough styles. The chants that drifted down from the balcony were often priceless and reflected a frontier spirit that permeated the cheap seats.

This spirit was also reflected by the "cup hockey" played along the topmost reaches of the balcony. Fans would crush a paper soda cup and kick the makeshift puck around in games that sometimes included as many as 20 participants.

A major balcony operation involved saving seats for late arrivals. One venerable fan named Tim Murphy specialized in seat saving in the unreserved side balcony section. According to those who knew him, Murphy and his corps of sidekicks would control sections of the balcony for which they would receive 50 cents apiece per seat saved. This practice ended with the closing of the old Garden.

Once the Islanders entered the NHL and became a force, the rivalry between Rangers fans and their Nassau counterparts became more intense than the one involving the teams.

A major turnabout in their relationship occurred when the Isles upset the Blueshirts in the 1975 playoffs. As Al Arbour's sextet

ABOVE: Angela Sarro and her late husband, Tom, first began to attend Rangers games in the 1950s. *From the Stan Fischler Collection by Barry Alperstein*

became dominant and the Rangers slipped in the late 1970s, a more vehement tone developed between the two blocs of rooters. It was further intensified after the Rangers unexpectedly beat the Isles in the 1979 playoffs.

Two major developments in the 1980s further enflamed passions. When the Isles won four straight Stanley Cups, their fans took on an air of superiority. They would denigrate the Rangers and their fans with chants of "1940, 1940!"

The second episode involved the controversial bodycheck delivered on Rangers forward Ulf Nilsson. The Swede's leg was severely damaged, and Rangers fans accused Denis Potvin of deliberately injuring their ace. The next time the Isles visited the Garden, Potvin was greeted with chorus after chorus of the now-famous "Potvin sucks."

As long as the Isles had four Stanley Cups and the Rangers three—the last being in 1940—Isles fans had the ultimate squelch: "1940, 1940!" But that trump cheer ended in 1994 when Mark Messier and company finally brought the fourth Cup to Manhattan.

The balance of power was divided by thirds in 1982, when the Devils moved into the Meadowlands. Like their Island counterparts, Devils fans were mostly suburbanites, many of whom had previously rooted for the Rangers.

In both cases—in Island and Jersey—Rangers fans numbered up to half the crowd when the Blueshirts were in town. The result was cheering and counter-cheering until both sides were winded.

Historically, there have always been uprisings among the rival factions. Americans and Rangers fans battled as far back as the late 1920s, and Islanders and Rangers fans started getting physical in the mid-1970s.

The advent of high-salaried players followed by higher ticket prices somewhat altered the texture of local hockey spectators.

When the present Garden opened in 1968, its configuration changed the balcony as a rooting entity. But the balconyites of the Eighth Avenue Garden became the "Blue Seaters" of its successor.

Renowned for their humor and notorious for their vocal cords, the "Blue Seaters" created an image of their own with some of their original barbs. Their Nassau equivalent—if there could be such a comparison—would be a group of diehards from Staten Island who occupied the last few rows near the Coliseum rafters.

Clashes between fans and players have been infrequent, although some such episodes did gain media attention.

One of the most explosive erupted during the Islanders-Rangers playoff series in 1990. In the opening game at the Garden, Pat LaFontaine was simultaneously elbowed by James Patrick and checked by Chris Nilan of the Rangers. Knocked unconscious, LaFontaine was removed from the ice and was eventually taken to an ambulance in the bowels of the Garden. By this time, Rangers fans had been provoked by Islanders enforcers Mick Vukota and Ken Baumgartner, who had attacked two less belligerent Rangers players.

Enraged, a group of Rangers fans descended on LaFontaine's ambulance and began rocking it as it headed toward 33rd Street en route to the hospital. Both LaFontaine and the ambulance finally escaped.

That type of fanaticism is certainly the exception, but such enthusiasm has always been present. Among the most enthusiastic fans from the 1970s to 1980s was a Brooklynite named Bob Comas, otherwise known as "The Chief." According to Larry Sloman, author of Thin Ice: A Season In Hell with the *New York Rangers*, Comas was borderline unique.

Said Sloman, "'The Chief' was New York's wholesale answer to Baltimore Orioles cheerleader 'Wild' Bill Hagy. They were both from a long line of official and unofficial team mascots, average workaday fans who somehow lived out their fantasies by dressing up—or down—and rallying the troops behind the home team. The Garden had been blessed with another quasi-official cheerleader years earlier, 'Dancing Harry,' who would tap dance around at courtside during the Knicks' games, putting the hex on the opposing team."

During games, "The Chief" would do an NHL version of Geronimo. He would wear an Indian headdress at the games and deliver a play-by-play of the action from his seat. When the Rangers scored, "The Chief" would leap from his seat and dash down the aisle, shrieking something akin to a Cherokee war chant.

Some Rangers fans actually became authors. Ira Gitler, a native of Manhattan, began going to Rangers games at the start of the 1940s and was a member of the Rangers Fan Club when it was organized a decade later. An accomplished jazz writer, Gitler also turned to hockey writing and has been a press-box regular for more than a dozen years.

Sloman became a Rangers fan when he was in junior high. After one visit to the Garden, he had become a fan for life. Like so many balconyites, he would play cup hockey with other fans in empty areas of the old Garden. He later graduated to roller hockey in Queens and, finally, the ice game.

Islanders fans developed an intensity all their own, first suffering through the early hapless years and then enjoying the rise of a dynasty. Similar uprisings to those at the Garden occurred at Nassau Coliseum.

The *New York Times* once described the following incident that took place in the late 1970s at a Blackhawks-Islanders game: "One incensed fan threw a container of beer at Dave Newell, the referee, and at the buzzer, spectators mobbed the visiting team's exit ramp, threatening the players and throwing debris at them. Two men were arrested and charged with disorderly conduct."

The *Times* went on to add, "At one time, Nassau Coliseum rooters were indulgent and parental. But this season, whenever the Islanders are losing a game, the fans turn with chameleon-like quickness into a raucous and dangerous crowd. The Islanders organization and its players point ironically to the young team's success as the source of the problem."

But for the most part, decorum has been maintained at the Garden and Nassau Coliseum, as it was at Continental Airlines Arena in New Jersey before the Devils moved to a new arena in Newark.

Both Islanders and Devils followers approximated the pattern of the Garden faithful. An Islanders booster club was organized soon after the franchise entered the NHL and highlighted every season with an annual dinner and dance. The Devils did likewise. Fans of all three clubs can be found at various NHL geographic points doing road trips, just as the Rovers' Blue Line Club did in the 1940s and early 1950s.

The enthusiasm generated by fans, whether from a front-row seat or the highest pew in the arena, also continues today.

The fans don't have Red Storey to dump on anymore, but it would not surprise anyone to hear the chant, "KOHARSKI, YOU'RE A BUM!"

That's the privilege that comes with being a Met-area hockey fan.

One of the most lovable of all such rooters dated back to the earliest days of the Rangers Fan Club. Petite, ever smiling, and always generous, Cecile, or Ceil, Saidel was the type of person you always felt like hugging because she was so nice.

A resident of the Bronx, Ceil had endured years of Rangers hardship with her own special dignity. Always present to support the team, she rarely missed a home game. During the 1993-94 season, Saidel had closely followed the Rangers, her favorites, in their quest for the Stanley Cup in the spring of 1994.

While the Rangers were beating the Capitals in the second playoff round, Ceil's friends noticed that she had not attended Game 5 of the series at the Garden. They became concerned and notified the police. Her body was found in her apartment. Ceil Saidel had been murdered a month before the Rangers won the Stanley Cup.

On June 14, 1994, the night that the Rangers annexed the championship, Adam Graves took time out to remember one of the club's most ardent supporters. "Ceil," said Graves, "took the Garden ghost and kicked it out of the rafters."

Why Rangers Fandom is Genetic

When Dr. John McMullen bought the New Jersey Devils in 1982, he made a two-part promise: 1) The Meadowlands Arena would sell out every game and 2) Rangers fans that called Jersey home would soon immediately switch their allegiance to the Garden State sextet.

Even a decade later, Dr. McMullen realized that this promise was one he wouldn't be able to keep. New Jersey residents, who had been Rangers fans before the Devils arrived in East Rutherford, maintained their support for the Blueshirts—and so did their children and their grandchildren.

And when Doc Mac was asked to explain this phenomenon, he tersely explained: "It's genetic!"

No family exemplifies this devotion to Rangerville more than the Gelman Family.

It all began with Sam Gelman, who became a Rangers fan during the 1930s. In time, Sam would pass on his hockey devotion to his son Harold who, in turn, passed it on down the line to his own son Randall.

Like many Rangers' fans, the Gelman gentlemen regard the Garden, where they still hold season tickets, much as a second home.

Reminiscing with his family, Hal remembers the olden days, throwing it all the way back to the 1940s, when it was actually possible to see three good hockey games in one day at the old Garden.

"In those days," Hal remembers, "There was a doubleheader on Sunday afternoon. It started with a Met League game at 1:30 and when that was over the Rangers farm team, the Rovers, played an Eastern League game...Once that was over, we would go down to Eighth Avenue and get spaghetti at Buitoni's and then hustle back for the Ranger game at 8:30."

Like other aficionados, Gelman had to line up at the 49th Street balcony entrance for the cheapest seats. When the doors opened, he would race up the stairs hoping to get one of the best seats in the house—in the first two rows of a side balcony pew. Anything available after that offered an obstructed view of the near side boards.

"In those days, the fan-favorite was Alex Kaleta," Hal chuckles. "His nickname was 'Killer Kaleta' and he was a little on the nutty side. The ironic part of it was he really didn't like to get hit at all, and was the furthest thing from a killer on ice."

In the old Garden days, the Rangers practiced in an enclosed rink called Iceland, which was on the top floor of the arena. Hal's dedication to the team took him to as many practices as he could manage. Eventually his loyalty drew the admiration of both the boys on the ice and the men behind the bench. When former Rangers star Phil Watson became coach in 1955, Hal and the new mentor became close friends. From time to time, Watson would allow Hal to put on the goalie equipment and practice with the team.

As Hal explained, "These were the days before any goalie wore face protection, but there was a see-through plastic covering that could pass for a mask, and I wore one of them. What I remember is Hall of Famer Andy Bathgate taking some shots at me, and some other guys such as defenseman Larry Cahan and Gerry Foley who were close friends of mine. That was a lot of fun."

Gelman was a charter member of the Rangers Fan Club, which was organized during the 1950-51 season. From time to time, the fan club took excursions to Boston to watch their favorites go up against the Bruins, at Beantown's *Gahden*.

One of Hal's favorite memories was a pair of home-and-home games against the Bruins

– Saturday afternoon in Boston and Sunday night in New York.

According to Gelman, Lorne "The Gump" Worsley had thrown a party the night before the afternoon tilt in Boston. Although Watson told Hal to be sure the players watched their curfews, Gelman made an exception for one of his favorite Rangers.

"So, now it's Saturday afternoon, a couple of hours before game time," Gelman remembers, " and I am standing by the Rangers locker room, when Gump comes over to me and says 'No way am I going to see the puck today—I have an unbelievable hangover.' "So I told Gumper to get his ass out there and not let Phil know, because these two guys really hated each other, and Phil would go nuts. Well, Gump suited up, went out there and made a bunch of unbelievable saves and beat Boston 2-0. It was one helluva [sic] shutout."

When the teams returned to New York on Sunday night, Boston lit up Worsley to the tune of 6 to 1.

"It seemed," adds Gelman, " that Gumper was still hungover."

While still a member of the fan club, Gelman also was Watson's unofficial *aide de camp*. When the Blueshirts started losing, Watson asked his general manager, Muzz Patrick, to send Worsley to the Springfield farm team and the GM obliged, only to recall the trouble-maker two weeks later.

Gelman: "Phil calls me and says, 'Go down to Springfield and bring Gumper back.' So I go to the Springfield arena and find Gump, and tell him Phil wants him back in New York. When Gump hears that he says, 'YOU tell Phil to go F— himself, I'm not coming back.' When I hear that, I go over to Eddie Shore, who ran the Springfield farm club, and tell him the Rangers want Gump back. In those days, nobody messed with Shore, so I bring Worsley back to the Garden."

While all of this was going on, Hal fell in love with his current wife Gina. At the time, Gelman managed to turn his girlfriend into an avid

Rangers fan, which at this point had become a family requirement. She easily became a convert after watching a Bruins-Rangers game in which Terry Sawchuk shut out Boston 1-0.

"I told Gina she was watching the greatest goalie ever, and on that night Sawchuk was at his best," Gelman remembers.

Hal cites that night as one of his most memorable games. But as far as sheer excitement goes, he vows he will never forget the Rangers-Canadiens playoff matchup in the spring of 1967, when Red Berenson started at center for the Blueshirts. On this night, the Gelmans were there with Hal's old friend Morty and his wife. When the game went into overtime, the fans were at the edge of their seats, especially Morty and Hal.

"Montreal was a heavy favorite against us," Hal recalls, "But when Berenson got a clean breakaway, it looked like we had it in the bag. Instead, Red hit the goal post and the puck didn't go in. When that happens, Morty got so excited, he leaped up, turned around, and swung his arms in disgust but wound up punching his wife and knocking her out cold. Shortly thereafter, Montreal's John Ferguson went around our defenseman Arnie Brown and scored to add to our misery."

In 1968, Hal and Gina welcomed the newest member of their Ranger-fanatic household: a baby boy they named Randall. . In no time at all, Randy joined the fandom.

"My favorite Ranger is Rod Gilbert," notes Randy, " He was the first Ranger I met, and from that time on, I followed his career until he retired."

When Hal suffered a heart attack in the 1970s, he was forced to miss every game till he recovered, but Randy maintained the family's Rangers romance in his father's absence.

Sick in bed again during the Rangers' 1994 Cup run, Hal glowed when Vancouver was defeated.

"Gina came into my room and popped a bottle of champagne for us to drink," he gleams.

Hal eventually recovered, and the bond that the sport had forged between him and his son took them as far as Toronto and even to Sweden for the Rangers' preseason games at Stockholm in 2011.

"Wherever we went," says Hal, "It was simply [about] enjoying a Rangers game with my son."

When Randy's wife, also aptly named Sam, gave birth to another Gelman boy, they decided to name the baby in honor of none other than the notorious Blueshirt, Sean Avery.

Randy explained, "We loved Sean Avery and I wanted to name him Sean, but Sam insisted on Shane. We settled this with a bet... Avery's number was 16 and if the baby was born on the 16th, the baby's name would be Sean, if not it would be Shane. When I told the original Sean Avery, he was all excited and wanted updates on the kid's birth.

"Now, I am having lunch with Sam at an Italian restaurant, and suddenly she goes into labor. That night, on September 13th, Shane was born. A few months later, Avery hosted us at his restaurant, Tiny's, and brought a bunch of gifts."

"My wife Sam and I," Randy concludes," Continue raising our family in a Rangers house with my daughter Anna and sons Zach—and of course Shane."

After all, as Dr. McMullen noted: *It's genetic!*

THREE
GREATEST
RANGERS
T E A M S

The defending Stanley Cup champs in 1933-34.
From the Stan Fischler Collection

DOUBLE DIPPING

THE CUP

1928 ◆ 33

Although they were born a year after the Americans, the Rangers immediately developed their own legion of fans, and an intense rivalry grew between the two New York teams. Lester Patrick and the Rangers had an advantage, having acquired Frank Boucher and brothers Bill and Bun Cook. Bill Cook led the NHL in scoring in the 1926-27 season, and the Rangers finished first in the American Division while the Americans finished fourth in the Canadian section.

According to Canadian hockey biographer Ron McAllister, the Rangers' (dynasty was actually born the first night Patrick's team skated on Garden ice that first season. They faced the Stanley Cup champion Montreal Maroons, who were loaded with such stars as Reg Noble, Hap Emms, Dune Munro, Babe Siebert, Nels Stewart, and Clint Benedict in goal.

To the astonishment of the veteran Maroons, neither team scored throughout the first two periods of play. As the third period rolled on, a stirring crescendo of cheers descended on the Rangers from the highest reaches of the Garden balcony, and the players responded.

Bill Cook stole the puck from the Maroons and sent a pass to Boucher, who relayed the puck to Bun Cook. The Montreal defense boxed Bun into a corner and seemed to have stalled the attack. According to McAllister, "Bun fought and dug like a terrier after a groundhog and sent a pass out to brother Bill. He grabbed it and raced straight in on Clint Benedict to beat the goalkeeper's dive with a slow shot.

"After what seemed years, the bell rang, and the game was over. Bill Cook and his Rangers had defeated the defending NHL champions! That was the real beginning of the New York Rangers as a hockey team."

In their first playoff test, the Rangers ran head-on into a hot Boston Bruins team for a two-game total-goals series. In the first game at Boston, the teams skated off with a 0-0 tie, but Boston annexed the round with a 3-1 win at Madison Square Garden.

Patrick realized that some building still had to be done if he was to win the Stanley Cup, and by the 1927-28 campaign, he believed that all the necessary ingredients had been added. All that remained for him was to heat gently and stir.

The Cooks-Boucher line was augmented by a rock-ribbed defense consisting of Taffy Abel, Ching Johnson, and Leo Bourgault. Other stars included Murray Murdoch, Paul Thompson, Alex Gray, Billy Boyd, and Laurie Scott. They formed the nucleus of a team that would be near or at the top of the NHL for years to come. That was the real beginning of the New York Rangers as a hockey team,

Bill Cook was supplanted as the American Division's leading scorer by linemate Frank Boucher, and the Rangers, after finishing second behind Boston, routed Pittsburgh in the first playoff round. Then they gained revenge against the Bruins with a 5-2 victory in a two-game total-goals series, which catapulted them into the Stanley Cup finals—a best-of-five showdown against the mighty Maroons.

To some observers, it was the hockey duel of the century. The powerful Montreal sextet represented the most hardened professionals on ice.

The Rangers were kids by comparison, but they were enormously skilled and determined. And they had wise Lester Patrick to orchestrate their clever moves.

Playing all the games at Montreal's Forum because a circus occupied Madison Square Garden, the teams squared off on April 5, 1928, and the Maroons muzzled the Rangers 2-0. That set the stage for one of hockey's most memorable moments.

During a play in the second game, Rangers goalie Lorne Chabot was severely injured and unable to continue. With no substitute goaltender on his roster, manager Lester Patrick himself decided to skate between the pipes and replace Chabot.

This seemed preposterous. Patrick was all of 44 years old, and his experience as a player had basically been in a defensive position. Only once did he play goal, when Hec Fowler, his goalie on the Victoria Cougars, was thrown out of a game.

Bill Cook scored for the Rangers early in the third period, but the Maroons tied it up. The game went into overtime, and Patrick held fast until Frank Boucher sank the winner at 7:05 of the first sudden-death period.

The Maroons won the third game 2-0, and it appeared that they would dispose of the Rangers. However, the gallant New Yorkers would have no part in any defeatist talk. Chabot was replaced in goal by Joe Miller, who surprised the hockey world by shutting out the Maroons 1-0 in the fourth match.

On April 14, 1928, the climactic fifth and final game was played at the Forum. Once again, the lithe Frank Boucher, considered the cleanest player ever to skate in the NHL, was the hero, scoring the winning goal in the Rangers' 2-1 triumph. In some respects, it was one of the most exciting scores ever made. The Rangers were playing shorthanded at the time, and Boucher had been dispatched to the ice by Patrick simply to rag the puck and kill time. Nobody anticipated a Rangers goal.

But Boucher controlled the puck at center ice and played it off the boards in the direction of Maroons defenseman Dune Munro. The quick-witted Boucher realized that the puck didn't have much speed on it and was slowing down midway between himself and Munro. When Munro dashed for the rubber, Boucher realized he had his chance.

Boucher raced against Munro for the puck and fooled him to gain possession. He made a clean breakaway, took aim against

Benedict, and scored. Thus, in only their second year of competition, the Rangers were the world champions of hockey.

The Rangers didn't win back-to-back Stanley Cups, but they continued to be a threat, mostly because of Boucher and the Cook Brothers. "Bill Cook," said Patrick, "is the brainiest player I ever saw and the greatest right-winger of all time."

They were good enough to develop into one of the foremost hockey clubs at a time when the NHL was still establishing itself in New York. The Broadway Blueshirts, as they were known in those days, rightfully earned the title of "the classiest team in hockey."

Lester Patrick's adroit orchestration of the roster had provided his Blueshirts with the nucleus of a contender for years to come.

The Cooks-Boucher line remained one of the league's best into the 1930s. Ching Johnson continued to be the defensive cornerstone, while John Ross Roach had become the new goalie.

By the fall of 1932, Patrick had replaced Roach with Andy Aitkenhead as starting goalie—a fortuitous move, particularly in view of the fact that Lester had traded Lorne Chabot to Toronto after the 1928 Cup win. As luck would have it, Aitkenhead and Chabot would face each other in the 1933 Stanley Cup finals.

A native of Glasgow, Scotland, the blond-haired, blue-eyed Aitkenhead caught the attention of fans because he enjoyed wearing a tweed cap while playing goal. Coach Patrick had no problem with it since Andy proved to be an excellent puck stopper.

While Johnson's 1928 Cup partner, Taffy Abel, had been dealt, the Blueshirts still had a formidable backline, including a new ace, Earl Seibert. The Rangers also had another Siebert, Albert Charles. Better known as Babe, the left wing would win the Hart Trophy with the Montreal Canadiens in 1936-37. It's noteworthy that Earl Seibert, like Babe, is a member of Hockey's Hall of Fame.

Complementing the Cooks and Boucher was a corps of gifted young forwards, including Cecil Dillon, Butch Keeling, Art Somers, and Ott Heller. One of the best of all was Murray Murdoch, a dedicated, tenacious forward who would one day set an NHL Iron Man record.

Although Murdoch broke in with the original club, he matured in the early 1930s and would eventually complete 11 seasons without missing a game. He played a total of 508 consecutive games and played in every one of the Rangers' 55 Stanley Cup playoff contests in that span.

"Lester was getting us ready for another run at the Stanley Cup," Boucher remembered. "Earl Seibert was just past his teens, but you could see that he was going to be a star. Ditto for Ott Heller. Earl was 6-foot-2 and Ott was a 6-footer, big for their time."

When the 1931-32 season ended, the Rangers had won their division but were swept in three straight games by the Toronto Maple Leafs in the Stanley Cup finals. It was somewhat of an embarrassment to Patrick because Chabot had won all three games for Toronto.

ABOVE: The Rangers celebrate winning their first Stanley Cup at New York City Hall. Mayor Jimmy Walker is at the center behind the Cup, with goalie Lorne Chabot to the immediate left and coach Lester Patrick to the right. Other stars include Bill Cook (fourth from left) and Frank Boucher (fifth from left). *From the Stan Fischler Collection*

A year after their first-place finish, the Rangers wound up third in the American Division with a record of 23-17-8; they were only four points behind the division-leading Boston Bruins and actually had the same number of points as Toronto, which led the Canadian Division.

In the early 1930s, the NHL had several ways of determining playoff winners. In the spring of 1933, the first round comprised two games, and the team that scored the most goals was determined the winner.

The Blueshirts faced the Canadiens in the first round and bested them 5-2 at the Garden. The second game finished in a 3-3 tie, giving New York an 8-5 series win.

Detroit faced the Blueshirts in the semifinal round, and this, too, was a total-goals series played in New York. The Rangers won 2-0 and then 4-3, which catapulted them into the Stanley Cup finals.

In those days, the finals were decided in a best-of-five series. As luck would have it, the Rangers faced Toronto, which had I just played the second longest game in NHL history against the Bruins. It had lasted through six overtimes plus change before the Leafs won.

"When the Toronto players came to face us at the Garden for the opener [on April 4, 1933], they were dead on their feet," said Boucher. "We had no trouble beating them 5-1."

After Game 1 at the Garden, the next three contests were played in Toronto starting four days later, giving the Leafs a much-needed rest.

A refreshed Toronto squad took a 1-0 lead early in the first period of Game 2, but after that, Aitkenhead shut the door, and Heller, Bill Cook, and Earl Seibert scored for New York.

The Leafs finally broke through in Game 3 when Red Horner shattered a 2-2 tie at 8:29 of the third period, forcing a fourth game.

Chabot played well for the Leafs in Game 4, but Aitkenhead was even better.

After three periods of regulation play, neither team had scored, and the contest went into overtime.

With seven and a half minutes gone in sudden death, the Cooks-Boucher line was on the ice. Patrick decided that it was time for a change, and Bun Cook skated to the bench while Butch Keeling took his place.

Boucher remembered the following sequence well: "Bill and I were heading for the bench, too, when suddenly, Butch came up with the puck and fired a rink-wide pass to Bill, who, seeing an opening and Butch with the puck, had quickly switched direction."

Bill nabbed the puck close to the right boards at the Toronto blue line and then swerved left toward the goal.

When the Rangers right wing looked up, he could see air on Chabot's right.

"Lorne gave me the whole stick side," Cook recalled. "I shot the puck at that opening."

The Toronto goalie moved too late; the red light flashed, and the Rangers had won their second Stanley Cup in only seven years.

As it happened, the second championship would be the last shining moment for future Hall of Famers such as Boucher, the Cook brothers, and Ching Johnson.

The next two seasons saw the Blueshirts ousted in the first round by teams from Montreal, first the Maroons and then the Canadiens.

Age had caught up with this singularly outstanding inner core of stars, and by 1935-36, the Rangers failed to make the playoffs all together.

Lester realized that it was time to rejuvenate his team, and soon players such as Babe Pratt, Phil Watson, Alex Shibicky, and even the manager's two sons, Lynn and Murray Patrick, were being developed in the Rangers' farm system.

Each would be pivotal in leading New York to a third Stanley Cup in 1940, following in the skate steps of their Cup predecessors in 1928 and 1933.

THE SUDDEN-DEATH VICTORY

◆ 1940 ◆

Had Rangers president, general manager, and coach Lester Patrick succumbed to charges of nepotism, his club would never have blossomed into a dominant team in the late 1930s and early 1940s, and it certainly would never have won the Stanley Cup in 1940.

But in his sons, Lynn and Murray, or "Muzz," Lester saw two gifted hockey players who belonged on the team whether the fans and newspaper critics liked it or not and whether Lester liked it or not—because he, above all, was extremely wary of having even one, let alone two, of his boys skate for the Rangers.

Patrick had carefully watched his sons' development from their days as amateur athletes. "The most amazing thing of all," said Lester, "was that the situation was never planned or even dreamed. I never steered or pushed the boys. It just happened."

When Lester opened the Rangers' training camp that autumn of 1933, Lynn had earned a starting assignment with the strong Montreal Royals' amateur team, a farm club of the Maroons.

Muzz was not inclined toward hockey at that time. An 18-year-old who weighed in

at 215 pounds, Muzz preferred pro football and six-day bicycle racing. When watching the competitor in action, an insightful athletic critic could tell that Muzz had the rare spirit of a winner.

His father was just such a critic.

"Muzz," said Lester, "had started that six-day race with Gerard Debaets of Belgium. He was pushed around, bounced on and off the track like a handball. He was big and fast and game, but he wasn't a six-day bike rider. Well, he was for a while. He stuck it out gamely through the fourth day, but injuries made him quit. I hoped this had cured him of six-day riding, and it did.

"Now, he decided to become heavyweight champion of the boxing world. When? As soon as the track season was over. He had promised to run the half-mile. He did, too, in June, and he set a new record."

Meanwhile, Lynn had played so well for the Royals that Lester invited his son to the Rangers' training camp in the fall of 1934. Lester was critical of Lynn. The last thing he wanted was to be accused of favoritism. Above all, Lester wanted a winning team, and he certainly didn't think that Lynn had matured enough for the Rangers. But when he told some of his associates so, they disagreed.

"Are your eyes going bad, Lester?" Frank Boucher asked. "Lynn is a pro. He's ready."

Boucher wasn't alone. Several of the Rangers pestered Lester, but Bill Cook's opinion was the one that mattered most. The team's captain was persuasive. "You'd better sign the boy to a contract before somebody else does," he warned.

That did it. Lynn was signed to a Rangers contract and assigned to the third line.

Lester's son was to be tested by opponents and fans alike. They reddened Lynn's ears, calling him a prima donna and a daddy's boy, but Lynn was too strong a character and too good a hockey player to be thwarted.

Perhaps the best proof of Lynn's ability was provided by none other than Conn Smythe, who offered Lester $20,000—at that time, a lot of money—for Lynn less than two years after he made his New York debut.

That left only Muzz on the sidelines, and Lester worried about him, concerned that the big fellow would get hurt as a boxer.

But Muzz could take care of himself. He knocked out 203-pound Phil Keating in two rounds and won the Amateur Heavyweight Championship of Canada all before he was 21.

Muzz studied under veteran trainer Jimmy Bronson at Stillman's Gym in New York City. The plan was to move Muzz into the pro ranks on June 28, 1936, but first he was scheduled to meet Bill Gould for the Catholic Youth Organization's championship. The date was May 11, 1936, and Muzz ousted Gould. He was ready to go pro, or so Bronson thought.

What Muzz neglected to tell the trainer was that he had made a promise to his mother that he would quit the sport after he fought Gould, and he kept his promise.

Bronson's heart was broken, but boxing's loss turned out to be hockey's gain.

Lester was as careful easing Muzz into the NHL as he had been with Lynn. The youngster was broken in with the Rovers, the Rangers' top amateur team, then Philadelphia, a strong minor-league pro club. By the 1938-39 season, the two Patrick boys were Rangers teammates: Muzz played defense and Lynn left wing.

The Patrick boys lifted the Rangers to heights experienced only by the Cook brothers and Boucher. The Cooks were gone, and Boucher had moved behind the bench to coach the Rangers while Lester handled the managing.

They were a marvelous crew, finishing second behind Boston in the 1939-40 season, but knocking the Bruins out of the playoffs in a six-game opening round. Some observers believed that Muzz provided the inspirational lever over Boston. Until then, the Bruins had been a hard-rock crew, dominated by the ever-rough Eddie Shore. But Shore overdid it on one occasion, and Muzz moved in on Shore and battered him to the ice. The Bruins were never the same.

The Patricks were not the only brothers making the Rangers a winning team. Neil and Mac Colville worked the second forward line with Alex Shibicky. The trio would have been a first line on any other team but on the Rangers, whose top unit comprised Lynn Patrick, Phil Watson, and Bryan Hextall.

Boucher once described that line and some of his other aces thusly: "Phil, the center, was a very unusual fellow with a most unusual temperament. Despite his Scottish name, he was a Frenchman, either laughing in a high-pitched squeal or so low in spirits as to be in tears. His volatile nature surfaced particularly later on, when he became the Rangers' coach in the early 1950s. If the team was doing well, he'd beam and preen and shout, 'That's my boys!' When we lost, though, he'd grow bitter and shriek at his players, often in front of the writers.

"When he was excited, Phil's English grew confused, and he was almost always excited in his early years with our club. Once, Johnny Gottselig, the great old left-winger of the Hawks, was needling Phil on the ice, and finally, in exasperation, Phil screamed at him, 'You . . . you . . . you been-has, you!' Gottselig was leading the Hawks in scoring at the time.

"Hextall was Watson's right-winger; though a left-hand shot, [he was] a hard rock of large bone structure and taciturn nature who could score off his forehand or backhand equally well. I always dreaded playing Detroit when the Wings had a body-thumper named 'Black' Jack Stewart on the defense. Every time they met, 'Hex' and 'Blackjack' belted each other. Neither would give ground, so it was a succession of hammerings which could be heard all over the arena. Surprisingly enough, neither ever seemed to lose his temper; they simply reveled in the bumping.

"We used to alternate Clint Smith, Alf Pike, Dutch Hiller, and Kilby MacDonald on our third line. Smith, called 'Snuffy,' was a small fellow but exceedingly clever.

He was hard to hit and was an expert on face-offs and digging the puck from the corners. Pike, who, like Lynn and Neil and Phil, would coach after I was named general manager, joined us in my first season as the team's deep thinker. He'd been an outstanding Junior player in Winnipeg.

"I remember that a few days after he reported to training camp in the fall of he and Lester got bogged down on contract negotiations. When Alf told me that the difference was $500, I told him that if Lester didn't give it to him, I would. As I've said, I was making $4,500 then, but I was determined to succeed and was convinced Pike would help us. And so Alf went to Lester and told him he'd decided to sign. Lester was puzzled, naturally enough, and probed Pike to find out why the boy who'd been so stubborn had suddenly relented, and finally Alf admitted I'd said I'd give him the $500. Lester bawled the hell out of me for being soft, but my gamble—for it really had been that, I suppose—paid off; Lester came up with the $500.

"Dutch Hiller was the best skater on a club that could fly—a team whose skating and puck-handling abilities often have reminded me, in retrospect, of some of the best Montreal Canadiens freewheelers. Dutch wasn't too big, but he simply glided with an unusual gait in which he seemed to lift himself above the ice with each stride, and he became a consistent scorer, too. Kilby MacDonald was also a smooth, assured skater with a gliding stride. He could play on any line, filling in if players were injured, and was great to have around—pleasant, friendly, outgoing. All in all, it was a wonderful team. In fact, I'll say it now: it was the best hockey team I ever saw."

The semifinal victory over the Bruins sent the Rangers into the Cup finals against the Toronto Maple Leafs, a team that had finished eight points behind New York during the regular schedule but was capable of winning big games. Because of commitments at Madison Square Garden, the NHL decided that the first three games of the best-of-seven series would be played on New York ice, and the remainder would be fought in Toronto. But after the second game, the circus showed up a day early through some misunderstanding, and the Rangers and Leafs were forced to finish the series in Toronto. This change unnerved the New Yorkers, who had won the first pair of matches at home by scores of 2-1 and 6-2.

Playing before their home crowd, the Maple Leafs rose to the occasion, tying the series on 2-1 and 3-0 triumphs. The Rangers appeared to be in trouble—until the Patrick boys took over.

The fifth and pivotal game went into sudden-death overtime tied at 1-1. Back and forth the players raced in the extra period, desperately trying for the score. More than 10 minutes had passed without a red light when Lester Patrick watched his son, Lynn, clamber over the boards with linemates Phil Watson and Bryan Hextall.

A masterful playmaker, Watson dispatched a neat pass to Lynn Patrick, who hurled the puck past Toronto goalie Turk Broda at 11:43 of the overtime period. The Rangers were winners, 2-1.

New York needed only one more win to capture their first Stanley Cup since the halcyon days of Boucher and the Cooks, but Toronto wasn't about to play dead. The Leafs held the Rangers to a 2 tie with only three minutes remaining in regulation time.

At that point, Watson appeared to have beaten Broda cleanly, but the referee disallowed the score on the grounds that a Rangers player had one foot in the crease, the line that runs a yard in front of the goal. Watson was so piqued by the decision that he spat in the referee's face and somehow managed to get away with it!

Once again, sudden death was required. Both Lester Patrick and Boucher valiantly tried to keep the players motivated after the depressing setback on Watson's near-goal. Apparently, they succeeded. Lynn Patrick's line took the ice, and with 2:07 left in the period, Watson passed to Bryan Hextall, who fired the puck past Broda. This time, the goal was irrefutable; the Rangers had won the Stanley Cup!

The next season, 1940-41, was virtually the last Lynn and Muzz played together. World War II had begun, and Muzz had joined the U.S. Army. He was the first NHL player to do so. Starting as a buck private in Italy and France, he came out five years later as a captain.

Lynn played on, recording his greatest years. In 1941, he scored 44 points and tied Hextall for the most points scored on the club. The next year, he scored what was then a remarkable total of 32 goals, second only to Bill Cook in Rangers history at that time. In 1943 he led in assists with 39 and points with 61. Then he entered the army as a private, emerging two years later as a first lieutenant.

The 1940 Stanley Cup victory was the Rangers' last for a long time. When Muzz left for the armed forces, a good chunk of the New York spirit departed, and Lynn's exit severely depleted the team's resources. When the war ended, the brothers tried to pick up where they had left off with the Rangers. But they just didn't have it anymore.

It was appropriate that soon after Lynn and Muzz retired as players, their dad, Lester, the illustrious "Silver Fox," retired from the Garden after 20 memorable years.

Who would have believed that it would be 54 years before the Rangers would win another Stanley Cup?

THE GREATEST CUP TRIUMPH
◆ 1994 ◆

By the start of the 1993-94 season, Rangers fans had become sick and tired of hearing the chant "1940," which had been constantly uttered by their rivals on Long Island.

Of course, the taunt referred to the last time the Rangers had won the Stanley Cup. The number of years had reached 53 once the season began in October of 1993.

In a sense, the philosophy of Rangers rooters echoed the sentiment of former National Hockey League president John Ziegler. It was Ziegler who once observed of every NHL team, "What we sell is hope!"

And Rangers fans had considerable reason for optimism as the 1993-94 season unfolded.

Under GM Neil Smith and head coach Mike Keenan, the Blueshirts had crafted a solid lineup with a three-part foundation—captain Mark Messier at center, Brian Leetch on defense, and Mike Richter in goal.

With the likes of Sergei Zubov, Adam Graves, and Alexei Kovalev, the supporting cast was formidable as well, although it would be significantly improved by a spate of late-season trades.

The season began quite well for the Rangers—there were no injuries to speak of, and the players seemed to be in cohesion with each other. Keenan's squad was in position to make the postseason. However, the Blueshirts still felt something was missing and made key swaps to pick up Craig MacTavish, Glenn Anderson, Brian Noonan, and Steve Larmer.

By the end of the season, Richter had set the mark for most wins in one season by a Rangers goalie (42), Graves had set the mark for most goals in one season by a Ranger (52), and the Blueshirts had won the Presidents' Trophy and were favorites to win the Stanley Cup.

But before reaching that point, the Rangers had to win a couple of preliminary rounds. The first was against the Islanders, and it was during this series that the Blueshirts exacted revenge for their 1993 playoff elimination.

Although Ron Hextall had played erratic goal for the Isles during the 1993-94 campaign, he was sensational, shutting out Tampa Bay in the final week of the homestretch and guaranteeing the Isles a playoff berth. Hextall's experience and competitive fire were considered assets for an Islanders team that entered the postseason round as distinct underdogs.

Inexplicably, Hextall turned sieve in the opener at the Garden. He was beaten early and often, and when the dust had cleared, the Rangers had six goals and the Islanders none. This time, the final score was a precise barometer of play on the ice.

For Game 2, Islanders coach Al Arbour tried young Jamie McLennan in goal. He

was more sacrificial lamb than netminder. The final score read Rangers 6, Islanders 0. Once again, the count fully reflected the play. The Isles were totally humbled. There was nothing—absolutely nothing—positive to say about them. The Rangers, on the other hand, played like a perfectly balanced machine.

In a one-sided series such as this, the dominant club usually suffers a letdown, but such was not the case as the teams moved to Nassau. Hextall was futile again in Game 3—a 5-1 Rangers triumph—and then went down in flames 5-2 as the Blueshirts mercifully sent the Islanders on vacation.

In the next round, Washington at least won a game—but only one—as the Rangers took the opener against the visitors, 6-3, and followed with another Garden victory, 5-2, and a Mike Richter shutout in Game 3, 3-0. Finally, the Caps interceded with a 4-2 edge before the Rangers ended it with a 4-3 clincher on Seventh Avenue.

Thus, the Rangers now collided with the Devils in Round 3. Here was a match made in promotional heaven, and the good news for Rangers fans was that the Stanley Cup favorites had won all six of the games played against the Devils during the regular campaign.

"But," noted Devil's captain Scott Stevens, "that was one season, and this is a new one."

"We have a great deal of respect for the New Jersey Devils," said Keenan when a reporter suggested that his club might continue its mastery and sweep the series in four.

The respect was well founded. Down a goal to New York in the opener and seemingly out, New Jersey refused to wilt. With Martin Brodeur replaced by a sixth skater, the Devils stormed the Rangers' zone in the final minute and tied the score when Claude Lemieux knocked the puck past Richter from a scramble in front.

The stage was set for New Jersey's Stephane Richer's magic stick, and it delivered. Having spoiled a Leetch assault after 35:18 of sudden death, Bobby Carpenter flipped a delicate pass to Richer along the left boards. With only Adam Graves between him and Richter, Richer went into overdrive, outflanked Graves, and flipped the rubber over Richter just as the goalie attempted his poke check. The red light flashed at 35:23 of overtime.

The 4-3 New Jersey triumph brought many ramifications. Most of all, it served notice to one and all that the Devils were prepared to give their rivals from Manhattan an intense run for their money.

Not that the Rangers didn't expect it. They sprinted from the gate in the opening minutes of Game 2 at the Garden, scored an early goal, and then repeatedly repulsed the onrushing Devils. The score remained 1-0 into the third period, but Lemaire's shooters couldn't find an opening, and New York eventually pulled ahead to win 4-0.

One thing was certain: an immensely entertaining and pulsating series was now well underway, even outdoing its early promise. Game 3 fulfilled the script with yet another Devils comeback and more overtime. But this time, the other team won. Stephane Matteau swatted a loose puck, which found its way through the labyrinth of legs and behind Brodeur at 26:13 of overtime.

Everyone agreed that Game 4 would set the tone for the rest of the series. A Rangers win would put the Devils in a precarious position, whereas if the home club victory could tie the count, anything could happen.

It was a vintage win for the Devs. Brodeur was immense; the defense had a Gibraltar-like quality, and the forwards, when not tending to their checking, sallied forth and produced three goals to the visitors' one.

The Devils' optimism was now on the rise. They returned to Manhattan and spanked the Rangers 4-1 in a game that they had led 4-0.

One game away from the Stanley Cup finals, the Devils were not receiving the media space that one would have expected under the circumstances. Much attention was given to the Rangers' front office turmoil and Messier, who had captured the imagination of New Yorkers with a daring ploy. The star had gone on record predicting a New York victory.

Game 6 took place Wednesday, May 25, 1994, at the Meadowlands. It was a contest filled with amazing twists and turns and with for a single constant—excitement.

The capacity crowd of 19,040 was treated to a first period dominated by the home club. New Jersey exited with a 2-0 lead on goals by Scott Niedermayer and Lemieux. Every aspect of coach Jacques Lemaire's game plan was working, a fact not overlooked by the New Yorkers. They were a dispirited lot heading into the dressing room, and their mood was reflected in the first half of the second period. Wave after wave of Devils poured through the Rangers' defensive lines, hurling innumerable volleys at Richter. The third—and very likely series-crushing—goal appeared imminent. But alas, it never came.

Still, if New Jersey could carry a two-goal lead to the dressing room with 20 minutes remaining, it would be tough for the Rangers to rebound. However, one Devils mix-up allowed Alexei Kovalev a bit of skating room, and the sharp-shooting Ranger rifled a shot past Brodeur. Instead of a three-goal cushion, the Devils had to contend with a fragile one-goal lead going into the third period.

Sure enough, the Rangers broke loose for three unanswered third-period goals to annex the game 4-2. Messier had made good on his promise with a hat trick, including the turning-point third-period goals.

Along with Game 6, Game 7 is now regarded as one of the finest playoff games in the NHL's long history. The Rangers took an early lead and carefully defended Richter's one-goal margin through the first, second, and most of the third periods. Still, the Devils fought back and finally removed Brodeur for a last, desperate effort.

The final thrust began when Bernie Nicholls won a face-off in the New York end. Suddenly, a play was in motion that culminated with Valeri Zelepukin camping in front of the net in position to deposit the puck behind Richter with only seven seconds remaining on the clock. It was overtime yet again.

"I told my players to be patient," said Lemaire, "and not make any mistakes that would give the Rangers a scoring opportunity."

At one point, the Devils appeared to have the winner. Richter skated to his right boards to field a loose puck, but the Devils' Billy Guerin lost sight of the biscuit. By the time he took possession, the Rangers' net was covered and the threat nullified, enabling the game to grind into a second overtime.

The series finally ended after an attempted Devils clearing pass was retrieved by Matteau, who moved down the left side and then swerved behind the net. Being checked by Scott Niedermayer, the Ranger attempted a desperation centering pass, yet somehow jammed the puck in the corner of the net.

For the Rangers, the moment was sheer ecstasy. The Blueshirts knew they had defeated a formidable opponent. More than that, Messier had lifted himself to the legendary status of Babe Ruth when he predicted the sixth-game victory and then captained his club to wins in both Game 6 and Game 7.

But for Blueshirts fans, the best was yet to come. They had now reached the Stanley Cup finals. For the first time since 1979, they were only four wins away from winning the championship. Their opponent would be the Vancouver Canucks, who, despite the presence of superstar Pavel Bure and dynamic leader Trevor Linden, seemed less threatening than the Devils.

If ever there was a strange scenario leading up to a championship, this was it. The Rangers' general staff—coach Mike Keenan and president/general manager

Neil Smith—were at war with each other. For the most part, the battles were subdued and contained behind closed doors. But enough leaks reached the media to inform both print and electronic journalists that a struggle existed between the two power brokers of the Blueshirts.

Nevertheless, a Cup had to be won, and that took precedence over everything else. The series opened in New York, and Vancouver rallied to tie the score 2-2 late in the third period. To the utter deflation of the Garden crowd, Greg Adams beat Mike Richter in overtime and the Canucks had a one-game lead.

The Blueshirts rebounded for a 3-1 win and then swept both games in Vancouver for a three-games-to-one lead. If ever there was cause for premature rejoicing, this was it. Coming home to a wild, madly deafening Garden crowd should have been enough to deflate the Canucks.

In his book, *Losing the Edge, New York Daily News* reporter Barry Meisel summed up the feeling along Broadway as well as anyone: "The city of New York considered Game 5 a coronation, not a contest. The monster of MSG did not consider defeat even a remote possibility. The wildest party in 54 years was scheduled to begin a few fashionably late minutes after 8:00 p.m. on Thursday, June 9, 1994, at the corner of 33rd Street and Seventh Avenue in Manhattan. No RSVP was necessary.

"The players who weren't too excited to fall asleep for their afternoon snoozes made their celebration plans in the morning. Tickets had to be distributed, family gatherings planned, friends alerted. The PR staff

fielded calls from the *Late Show with David Letterman, Good Morning America*, and every other self-respecting media outlet that hadn't hopped aboard the bandwagon. The mayor's office wanted to make parade plans. The New York City Police Department had to prepare for a jubilant riot"

The riot was not to come, nor was the Rangers victory. What appeared to be a fait accompli turned into a letdown. The Canucks won 6-3, sending the series back to Vancouver. On top of that, a report had surfaced that Keenan had agreed to become general manager and coach of the Red Wings after the season. In fact, no deal had been completed, but the rumor was enough to set off a chain reaction of assertions and denials that lasted through the series and beyond. As for Game 6, it kindled the worst fears of any Rangers fan. The Canucks won 4-1, sending the series back to the Big Apple.

"If they beat us three straight," said Messier, "the Canucks deserve to win the Stanley Cup."

Keenan delivered what some considered his most arresting speech before the final game. The Rangers then took the Garden ice and the game into their hands. They jumped to an early lead and built on it. They had a 2-0 advantage five minutes into the second period, and the situation seemed well in hand until Trevor Linden scored a short-handed goal at 5:21. But Messier fattened the lead to two and the Rangers took the ice to start the third with what appeared to be a thick cushion.

However, the ubiquitous Linden scored on a power play at 4:50 of the third, sending the Rangers into a defensive shell. Often, such ultra-conservative play is a prelude to disaster, but the Rangers were willing to gamble. The lead remained intact as the clock ticked down below the five-minute mark. At that point, a Canucks youngster named Nathan LaFayette came within an inch of bursting the balloon. His shot hit the right post behind Mike Richter but bounced away without causing any harm.

As the overflow crowd bit fingernails, held its breath, and prayed, the Rangers ran through four more face-offs in their own end before the clock ran down to 0:37.8 and then 0:28.2 following two more face-offs. Once again, the puck was iced, and the last face-off was held between Craig MacTavish and Pavel Bure. The Ranger won the draw, pushing the puck into the corner, where Steve Larmer pinned it against the boards.

That did it. The Rangers had won their first Stanley Cup in 54 years, and their followers no longer had to listen to chants of "1940, 1940!" from their Islander counterparts.

The cheering was clocked at seven minutes minimum, after which the Stanley Cup made its appearance. The time was 11:06 p.m. when commissioner Gary Bettman proclaimed, "Well, New York, after 54 years your long wait is over. Mark Messier, come get the Stanley Cup."

Thus, the 1994 champions moved alongside the Rangers' 1928, 1933, and 1940 Cup winners as one of the outstanding clubs in New York hockey history.

INDEX